# THE ECONOMICS
# OF WELFARE

# THE ECONOMICS OF WELFARE

## A Contemporary Analysis

David Z. Rich

PRAEGER

New York
Westport, Connecticut
London

**Library of Congress Cataloging-in-Publication Data**

Rich, David Z.
   The economics of welfare : a contemporary analysis / David Z.
Rich.
      p.   cm.
   Includes bibliographical references and index.
   ISBN 0-275-93309-1 (alk. paper)
   1. Welfare economics.   I. Title.
HB846.R53   1989
330.15'5—dc19          89-30899

Library of Congress Catalog Card Number: 89-30899
ISBN: 0-275-93309-1

First published in 1989

Praeger Publishers, One Madison Avenue, New York, NY 10010
A division of Greenwood Press, Inc.

Printed in the United States of America

The paper used in this book complies with the
Permanent Paper Standard issued by the National
Information Standards Organization (Z39.48-1984).

10  9  8  7  6  5  4  3  2  1

This work is dedicated to my mother, Vanessa,
to the memory of my father, to my sisters, family,
and friends, and especially to Diana Lerner,
for being with me.

Things could get a lot worse without any return to the condition of the 1930s. It seems more likely that the world will continue to teeter along from one crisis to another at a disappointingly low level of activity, but avoiding a catastrophic fall. The more serious risk is to morale. The public mood may become less tolerant, more impatient, more heated, more receptive to magical and mistaken remedies.... If of necessity we must say farewell for a time to full employment, do not let us turn our backs on it or imagine that the world will be a better place without it.

Sir Alec Cairncross
"Farewell to Full Employment"
Ellis Hunter Memorial Lecture
York University, 1978


And if thy brother be so waxen poor and his means fail with thee, then thou shalt uphold him....

Leviticus, XXV:35

# Contents

# Acknowledgments

I would like to express my thanks to my editor, Jim Dunton, and to my project editor, Bert Yaeger, and their staff, for working with me. These are ideas that have been developed since the publication of my first book, *Contemporary Economics: A Unifying Approach* (Praeger, 1986). With respect to the chapter on the United States welfare system, I would like to express my appreciation for the discussion and clarification received from Professor Avraham Doron, of the Social Welfare Department of the Hebrew University, Mt. Scopus campus.

# Part 1

# THE PROBLEM
# SITUATION

# 1

# On the Nature of This Work

For the person not trained in the discipline of economics, this field of social inquiry and policy making is certainly baffling. Economics deals with the generation of wealth and the allocation of scarce goods, resources, and services among competing forces. The purpose of this is to establish a strong industrial base that provides employment and promotes the general well-being of the populace. However, to the untrained person economics may seem a discipline in which discussions held among its practitioners lead to nowhere and in which the processes of business activity continue regardless of what the professional economists say or do.

For example, proposals are stated by government leaders for generating growth, yet business cycles come and go as if immune to these proposals. Economists, employing extremely sophisticated econometric models, attempt to determine the frequencies and intensities of these cycles, but more often than not are kept off guard by the intensities and influences of the real cycle. A speech by a leader of a big corporation can send shock waves through the economy and influence activity in ways not previously considered. The policies and activities of a foreign country can influence the home country's markets with the economist being able to understand these influences only after they occur; moreover, the extents of their secondary influences can be evaluated only after they have made their impacts on the economy.

It is equally puzzling to the lay person that economists prefer to relate to their discipline as a science, while the very nature of economics does not make for the precision of prediction and analysis which exists in the physical sciences.

The lay person may open an academic text on economics and find advanced mathematics therein that seems to endow economics with the semblance of being scientific, but then may read about poverty, unemployment, and the homeless in newspapers and magazines; indeed, should the lay person walk the streets of any big city, that person would discover these very same people to be a social reality, and their dissolute existence a scathing comment on society and economics.

In spite of this baffling situation, however, the lay person should understand the economist's position. Economics is not unlike the study of medicine, a discipline in which a degree of uncertainty exists in both diagnosis and prognosis. Indeed, in medicine, the well-being of a patient often depends on the doctor's abilities, sensitivity, and understanding in prescribing treatment geared to the particular needs of that patient. A person who is ill may affect other people nearby, including loved ones, but this certainly does not determine the well-being of the entire society. Nevertheless, economic activity is a general social condition and the isolation of an economic malaise cannot be conducted in a single sector of the economy but on a large scale, embracing various sectors. The understanding of the malaise—its causes and consequences—depends on the economist's training, skill, and sensitivity in dealing with a given problem.

Since the end of the Great Depression, economists have become increasingly aware of the difficulties of their discipline. Indeed, during that economic upheaval economists argued among themselves over issues of full employment and economic growth. Perhaps only John Maynard Keynes pointed to the real problem: that the neoclassical assumption of full employment as the basis of economic theory and policy-making was inadequate, indeed invalid. It is correct to maintain that the lessons of the Great Depression have been learned well, that taxation and especially the social security tax have been established to alleviate economic distress, that the government has assumed the role of the economic protector of the banking system, that unemployment insurance is a form of buffer against personal poverty. Nevertheless, as the lay person will readily point out, poverty still exists and in our postindustrial society taxation is a burden, the social security system provides little assistance in assuring a living standard reasonable in our time and unemployment insurance is far from adequate as a means of combating the ravages of personal poverty. Granted, these measures are better than being without them as was the situation which existed prior to and during the Great Depression; the question which has to be addressed now is, are these measures still appropriate to our contemporary economic reality?

This question has to be considered not only in light of the advances made since the Great Depression, but specifically with respect to our current economic situation. Economists and statisticians are amassing empirical material concerning labor, unemployment, housing and health and education, as well as the effects of international trade on the economic situation. These statistics are supposed to clarify the current situation and provide material for the economist to treat in theory-form.

Hence, the economist *is* a scientist in the sense that he or she seeks to make sense of the amassed information about the economy in general and its various sectors in particular. The economist must consider the overall operations of business and the government's activity as a regulator; the economist must construct theories and seek to apply them to the subject matter of economics. But economics cannot be restricted to a laboratory because it deals with the social dynamics of the allocation of scarce resources among competing ends, the alternative uses of these resources in the manufacturing of goods and services, the investment of the profits on sales after expenses are deducted. The problem with testing economic theory is that there is a marked absence of laboratory conditions for testing; theories can only be tested for their internal logic and the contributions they make with respect to other theories to the body of economic knowledge.

The nature of economics tends to render the discipline as somewhat of an esoteric field of inquiry, open mainly to its practitioners. The consequence of this is that economists converse mainly among themselves and government and business representatives who have some orientation in the discipline's language and theories, to the exclusion of most laypeople. However, as Wassily Leontief stated:

We, I mean the academic economists, are ready to expound, to anyone ready to lend an ear, our views on public policy; give advice on the best ways to maintain full employment, to fight inflation, to foster economic growth. We should be equally prepared to share with the wider public the hopes and disappointments which accompany the advance of our own often desperately difficult, but always exciting intellectual enterprise. The public has amply demonstrated its readiness to back the pursuit of knowledge. It will lend its generous support to our venture too, if we take the trouble to explain what it is all about.[1]

Leontief's approach is difficult to put into practice even in the best of circumstances. One reason for this is that while of all the academic disciplines, economics most directly touches people's everyday lives, the way it works remains widely misunderstood if not utterly confusing. Moreover, people are most reluctant to discuss economics with academicians when they realize that the debates among economists seem not to lead to resolutions and the economy continues with its cyclic movements regardless of what the economists say or do.

The most confused and confusing branch of economics is that of welfare economics. Other branches of the discipline are value-laden, but they incorporate values as economic theorems to be tested within the confines of a theory. They may reflect the prejudices of a specific economist or school of economic thought—prejudices that can be assessed within the theory and its workings. There is no consideration of the "common good," the "benefit of all concerned," and of "social justice," which are the central considerations of welfare economics.

Moreover, these are philosophical considerations that have been debated at least since the time of Socrates and, as with all philosophical considerations, there have been no accepted and permanent resolutions. The difficulty is compounded still further when philosophy meets economics in the field of welfare. A priori, we cannot accept unemployment as beneficial for society; we consider repugnant the thought of an able person being without employment because of the mysterious forces of economics, cold and impersonal as they are. Yet, an argument can be presented for unemployment, as it allows for labor mobility and the seeking of opportunities which would not exist if employment is full, as there would be every reason for people to maintain their status quo and there would be no place to move to, should a change be desired.

Welfare economics also pertains to the side issues of mainstream economics, such as the environment, the justice system, education, and the allocation of businesses in areas and locations that provide the most efficient services. This special branch of economic endeavor is thus concerned with what Joan Robinson termed, the second crisis of economic theory, that of relating theory to the issues and problems of contemporary society.[2]

According to classical and neoclassical economists, the individual is the best judge of his or her own economic welfare. Is this still the case, or has the government's size become so overwhelming and society's problems so complex, that the individual has to relinquish his or her personal interests to those of the greater good? Indeed, in our contemporary socioeconomic situation, what is the greater good and which authorities are responsible for its determinization and realization? The philosophical foundations of welfare economics are inescapable.

Welfare economics joins the issues of policy with the social dynamics of production, consumption, and living. While the subject of welfare economics is certainly not new to the body of economic literature, it gained its present significance during the Great Depression. Prior to the depression, welfare economics occupied a place in the literature mainly as a wayward son, a part of economic thought that joined economics with its philosophical roots, but little more than that. The main body of economic thought pertained with issues of marginalist production, foreign trade and theories of microeconomic competition—the exception being the socialist writings that gained new respectability since Karl Marx's *Capital*.[3] With Jeremy Bentham and John Stuart Mill,[4] the concepts of utilitarianism and the "hedonistic calculus" placed the issues of welfare economics in the literature, showing their relationships to prosperity and economic growth, and presented the conflict between individual rights and the greater social good. These issues are still very much alive and are certainly relevant when the economic decisions are enacted into policies.

Moreover, with Marx's *Capital,* a new face was given to the "dismal science" of economics. Marx sought to humanize economics by placing it in a dynamic of dialectical materialism, to show that the dislocations of human living, the ties to the market place and the subjugation of the worker to the businessman who paid the wages, would be relieved and the economic situation redeemed in the "future." This future has yet to arrive and surely enough has been written on Marx's method and theory to show both the merits and faults of his reasoning.[5]

Indeed, the impact of his theory is so great that it serves as the watershed dividing classical from neoclassical economic reasoning.

It was during the Great Depression, however, that the issues of economic welfare became the prime concern of government leaders. Moreover, the paradox of capitalism became glaringly apparent during this period: there was extensive capital equipment existing side by side with high unemployment, with the instruments of capitalism unable to bring them together.[6]

However, with all the benefits of the post-Depression era, with social security, unemployment insurance and welfare plans, there exists still unnecessary unemployment and people who cannot fend for themselves economically. Taxation has become questionable as a method for redistributing funds and redirecting monies, and social security payments are most certainly inadequate in preventing serious economic disadvantages among their recipients.

Both the theory and practice of welfare economics have to be reconsidered; indeed, welfare economics will be approached with respect to dynamic disequilibrium, in terms of a theory of economics that the present writer has formulated elsewhere.[7] The object of this work is the formulation of a theory of welfare economics incorporating this aspect of economics into the mainstream of micro-macro reasoning. There can be no rationality for the paradox of capitalism to exist to any extent today. Nor for that matter should the symptoms and conditions of this paradox be found in any country regardless of its economic and political orientation. The means of production and the elimination of poverty are available, and in our contemporary era they should most certainly be utilized. A theory describing and explaining the mechanisms for this utilization will be presented in this work and the applications of this theory for the developing and emerging countries will be discussed. Poverty is both cruel and debilitating, no matter the geographical locations in which it exists and regardless of the political system which fosters it. A reconsideration of welfare economics with the attempt to remove poverty from our economies is the concern of this work.

# 2

# General Comments on the Modern Economy

Since Adam Smith wrote his great work, *The Wealth of Nations*,[1] economists and political theorists have for the most part accepted Smith's teaching that the specialization and division of labor generate the maximum level of economic efficiency. However, since the development of the capitalistic system it has become increasingly clear that specialization and division in the work processes require the resignation of one's personal identity as a worker to the greater scheme of the overall production plan. This, of course, is necessary, for without this personal submission there would be no production but only chaos as each individual attempts to assert his or her uniqueness and numerous conflicts would result which would most certainly bring to an end any attempt at a unified production scheme. It has become also clear that in spite of this resignation of one's personal identity to the production processes, the division and specialization of labor are limited by the state of the technological arts and are restricted by the types and levels of consumer demand which bring the production processes into fruition.

Indeed, the dependence of economic activity on the two factors of technological limits and the levels of consumer demand can be seen by comparing our decade's goods and services with those of the previous decade to realize the impact that technology has made on the economy. The development of consumer awareness and the diversification of tastes and wants have made their influences felt on managerial decision making and the resulting allocation of resources to satisfy consumer tastes and wants. The utilization of technologies for better production and for the development of new products also stimulates consumer demand and brings about shifts in consumption patterns, resulting in previous demand schedules being no longer accurate, thereby shifting aggregate production schemes accordingly.

In retrospect, our present economic situation in our contemporary era is more responsive to the dynamics of economics than at any other time in industrial history. Not only is the consuming population aware of the impact of technology on the production processes; they are also aware that the industrial decision makers will utilize new technologies in the manufacturing of new products and in the production processes of existing successful commercial products, for stimulating new demand and to enter profitable competition for existing markets. This has resulted in greater sophistication in marketing and the distribution of goods and services and requires the consideration of alternative methods of advertising, to reach the various target and secondary consuming classes with the intention of spin-off being generated, thereby influencing other consuming groups in their purchasing patterns.

In the post-Depression era the government has taken an active role in the economy, serving as a regulator and performing in a counter-cyclical manner to stem inflation or to rejuvenate a slowing-down economy as the case may be. The government also performs by enabling the development of necessary infrastructure which allows economic activity to take place. Without sufficient road systems and ports, goods and services are moved with great difficulty, supply and demand responding accordingly. The government has thus assumed the role of underwriter for the economy and seeks to take the necessary steps to ensure the economy's well being.

With respect to business activity there seems to be a fairly good coordinative relationship between business and government policy. The economy generates business cycles and the government acts counter—cyclically to reduce the pressures on the economy when the peaks and troughs become too extended. Such counter-cyclical policies are, however, undertaken without the considerations for welfare. This is so because of the basic assumption that if the economy is healthy, the social welfare is also healthy. As appealing as this may sound, unfortunately it is not the case. For in our era and with our highly sophisticated knowledge of economics, there should be no longer pockets of chronic—as opposed to frictional—unemployment; nor should hunger and deprivation be the case. But these do exist and are blights on our contemporary society. The policies of government must be questioned.

Standard government policy with respect to welfare was formulated during the Great Depression and shortly after World War II, while these policies were adequate then, they are in need of reconsideration now. The concept of social security—or national insurance as it is called in Great Britain—is most certainly sound. The difficulty with the systems which handle social security is that they have become over-bureaucratized, to the point of operating inefficiently and to thus be out of real contact with the issues to which they were supposed to relate. Social security payments are insufficient and beneficiaries have to supplement their incomes with outside employment, if possible at the recipient ages; this employment being often illegal with respect to the welfare system and, as it is most usually taxed, the person's economic welfare and purchasing power are reduced that much further.

Taxation itself is a method for regulating the amount of currency in the economy and is a means for dealing with the cyclic dynamics of inflation and deflation, with the purpose of keeping the economy on what is considered to be an even keel of growth. It is contended that in this manner unemployment can be kept to the minimum under the given conditions. However, in the contemporary economy, taxation as it is being used is ineffective, given the situation of dynamic disequilibrium, so that instead of being a method for revitalizing the economy or cooling it down as the case may be, it serves as a disincentive for extra work and a hindrance to growth. This point will be treated further in Part 2.

There is still another aspect of welfare economics which must be considered and that is the changing complexion of the employment situation. With the impact of ever-increasingly sophisticated technology on the production processes, the requirements for industrial employment vary correspondingly. With the introduction of robotics and other aspects of artificial intelligence in the production processes, for example, jobs that were once the mainstay of a goodly portion of the working population in some areas of industry are being phased out with workers being replaced by robots, programed to operate efficiently with a minimum of off-time and mechanical difficulty. There is, of course, resistance to this type of job replacement, but with the technological impact on industry and international competition, the resistance will yield to the new methods and labor will be reoriented accordingly.

It might seem that the tone of the argument so far is pointing to the advocacy of a welfare state, where the distortions of the employment situation are padded by compensation in several forms by the state, where the individual will not suffer as a result of economic fluctuations because his or her well-being receives the concern of the state, where all will be cushioned and be made soft. Such, however, is certainly not the direction to be taken in the argument to follow. We have not to look too far afield to see where such welfare states are economically. The revolutions in Hungary, Poland, and the Prague Spring during the short-lived Dubcek regime attest all too well to the failures of these systems. Moreover, in the Soviet Union and People's Republic of China—those self-proclaimed bastions of socialism and the welfare state—the leadership has openly admitted to what the citizenry had to cope with all along: that the systems do not work as they are supposed to and the economic distortions far outweigh any benefits accorded to the citizenry by these systems.

On the contrary, the argument to be presented here will attempt to demonstrate the benefits of the current system as it exists—with modifications due to cultural differences and internal circumstances—and to provide an approach to our contemporary economies that will eliminate the necessity for welfare payments and will reduce unemployment to its frictional condition.[2] This may sound somewhat utopian, and hence unrealistic, given the history of welfare since the Great Depression and the entrenchment of such policies as taxation and social security as well as unemployment compensation designed to assist the citizenry. Our contemporary economy is, however, unique in that it allows us opportunities which hitherto were nonexistent or nonconceivable. The challenge is thus to use our contemporary economy to absorb welfare recipients and to make them productive. It is a shame on our contemporary economy and our levels of knowledge that unemployment and pockets of poverty exist, when the possibilities are so great of eliminating these conditions that are indeed throwbacks to the earlier era of industrialization. We have the opportunities for achieving economic strength never before existing. We should not let these opportunities lie idle and perhaps disappear because we approach our economies and formulate our policies with inadequate conceptual tools.

# 3

# Edgeworth and Pareto: The Neoclassical Foundations of Welfare Economics

Practical men, who believe themselves to be quite exempt from any intellectual influences, are usually the slaves of some defunct economist. Madmen in authority, who hear voices in the air, are distilling their frenzy from some academic scribbler of a few years back. I am sure that the power of vested interests is vastly exaggerated compared with the gradual encroachment of ideas. Not, indeed, immediately, but after a certain interval; for in the field of economic and political philosophy there are not many who are influenced by new theories after they are twenty-five or thirty years of age, so that the ideas which civil servants and politicians and even agitators apply to current events are not likely to be the newest. But, soon or late, it is ideas, not vested interests, which are dangerous for good or evil.

John Maynard Keynes
*The General Theory of Employment Interest and Money*

## GENERAL COMMENTS

Because of the demands of their professions, politicians have to be practical people, for they deal often with urgent problems requiring swift and appropriate decisions. Politics indeed makes strange bedfellows because the expediency of the moment requires the commital of obligations with differing political factions and with people of different views.

Politicians, however, are not, by the demands of their pragmatic profession, excluded from the recptivity and understanding of new ideas. Indeed, more so than ever, budding politicians and those already established in office receive university educations and are relying on academic advisers, because of the demands of understanding technologies and their impacts on society and the manner in which society responds. While the practicalities of politics require pragmatic skills, it is now considered practical to be involved with the new ideas and their ramifications. Keynes's comment is therefore correct in our time: that the practical people of politics (and of course business) are influenced by academic scribblers of a few years back, but it is not the case that the contributions of these academics are absorbed by some form of osmosis, gathered from a rarified mixture of hearsay and popular opinion.[1] These works have been read, even studied and comprehended, if only for the hedonistic reason that these practical people can apply these ideas to their profession.

That madman in authority hear voices in the air is certainly not new to our era nor to the period in which Keynes wrote. History is replete with leaders who were mad and claimed to have received their authority from higher up, and who distorted the theories of academic writers of earlier times. Many of these leaders surrounded themselves with the learned men of their time and often listened to their ideas—even though they were more often discarded than heeded. History is also replete with the lack of guarantees that a valuable academic writer will have his or her works receive the noteriety they deserve. Economics is certainly no different as the subject matter of economics relies on those economists who have, either through the merits of their works or through the strange and uncertain paths that personal and public history take, had their works brought into the mainstream of economic thought and have influenced the political conceptualizations of managing the economy.

Two such economists are to be considered here because their works have been influential in welfare economics. Indeed, so great are the influences of Edgeworth and Pareto that all welfare considerations on which practical people of politics seek advice from their academic advisers are answered from the viewpoints derived, either overtly or tacitly, from the Edgeworth-Pareto considerations.

It must be made clear that the present writer, when discussing the ideas of other economists, has made a demarcation other than that which is accepted. The accepted demarcation in economics separates the classical school from the neoclassical school with the writings of Karl Marx, especially his *Capital*. This is because Marx concentrated on issues that were not the main concern of classical economics, such as the mechanisms of historical dialectics and the considerations of value in the industrializing economies. Marx also expressed concern for the working classes, a subject outside the scope of the new science of economics in its classical period and, while guilds and professional associations were certainly not new when Marx wrote, he emphasized another type of "association" that was foisted on society by the dynamics of industrialization in the form of the amorphous working class having no professional identity but whose influence was essential for keeping the processes of industrialization in motion.

The demarcation which the present writer wants to establish is that between the neoclassical and Keynesian schools and contemporary economics, post-Keynesian in orientation because of the types of problems which arose with and after the termination of World War II. During this period the advent of a new type of economics came into existence corresponding to the development of industrialization. This was managerial capitalism[2] together with the penetration of multinational companies forming markets in the developed and developing economies. Indeed, the very conception of economic development is contemporary and it deals with issues touched on vaguely by the classical economists but not dealt with at all by the neoclassicists. Edgeworth's and Pareto's contributions fall within the scope of the neoclassical school; they nevertheless serve as the basis of current welfare economics. The roots of economic theory go very deep in society, but sometimes they yield inappropriate fruits.

## EDGEWORTH'S CONTRIBUTION

Francis Ysidro Edgeworth's main concern in the field of economics was the transformation of this discipline into an exact science. To accomplish this, he sought a calculus "by whose scale moral questions could be determined and happiness thus maximized." [3] That is,

. . . to compare the happiness of one person with the happiness of another, and generally the happiness of groups of different members and different average happiness. Such comparison can no longer be shirked if there is to be any systematic morality at all. . . . You cannot spend sixpence utilitarianly, without having considered whether your action tends to increase the comfort of a limited number, or numbers with limited comfort; without having compared such alternative utilities.[4]

Consumption—even the spending of sixpence in old British coinage—is not a continuous affair, so that the measurement of utilities is not, for Edgeworth, an ordinal computation. What he termed "atoms of pleasure" could certainly not be counted, just like we cannot count the grains of sand on a beach. Yet we have an awareness of experiences, situations, and purchases that provide us with greater or lesser pleasure when compared ordinally.

For Edgeworth, the concept of pleasure and its degrees can be interpreted by the use of indifference curves, where two products or two people bargaining for the same product at differing prices come to an agreement on the basis of eliminating their degrees of indifference according to price. For example, the graph (the Edgeworth Contract Box) is to be viewed from either A's or B's position to determine each contender's bargaining position. Two persons consume both commodities A and B and person I's consumption of A is measured along the horizontal axis and I's consumption of B along the vertical axis. Person II's consumption of A is measured along his or her horizontal axis and the consumption of B measured along the vertical axis. The midpoint of the box shows an equal distribution of A and B for persons I and II; point P shows that

**Edgeworth Contract Box**

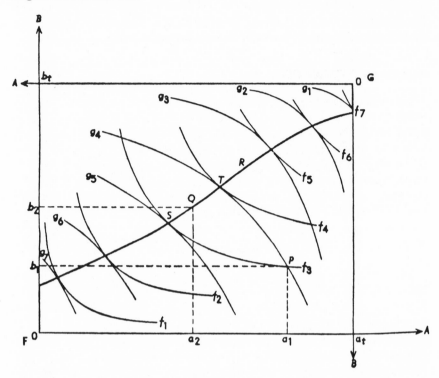

I gets $a_1$ of A and $b_1$ of B, whereas II gets $b_1b_2$ and $a_1a_2$ of B and A respectively. Movement from one point to another on the diagram represents an exchange of commodities (or money) for commodities between the participants and movement occurs when the participants expect to and seek to better their positions. There is, however, a point at which no movement will benefit the parties, such as point T where the indifference curves $f_4g_4$ are tangential to one another. Moving from T would benefit either I or II, but only at the cost of the other, reducing the other's satisfaction.[5]

Edgeworth's contribution of indifference curves and the contract curve at which the actual exchange takes place has shed much light on bringing the bargaining process from the level of psychological computation on the part of participants to the actual process of exchange that will occur when parity between each party concerning satisfaction from the bargain has been achieved. Of course, in the real world there is no guarantee that such a position will be struck and that the terms of the initial bargaining will remain throughout the process. Nor is there certainty that in the face of disappointment the original parties will most likely continue bargaining. These uncertainties limit the efficacy of Edgeworth's contribution.

It is significant to point out that Edgeworth's contribution is based on the premise that the individual is the best judge of his or her own well-being, or to use Paul Samuelson's expression, "individual preferences are to count." [6] It was Pareto, however, who moved the concept of individual preferences from the bargaining process to the realm of general welfare policy.

## PARETO'S CONTRIBUTION

Edgeworth was concerned with bringing the hedonistic calculus of Jeremy Bentham and the other Utilitarians from a strict expression of personal wants to a graphical and mathematical formulation in a more general sense and usage. Edgeworth sought to objectify the subjective and to translate this objectivity into the language of economics. For if economics is the science of the allocation of scarce resources among competing ends, and as humanity has manifold needs and wants and therefore competes for these resources according to each individual's tastes, then these needs, wants, and tastes, can be given expression in economic terms in the form of the bargaining contract curves Moreover, by objectifying the subjective, the status of "science" is still that more secure for economics.

The individual's supply and demand functions, as determined by the contract curves described by Edgeworth, constitute a small but nevertheless significant part of economics. Other factors, such as industrial output, transportation, and the movement of goods and services according to generated demand, together with the government's role of economic underwriter and builder of social infrasturcture and regulator of business cycles, tend to complete the economic picture. Welfare economics enters the picture when the government operates, together with business and labor, to counteract the cycle's movement, or when it appropriates property to construct infrastructure, or when business phases out a product or set of products and begins research into a new line but laying off employment in the interim, or when transportation becomes inefficient and has to reconsider its routes and costings. Pareto sought to deal with these circumstances.

Vilfredo Pareto (1848–1923) elaborated a general theory of economic interdependence which, as Leontief pointed out, is "gradually being combined—into what promises to be a unified logical structure—with two other fields of analytical inquiry, the theory of market mechanism and the analysis of the behavior of an individual firm and of a separate household." [7] This is a grand program indeed and Pareto's concern with economic welfare was that of keeping the economy on a growth pattern in which the essential services are provided by government.

Pareto objected to Edgeworth's attempt to mathematize the utilitarian hedonistic calculus by placing it within the impersonal relations of the indifference curves and mathematical formulations. He went a step further than Edgeworth by calling his curves of indifference, curves of "opthelimity"—a word with a Greek root meaning the same as the Latin-based word, "utility." Moreover, by using a different term than Edgeworth, he was able to take his theory further and deal with both the micro and macro economy, while Edgeworth's concern with mathematical psychics, the attempt to treat in scientific terms the dynamics of personal utility, forced him to focus more on the individual and his or her relations with others in the realm of economics than on the ramifications of the economy in general.

While accepting the premise of Edgeworth's analysis that the individual is the best judge of his or her own well-being, Pareto sought to generalize this premise, making it relevant for the macro economy. The Pareto Optimum is defined as a position in which no individual is better off or worse off by a reallocation of resources, or the distribution of goods and services, or by government policies or shifts in economic orientation.

This does not mean that Pareto considered that shifts in the economy are to be prevented to maintain the optimum status quo, nor that the the dynamics of the market mechanism should not act to reallocate resources or bring about structural changes in the long run once optimum is reached. Pareto's concern here was for the cardinal ophelimity of each person in the economy and with the workings of the economy's institutions and the way they influence the individual. Thus, for Pareto, an economy is in its optimum position when it is efficient to the extent that any shift from the optimum is a shift from efficiency. In the contract graph, for example, the Pareto Optimum between two social goods—goods which have become widely demanded—is represented by PP'ST, and that any movement within this area which brings S and T closer leads to ophelimity. Optimality is achieved when these curves can no longer be brought closer and consequently, as they move farther apart, their optimality declines and efficiency decreases accordingly. Pareto's concern was, therefore, with achieving the optimum in the allocation of resources among the manifold competing ends and, as the trade-off between one such end and another reaches the PP'ST positions and they move closer to each other, then for these ends the efficiency in resource allocation is at its maximum. Expanding this trade-off position to the entire economy brings the economy to its maximum so that any movement from this position has to be set off by a corresponding movement toward it for overall efficiency to be maintained.

The difficulty with Pareto's theory comes with welfare considerations, for how is it possible to improve the general socioeconomic welfare, thereby increasing the purchasing power of the socially disabled within the prevailing social context, without reducing the position of another sector or sectors? For Pareto's Optimum to exist, three conditions must prevail. First, the marginal rate of substitution between any pairs of inputs must be equal for all producers using them. Second, the marginal rates of technical substitution must be the same for all producers employing technologies. Third, the marginal rate of transformation between two goods must be equal to the marginal rate of substitution for these goods. Only then can Pareto's ophelimity exist and according to his theory the economy will be in its maximum efficiency position. Welfare can be changed to compensate any sector by altering the marginal rates of product substitution and transformation and this influences the marginal rates of substitution according to the changes in demand resulting from the alterations in the welfare scheme.[8]

## A CRITIQUE OF THE EDGEWORTH-PARETO ARGUMENT

Much has happened in world history and in the development of economic theory since Edgeworth and Pareto wrote. There was the Great Depression in which the laws of neoclassical theory broke down and there was the rise of the unions that sought to redress the workers' situations and improve their lot. There was the Second World War with the allocation of vast resources for destruction instead of economic rejuvenation, and the consequent tremendous loss of lives and great human suffering. There have been new nations rising and old political orders reducing their own domains of rule. New requirements of welfare have developed within nations seeking to generate wealth and expand their influences. There is also a new type of economic imperialism in the form of the multinational companies, gathering resources and employment throughout the world under a single company banner.[9]

Of course, neither Edgeworth nor Pareto was blessed with the vision of prophetic foresight to formulate theories which could account for all the economic changes as a result of these developments. The difficulty for our era is that we are still under the shadows of these two great economists concerning welfare considerations even though our current situation is so different than that of the time in which they wrote. Moreover, the isolationist tendencies which prevailed during their time as Europe sought integration within itself and was unable to cope with this reality and as the United States rejected the League of Nations, which U.S. President Woodrow Wilson proposed to the world, are no longer relevant today. Now, the world's economies are strongly tied in international commerce, so that domestic events often have international reverberations. This condition also bears on the economies' welfare.

While Edgeworth's position is important, it is only relevant for localized bargaining positions. For in terms of consumer goods, the range today is extremely wide, with close substitutes nearly eliminating the closed dynamics of the contract-type situation that Edgeworth described.

Pareto's Optimum is clearly important as it represents an ideal case in a closed economic situation. It has been rendered irrelevant, however, because his three conditions are so severely weakened in our economic reality. For example, imputs are of such a wide variety and both production plans and consumer tastes so diversified, made even more so by the vast array of substitutes, that attempts to evaluate the marginal rates of substitution for more than one producer run into the greatest computational difficulties, which for the sake of ease of handling, can be reduced to the problem with which Edgeworth dealt: that of redefining personal utility for producers and consumers into a scientifically measurable quantity for each producer in each specific transaction.

His concept of the marginal rate of substitution also runs into difficulties, for such rates of substitution are determined by the productive abilities of the workers and their technological skills in relation to the target and subtarget groups for which production is geared and the possible state-of-the-art alternatives which will not alter the product. The difficulty is that these qualities are different for every business so that because of the differences in managerial ability, this affects business orientation and, to some extent, plant location with respect to the target groups. The marginal rate of substitution cannot, therefore, be measured with any degree of validity for the same technologies, because different businesses have different approaches and utility and production considerations.

Pareto's third condition, that of the marginal rate of transformation equaling the marginal rate of substitution, results in a tautology. To substitute goods so that their marginal rates are equal is to transform the substituted goods into the desired good; a good so transformed takes on the characteristics of the substituted good, so that no real information is imparted by this condition. Moreover, the substituted good on margin becomes the actually preferred good so that no real substitution will take place in the near future and therefore no such condition of equality can be measured.

There is another problem with the Edgeworth–Pareto approaches. Both maintain that substitution at the marginal rates is made on the basis of expectation. With Edgeworth's argument this can be seen as the bargaining positions draw closer, with each participant giving up an advantage on the margin to move closer to the desired result. With Pareto's argument, this is demonstrated by his use of marginalism for his three conditions. Substitutions made at marginal rates are based on expectations to be derived from substitutions and while economists attempt to quantify economic behavior, expectation and substitution operating together lead to a paradox in which an expected outcome from substitution is not the outcome expected because marginalism and expectation cannot exist together. The paradox is constructed in part 2; for now, it must suffice to say that the transformation of psychological motivations of which expectation is one, into economic language has resulted in more difficulties than clarifications in economic science.

The basic premise of welfare economics as accepted by Edgeworth and Pareto—that the individual is the best judge of his or her own needs—is accepted as the basic premise of this present work, provided that rational individuals only are considered. With this premise, welfare economics must be structured to cope with an economic situation unique to our contemporary era. The fact that the individual in our era has achieved a somewhat paradoxical position attests to its uniqueness.

The paradox is this: According to welfare economics the Edgeworth-Pareto assumption, that the individual is the best judge of his or her needs, still prevails. Yet, according to the same body of welfare economics the government determines

cities to take advantage of the culture and intellectual activity there. However,
the population in these cities grew, employment became harder to find after
industrial expansion reached its limit due to the economic situation that allowed
no further expansion, and as land for such expansion became scarce.

There was a corresponding shift in economic theory, which took into account
movement of the labor force into cities and the business cycle's effect on
employment as a consequence. Consider, for example, Edgeworth's contribution
to welfare economics. His argument was predominantly hedonistic, attempting
to provide a calculus of personal moral considerations as they operate in the
economic sphere. His argument moved from the individual to groups affected
by individual's economic decisions, back to the individual to measure the
satisfaction resulting from the economic trade-off situation between alternative
goods. Pareto generalized Edgeworth's argument to pertain to society in general with the optimum situation existing when no shift of resources will affect
the economic well-being of any other sector.[1] However, there was another approach that took into account the new economic realities at the time; this approach
was provided by Eugin E. Slutsky.[2]

Slutsky used theorems based on Pareto's opthelimity, so that a good desired
by a person has greater utility for that person than competing goods not so
highly desired. For a fixed income y, the consumer will choose from a list
of competing goods with prices $p(1, 2, \ldots, n)$; the good chosen or consumption
fit with both the consumer's desire and his or her budget alloted for this
sort of consumption. Hence, if the good purchased is n, then $op/oy = p/n$.
The consumer has to allocate his or her income according to his or her needs
and desires, then $y = \Sigma y(p_1 - p_n)$ for all these consumer's goods. As $y \subset Y$, that
is, personal income is a subset of national income, and as the consumer's
desires are ordered according to his or her needs and desires with respect
to available products, then $Y = y(\Sigma p_1^n)$, the consumption preferences for all
goods in the society. An upward shift in the price of the preferred product
causes the substitution effect, in which the consumer chooses the product
closest in quality to the preferred product at either the previous price
or one which is less than the increased price. Slutsky's substitution effect
allows consumer to maintain his or her consumption preferences with little
change so that consumption patterns can remain fairly stable. With this situation
stable, the economy will remain fairly stable, with price shifts being compensated the substitution effect.

Thus, from this argument, the general position of national income—
Y—can be assessed for its utility (opthelimity) on the basis of macro
spending patterns. So that should the government require, it can introduce
policies which alter consumption patterns according to the economy's requirements without seriously disrupting consumption patterns because of the substitution effect. When the business cycle turns downward, according to this
theory, incomes are restricted so that a corresponding increase in the money
supply will stimulate business again and the downward motion will be halted.

and sets policies which are best for the economy as a whole—and what constitutes
the economy if not individuals and their transactions? If the individual knows
his or her needs best, then the government's role in this respect is both redundant
and hindering, for the government cannot know each individual's tastes and
needs. Moreover, if the collective body of rational individuals operates according
to each individual's own needs and wants, then how can there be welfare economics? Should these needs and wants coincide to any extent that allows for
their objectivity and quantification, why should there be a need, nevertheless,
for governments to formulate and institute welfare policies?

Nevertheless, in the history of economic development since the Industrial
Revolution, it has been shown that even though people act according to their
own needs and wants, such conditions as poor education, slums, inefficient and
insufficient infrastructural services, and a chronically neglected class of people,
defined by the economic stratum in which they exist, remain in this stratum to
a large extent with upward mobility extremely difficult. This is dangerous for
society, especially because of the luxuries that the higher strata are able to afford
are denied the lower stratum due to its economic situation. This has set up a
conflict situation with the lure of "quick and easy money" of crime compared
to doing a good day's honest work within the society which pays just-above
subsistence wages. In the concept of welfare economics, the government is
expected to act as the prime economic mover and step in to rectify the situation;
how should it do so without violating the premise that the individual knows his
or her needs and wants best of all? Should the government seek to rectify social
imbalances through regulating the social strata's purchasing power?

The theory of neoclassical economic welfare as expanded from Edgeworth's
and Pareto's theories is no longer adequate in our contemporary era. Their
theories pertained to a different era, that of the Industrial Revolution, and since
then the terms of economic reference have changed. The basic premise of the
rational individual knowing best his or her needs is still valid and certainly
important in our contemporary era. With regard to the implementation of economic policies, however, the concept of compensation for the lower income
stratum has to be evaluated and the entire approach reconsidered. The aim of
contemporary welfare economics should not be to devise ways to compensate
the lower stratum with subsidies or other sophisticated approaches; the aim of
contemporary welfare economics should be the shifting of this stratum from
receivers to full participants in economic activity, to rid the members of this
stratum of the social blight of deprivation that is a virulent anomaly, a vestige
of the Industrial Revolution and the distortions which it had to generate in order
to be effective. A theory seeking to accomplish this will be stated in Part 2 of
this work; it will be a theory consistent with the conditions of our contemporary
era and its economic situation.

# 4

# Slutsky'
# Effect: The

During the Industrial Revolution there was a te
businesses. Cities developed along with indust
did the cities in which they were concentrated. V
and business activity tapered off many of the e
their work, which led to the deterioration of
become an integral part of industrialization a
the cyclic motion, good periods were bound
as fall follows summer. However, during th
olution a situation developed making the dow
than in the early days of industrialization.

In the early days of the Industrial Revolu
an influential component of the business co
expansion, industry assumed greater import
correspondingly; there was increased dema
industry. Hence, a greater proportion of th
cycle's upturn and a significant number s
unemployment when the cycle turned do
attracted people because of the manifold
the centers of culture, the arts and science
as well. They offered new and exciting st
to the traditional and more rural popul
reaching employment opportunities tha
that made them so attractive, but the

the
as t
indu
for
T
the
empl
to we
to pr
econo
econo
by th
satisfa
choice
eral, w
the eco
proach
was pr
Sluts
by a pe
personal
of comp
will mee
particula
As the c
and desir
is, as per
preference
to the ava
consumers
results in
which is c
or at a pric
allows the
deviation s
generalized
pensated by
Moreover
$Y(=\Sigma y)$—c
consumption
programs wh
ments withou
tution effect
reasoning, in
supply will st

The increased money supply will restore the general consumption patterns offset by the substitution effect as the money, as it works its way into the economy, will revitalize demand, bringing it to its previous level in the aggregate. As the cycle moves upward, government intervention is reduced accordingly as more goods and services are produced to meet the increased demand through employment and money in circulation due to the increased business activity. The substitution effect is limited as more people gain liquidity to purchase according to their needs and desires. The substitution effect does have a role as close competitors vie for the consumer's currency and seek to make such substitution profitable from both the consumers' and their own positions.

Slutsky therefore moved Pareto's concept of opthelimity still further by making it dependent strictly on prices and incomes. By so stating utility in this generalized form, Slutsky removed it from the hedonistic realm of Edgeworth's theory and from the slightly more objective trade-off argument posited by Pareto, and placed it in the realm of impersonal relationships of incomes and the market mechanism. According to Slutsky's approach, the economy is said to be at its maximum welfare position when consumers purchase strictly according to their tastes, as determined by their incomes allocated for each item of consumption.

The government functions in the market in this condition only as a corrective mechanism, keeping the economy on an even keel. As each sector is functioning efficiently—with each consumer acting economically in terms of his or her best interests, limited only by liquidity—the economy is performing in a quasi-Pareto optimum. Slutsky's contribution had the government acting in a Pareto sense of not depriving one economic sector in order to compensate another; the government must, however, keep the economy on an even keel to prevent serious disruptions of the market mechanism so that the market will operate according to consumer demand. This is maintained during periods of fluctuations by the substitution effect, by which consumer preferences are not seriously disrupted.

There are two difficulties with Slutsky's work. One is that it appeared in 1915, when much of the world was at war and another large part of the world was preparing to enter the fray. After the end of World War I, depression set in and there was a serious time-lag between the shifting of industry from a wartime to a peacetime footing with demobilized personnel unable to find employment. The very operation of the substitution effect was impossible, because there was very little income to make a serious impression on the market mechanism as an indicator of consumer preferences. Goods were limited and incomes so restricted as to limit goods substitution. The inflationary period that followed was not due to consumption and production, but to the "paper chase" based on money for money's sake. So his theory had limited importance and is most certainly not tested.

The second difficulty is, of course, the breakdown of the neoclassical system in the Great Depression. Slutsky's theory is based on a concept of near-full employment, allowing for marginal fluctuations in the employment rate, and with the money effect valuing the goods and services and allowing for substitution when available. These conditions did not prevail to the extent which would make Slutsky's theory workable because during the Great Depression productive capital lay idle and able-bodied workers were unemployed.

Thus, while Slutsky objectified the concept of utility in economics and developed welfare economics further than Edgeworth and Pareto, the market mechanism on which he constructed his theory and stated this objectivity broke down. Keynes's alternative of having the government shift from a passive to an active participant in order to stimulate employment provided a viable solution to the circumstances of the depression. Economic welfare was then transferred from an ineffective market mechanism to the full authority of the government, which established works projects—some without economic structural utility—to get employment functioning again. These works projects were to provide employment and income which would stimulate demand and get businesses active once again. Keynes's plan had much success but unfortunately it was interrupted by another war. When World War II ended, a new era of economics began and Keynesian depression economics was no longer viable.[3]

In the aftermath of the Great Depression the contributions of Edgeworth, Pareto, nor Slutsky are not valid, for they are based on the principles of utility which no longer hold. For the economics of welfare to be viable in our time, they must relate to the realities of our contemporary era.

# Part 2

## THE THEORY OF CONTEMPORARY WELFARE ECONOMICS

# 5

# Introductory Discussion

No other science illustrates better than economics the impact of the enthusiasm for mechanistic epistemology upon its evolution. Does the transforming of economics into a "physico-mathematical science" require a measure of utility which escapes us?

Nicholas Georgescu-Roegen
*The Entropy Law and the Economic Process*

## GENERAL COMMENTS

The reason for the enthusiasm for mechanistic epistemology in the development of economic theory was the progress in both productive terms and for the theoretical possibilities in economics for the development of mankind in the Industrial Revolution.[1] This economic revolution was, itself, an exploitation of machinery with the corresponding development of the labor force to work the machinery. As the mechanistic processes of production tended toward centralized locations in the cities which were being formed, the labor forces in these cities attracted not only further businesses that serviced the big industries; the labor forces brought into these cities education and medical services so that professional people such as doctors, lawyers, and teachers, also moved into the cities.

The Industrial Revolution was a historical era that not only broke down old ways and customs; it led to the establishment of new ways of life, appropriate to the conditions of industrialization. For example, there was the dissolution of the great emphasis on rural living and the beginning of systems of co-operation between the rural and urban sectors, with the population shift to the cities resulting in the urban centers' dominating their rural counterparts. Not only was the vast amount of foodstuffs shipped to the urban centers, but the very equipment used to plant and harvest, to tend the cattle and to move the farm produce, was manufactured in the cities and purchased by the agricultural communities. Cotton and other crops were harvested with less cost and greater efficiency through the use of machinery. The mechanisms that transformed the processes of manufacturing spread throughout the industrialized countries as the dynamics of the Industrial Revolution set in.

It was during this period that economics established itself as a science. It was not mere coincidence that Adam Smith wrote *The Wealth of Nations* at the beginning of the Industrial Revolution and that his description of efficient production turned on a mechanistic base. Smith understood the processes of production, applying the new science of Newtonian mechanics and the benefits of trade through increased productive efficiency and comparative productive advantages in, the various market sectors.

Mechanics was not new to the industrializing world; Archimedes wrote of being able to move the world with a fixed point and a fulcrum, applying the principle of leverage. Moreover, the ancient invention of the wheel had been exploited sufficiently as to form a relationship between the worker and his tools of labor. The wheel, the fulcrum and lever, and other mechanical devices such as the pulley were certainly employed efficiently prior to industrialization. But the Newtonian impact on manufacturing resulted in the development of gears with differentials, with the transformation of potential to kinetic energy and motions necessary to open new vistas of production, with this new conception of energy controlling the production processes that began the Industrial Revolution.

R. A. Gordon lists five great technological advancements since the Industrial Revolution. These are: (1) the development of textiles in Britain from the mid–1700s to the development of the railways; (2) the application of steam power to rail transportation; (3) the Bessemer furnace, and also the development of steel and the application of steel in industry; (4) the development of electric power, of the telephone, and the application of chemicals to industry and the development of management and marketing; and (5) the combination of advanced science with manufacturing that began intensively in World War II, with the results being new electronics in industrial conceptualizations and the harnessing of nuclear power, the development of synthetic fabrics, the development and expansion of light metals and of wonder drugs, all of which require new approaches to management and marketing.[2]

Hence, the impact of science on production that began with the applications of Newtonian mechanics to production continued into the nuclear age. New chemicals for production, new drugs, new concepts in electronics and computers—these were offshoots of the last world war because of their applications to both military and peaceful purposes in the postwar period.

Each of the processes by Gordon required the organization of people in the manufacturing processes, the mustering of capital and of knowledge to apply to production, the distribution of resources, the cost-efficiencies of the production methods and the consideration of alternatives, and prices that are competitive with similar products for the consumer. These considerations are well within the realm of economics and they affect people, employment, the dynamics of the urban-rural relationships, and the impact of foreign commerce through the international movement of goods and services.

The point is not that economics is a science that evolved under the enthusiastic approach of mechanistic epistemology. The discipline of economics is one which searches out interrelationships, their hermeneutics and their effects, which is often a complicated process that can be simplified somewhat by the use of the tool of mathematical thinking. There is, however, the tendency to make mathematics *the* language of economics; if this mathematization is carried too far, economics, as the study of the allocation of resources among competing ends, will become too technical to be of use to industrialists and businessmen, as well as government decision makers.

This search for interrelations and their dynamic effects contributes to making economics a science. During the Industrial Revolution, economists such as Adam Smith, J.-B. Say, David Ricardo, and Karl Marx sought to understand these interrelations and their impacts of industry on land and labor, and the impacts of land and labor on employment and industry. The population movements also had to be considered as well as the impact of foreign trade, and the comparative and absolute advantages in trading positions and the close competition in the production and selling of goods and services.

Science deals with knowledge, with the formulation of knowledge into systems that allow its practitioners to work and derive consequences, to apply the consequences and to reshape the fields to which the systems relate. Every science, from astronomy to biology, from micro-and macrophysics to medicine, performs according to this *esprit*. The philosophers of science may argue the methods of science, whether it is best to be pragmatic or positivistic, or whatever the school of thought.[3] But the spirit of science, with the impact of knowledge on the fields of inquiry and the subsequent changes that knowledge induces, cannot be argued as it is both historical fact and current fact, certain as science itself and the progress that science has made.[4]

Economics is a science because its practitioners construct knowledge systems to explain economic events and apply these systems to their respective branches of economic inquiry to derive consequences that lend themselves to applications in the real world of commerce and finance. A person claiming to be a realist may argue that businesspeople interested only in moving supplies and making profits have no time for the esoteric cantillations of the economist. The businesspeople, the argument may go, have little or no knowledge nor understanding of the Economists' terms marginal costs and marginal revenue, nor have they the need for the economists' graphs or the knowledge of advanced mathematics other than the business arithmetic necessary for calculating costs and profits, and for keeping books.

In fact, this is no argument but a pseudo-argument. The very same business people most probably have little or no knowledge of microphysics, but their merchandise, and indeed their very bodies, are composed of atoms and their substructures which are the subjects of microphysicians. While the economist may discuss the subject in terms of the field, the businessperson will discuss the same concepts but employ language to which he or she can relate. Should the businessperson find that the economist's prediction is correct, that is, that profits have increased while costs remained fixed or lowered as the economist dictates, that business person may become curious and seek to understand the mysteries of the economic discipline. The hard-headed businessperson may not be so hard-headed when economic knowledge helps his or her earning power.

It was such advice that Adam Smith offered the general business community when he discussed the division and specialization of labor in the *Wealth of Nations*. It has been the same type of advice which economists have offered as industries tended toward centralization, as competition increased and profits became more difficult to obtain, and as foreign markets opened up in competition and economists explained the utilities of currencies and the concept of comparative advantages in trade. Are not politicians realistic people who must know how to influence their constituencies and keep their rivals at bay? Do not these politicians in their capacities as finance ministers and secretaries of the treasury, as officials of central banks and as secretaries and ministers of health, education, defense, agriculture, and transportation, as well as welfare, turn to the economists for instruction and guidance in the conduct of their public affairs and responsibilities?

Economists have watched their theories shape economies; they have been observers to industrial centralization and of industrial competition, they have been witnesses to the many companies competing for consumers. They have watched economies change as their advice becomes incorporated into business and government policies, and have changed their theories when necessary as changes in the economies occur, and they have, as with every scientific discipline, engaged each other in debate when theories clashed and have sought clarification when their theories have faltered.

The economist is aware of the difficulty of not having laboratory conditions for testing and must therefore rely on the logical consistencies of his or her theory and for the slower dynamics of socioeconomic events for determining the theoretical results in their practical applications. The limitation of the absence of a laboratory, has resulted in strong reliance on a substitute, that being mathematics, with the consequence that sometimes the discipline of economics takes on the appearance of a physico-mathematical science to compensate, so that theories are as a physical science in appearance, as the expression of economic events is placed in mathematical relationships.

From the vantage point of history, however, the economist does have a laboratory of sorts, for the economist can observe the impact of theory on the economy and the impact of economic events on the formulation and statement of economic theory. The economist observes the forces that brought about the decline of mercantilism and physiocracy as doctrines and that brought about the Industrial Revolution in their places. The economist can study the short-run trade cycles that occurred over the period of the Industrial Revolution and can account for the failures of the theories during that period and the cessation of the Industrial Revolution with the Great Depression.

The contemporary economist realizes that since the end of World War II we have entered into the era of post-Keynesian theory, that the Keynesian conception was oriented for depression and is no longer viable, and that economists must formulate theories to account for the new reality. Our new era offers unique opportunities. We have to consider the economy not as a closed physico-mathematical entity, but as an open system, one which responds to and contributes to international trade and the needs and requirements of the developing economies. Our theories must therefore be appropriate for the post-industrial economies as those that are undergoing industrialization. Economists must consider the impact of one economy on another of similar growth and industrialization, for our world is no longer composed of isolated and somewhat hostile nation-states. Our tendency for internationalization, manifested in the various trading zones and the United Nations, requires new demands on economic theory and this situation is most assuredly unique to our time. The contemporary economist's laboratory is our situation, and the viability of economic theory depends to a large measure on how well the theory relates to these conditions and offers solutions to the unique problems which exist in our time.

## COMMENTS ON MARGINALISM

One aspect of neoclassical and modern economic theory which must be reviewed is the concept of marginalism. Marginalism was important in neoclassical theory of the firm, when it was necessary to consider the amount of revenue gained from producing an additional product. A cut-off period of production had to be realized so that revenues could be calculated and profits realized. Even though competition today is strenuous and that costing has become far more complicated due to the rigors of competition and the diversified production and manufacturing within each firm, marginalism still has a role to play in economics. This role is limited, however, because the calculations of additional quantities of a product, the revenues received, and the profits realized, are far from certain. We learn from marginalism that the most efficient use of a firm's resources in production is achieved when the receipts gained from the production of an additional product are equal to the added production costs involved in manufacturing that product, that is, when marginal costs equal marginal revenues. At this level the productive resources engaged in the product's manufacture are used at their maximum efficiency; should production fall below this level, facilities are still available for increasing production, and should production occur above this level, either production will be cut back because of losses sustained as revenues from the increased production are less than production costs, or the product will be eliminated due to the firm's limited resources.

Marginal cost can be stated thus: $MC = p - VC$, with $p$ being the price and VC being the variable cost of production. VC is the cost of improving the seller's—that is, the firm's—offer sufficiently by raising the sale by one or more production units; another way of considering the VC is the savings gained by offering the market less attractive terms of purchase, leading to a decline in sales by one or more units. For every sale there is a buyer, so that elasticity of demand is expressed by $e = p/VC$, which can be written as $e = p\Delta q/q\Delta p$, that is elasticity is equal to the price in relation to the change of quantity, divided by the quantity in relation to the change in price. In the MC equation above, $p\Delta q$ equals p, $q\Delta p$ equals the variable cost of a single unit with respect to its price. When $e > 1$, the MC is rising; when $e = 1$, the MC is unchanged; when $e < 1$, the marginal cost is declining.

Another aspect of marginalism that must be discussed is marginal outlay. This is the buyer's cost of persuading the seller to sell one more unit. The marginal outlay includes the buyer's variable cost, which is the price change, increasing or decreasing, in response to demand. Marginal outlay can be stated thus: $MO = p - VC$. The buyer's elasticity is also p/VC, so at the time of the sales transaction the price paid must equal the price agreed upon by the seller, so that [MC = MO] ≡ Marginal revenue is an identity relationship that must always hold for the marginalist doctrine.

This of course means that $(p - VC)_s = (p = VC)_b$, with the subscripts standing for seller and buyer. Since $e = p/VC$ for both sides of the transaction, the MC and MO equations can be written: $(p - p/e)_s = (p \neq p/e)_b$. From this identity derived from the above equations some unwanted consequences can be drawn.

One such derivation occurs when setting the elasticities to unity. The identity takes the form $Op_s \equiv 2p_b$, but this is clearly not the case, for a price does exist at which the transaction was made, in which the seller's and buyer's prices were equal. If the elasticity of one side is greater or less that the other, adjustments will be made until either the transaction is completed or abandoned. Equal elasticities, either greater or less than unity, result in similar difficulties, rendering different sale and purchase prices, when in fact only one price is set for the transaction to occur.

This difficulty represents one case where there is a clash between situational logic, in this case the logic of marginalism, and reality. According to marginalist reasoning, such a transaction price is set according to the marginal propensities to sell and to consume; on this point there is no clash. The difficulty comes when this price setting is derived from marginalism and results in a paradox of no transaction price according to the derivation and a real transaction price by which commerce is undertaken. This paradox is not a result of reality but exists because of marginalist logic.

Another difficulty with marginalism concerns the marginal efficiency of capital, a concept employed by John Maynard Keynes in *The General Theory*. The marginal efficiency of capital is the relationship between the prospective yield of an capital asset and its supply price. The prospective yield of an asset, such as an investment, is a series of annuities $A_1, A_2, \ldots, A_n$ that the investor expects to gain from selling the investment after deducting expenses. The asset's supply price is not the market price, but that price which would induce manufacturers of borrowers to produce an additional asset unit; this is sometimes referred to as the replacement cost.

Keynes defined the *mec* as being equal to the rate of discount that would make the present value of the series of annuities given by the returns expected from the capital asset during its life just equal to the supply price, that is, its replacement cost. Because the *mec* depends on the rate of return expected on money as if it were a newly produced asset, that is, a measure, neglected is the historical result of the asset's yield on its original cost if considered after the asset's life has ended.

From this argument, a paradox can be constructed. Let $M(mec\underline{X})t_a - t_c$ stand for the market value of an asset expected to have the mec of $\underline{X}$ over the life span of time a to c. If during this period only a few purchases of the asset are made, its *mec* from the investors' point of view is affected insignificantly, a fact judged with considerable accuracy, so that the real rate of return on the investment is that which is expected. Here no difficulty exists.

If, however, during the period a to c a large investment is realized in the asset, the *mec* will decline accordingly. Let this be represented by $M(mec - \underline{X})$, where $-\underline{X}$ is the mec of $\underline{X}$ lower than for its first investor and existing in time b. Thus, $M(mec\underline{X})t_a - t_c \neq M(mec\underline{X})t_a - t_c$, because during this time span the expected yield of $X$ was lowered in reality, so that the logical construction of the *mec* over time results in a paradox of not being the same *mec* over the same period of time.

It may be argued that the reasoning here is unfair, that the paradox does not hold because what must be considered is the entire investment schedule, which would show the aggregate increase in investment and the appropriate decline in the asset's *mec*. This is certainly what Keynes meant when he cautioned against the confusion that the *mec* has brought about because of the failure to understand that it depends on the *prospective* yield and not its current yield.

This can be best illustrated by pointing out the effect on the marginal efficiency of capital of an expectation of changes in the prospective cost of production, whether these changes are expected to come from changes in the labor cost, i.e., in the wage-unit, or from inventions and new technique. . . . Insofar as such developments are foreseen as probable, or even as possible, the marginal efficiency of capital produced today is appropriately diminished.[5]

In the real world where most things are probable if not possible, it may very well be that an investor does not foresee any changes and that the investor's personal expectation of the *mec* is held constant, while others who have invested in the same asset experience a decline in the *mec*. In any case the investment-demand schedule will be altered in reality whether such an alteration is expected or not. Keynes's point, instead of clarifying the confusion, only emphasizes it.

These arguments were stated in an earlier work by the present writer and they were resolved with the use of utility.[6] They were restated here to show the importance of marginalism in general for neoclassical economics, but their significance here is that welfare economics in the neoclassical period of thought relied strictly on marginalism for its viability. The Edgeworth Contract Box, for example, employs the marginalist line of reasoning with the use of indifference curves, for they are expressions of the marginal utility expected as a response of the bargaining opponent's offers, Pareto relies on the marginalist argument because his optimum exists when compensation for one sector does not affect— on margin—other sectors, so that relative positions remain unchanged as a result of compensation. This has its problems, for if a sector *is* compensated, while the other sectors remain unchanged, that very compensation is a marginal change upward. Slutsky's entire approach is based on marginalism as calculated by individual consumers with respect to their liquidity schedules and in light of closely competing products. If the margin in competition is considered by the consumer to be insufficient for changing consumption patterns, given liquidity restrictions, the decision may be made to continue the same patterns while reducing savings or, perhaps, by going into an anticipated short-term debt.

It is posited here that marginalism is of value, but only for small businesses operating in limited markets. For the macro economy, and specifically here for considerations of welfare economics, marginalism is of no value. The emphasis on programs must be on their utilities with respect to given objectives, with these objectives, in turn, being formulated on the basis of utility. This will be argued in the chapters to follow.

# 6

# The Utility Optimum

## FROM "ECONOMIC MAN" TO "CONTEMPORARY INDIVIDUAL"

In the literature of economics, the notion of the "economic man" is that of the individual who, in matters of economics, acts strictly in a rational manner. The economic man's judgments are supposed to be clear and he opts for the best among competing alternatives in the decision-making process. Thus, the economic man is one who acts according to his best interests, as only he knows what is best for him among the available choices.

The very notion of the person acting rationally and in his best interests forms the basis of neoclassical welfare economics. This notion is supported by a more basic concept on an economy fluctuating in dynamic equilibrium, so that at one time one set of alternatives are attractive as choices, and at another time a different set of choices will be available. Eventually, a set of choices resembling the first set will appear the better, while later a set resembling the second set will appear better and so on in a recurring cyclical pattern. The economic man, according to his current economic position at any one time, is confronted with these alternative choices and will act according to his best interests at the time, only to be confronted with different choices, the acting on which may negate the earlier decisions.

According to neoclassical welfare thinking, the economy is *not* at its optimum when the movement along the indifference curves is halted because of a a better bargaining position of one sector over its bargaining opponent (Edgeworth), or when a shift in resources worsens the position of one sector over another (Pareto), or when price changes do not result in corresponding shifts in the sub-situations of preferences (Slutsky). The economy is not at its optimum in each of these situations because economic man is restricted from behaving economically according to his best interests and the interests of the sectors to which he belongs. Neoclassical welfare economics relies on an optimum. But in each of of the situations discussed above, an optimum is not permanent. The Edgeworth optimum is a bargaining position for each situation. Once achieved, another situation takes its place. Sector bargaining is not static and the terms, on which agreement is achieved, change, requiring new bargaining periodically. The Pareto situation is also dynamic because the conditions in which all sectors of the economy are satisfied and that any compensation for one sector is at the expense of another or other sectors is also temporary. New policies, new internal conditions, require taking from one sector and subsidizing others—such as improving schools by way of taxation. The Slutsky position relies on personal and sectoral liquidity, which fluctuates according to monetary policy and to the economy's position on the cycle.

There is a further difficulty here, of going from the economic man to sectors in which he is considered to belong. In bargaining, the individual's position may be improved by threatening to break off the bargaining if he fails to get a deal better than that offered to him. Similarly, a shift in resources which affects economic man's position negatively can be rectified by his obtaining competitive resources to compensate for the shift.[1] Furthermore, economic man's income is fixed for any period of time, at which there are competing prices for goods and services. Price increases which, through the income effect reduce his purchasing power according to his present consumption patterns, can be rectified by shifting consumption to lower prices in competing products. The economic man as individual has much more flexibility in fending for himself and acts accordingly. To project individual economic behavior onto sectors is questionable because of personal tastes and opinions. The only advantage gained by sacrificing personal independence for sectoral belonging is that of strength in numbers, so that individual positions can be made forcefully and with impact.

Such force and impact may, however, not be very effective and indeed run counter to the person's requirements. For example, it may be advantageous for a union as a sector to strike for better pay and working conditions, but the individual who is both a union member and a private consumer will most likely suffer economically as the strike pay is far from sufficient to maintain his or her living standards and family support. It may be that should an agreement be reached, the increased benefits will more than compensate for the losses incurred. To this, there is absolutely no guarantee, as the printers striking against Rupert Murdoch's chain of newspapers in London in 1986 realized much to their dismay.

This does not mean that the concept of ''sectors'' is not useful; indeed, it is necessary, if only for the sake of government officials and policy makers. As it is impossible to consider the concerns of each individual in society, when discussing economics from the policy-making position it is necessary to treat people in groups formed around a common issue. To talk about the medical profession or the academic profession, the truckers and musicians—to place people into economic sectors—does not negate the differences and idiosyncrasies among the people, but discusses them with respect to their common bond, which allows them to be so sectorially classified.

In this case, if each economic sector were to operate according to its own best interest, all sectors will be at optimum and the economy will be operating at its maximum efficiency. In this situation, the need for welfare economics would be for marginal cases, such as people who are cut off from society, the ill and disabled to the extent that they are unable to provide for themselves, and those who are criminals. However, this is not the case, even under the tenets of neoclassical economics.

Whatever the styles of government, health and education have been the concerns of the public sector, that is, of the policy makers. Public health has been an issue since the Industrial Revolution and as a result of the pollution and working conditions of industrialization, standards have been set for the maintenance of public health. The education system has been subsidized by local and national governments, for the costs of construction, teachers and other infrastructure is too great to be financed privately on a large scale. Moreover, the changing technologies due to the introduction of science into industry and the fierce competition, both within a country and from abroad, require the employment of different labor conceptions, resulting in unemployment for those not trained (and perhaps, under the circumstances, not retrainable) to meet the changing demands of industry. As "economic men" these workers should seek retraining, but in the world or reality, this may not be possible. There is a correlation between the demands of industry, the skills and knowledge required for learning new techniques, and the basic education and upper levels of learning received. The absence of higher education makes the learning process that much more difficult when acquiring new skills is concerned. Those who have higher educations have the better chances of finding and holding jobs in the labor markets than those already employed and set in their ways but threatened with unemployment because of their lack of flexibility.

Indeed, the very concept of labor with respect to new technologies has been brought into question, especially with the increasing uses of robotics on assembly floors. These machines are not subject to union influence, they require no vacations or pensions, their initial costs are high but these decline over time and they are as sure in their work as the very computer programs that set their patterns. The phasing out of workers through retirement cannot compensate for newcomers to the labor force who cannot compete with the new working technologies.[2]

The neoclassical concept of economic man acting according to his own best interests brings about maximum economic efficiency has been brought into question by the contemporary economic realities. Should such a creature as the "economic man" really exist, his orientation would be different from that imposed on him by neoclassical thinking. Indeed, the very concept of "optimum" must be brought into question and its relevance for welfare economics be explained. An optimum position for one person may not be the same position for another; nor may such a considered optimum be obtainable, given prevailing economic conditions. Should such a position be obtained, however, it may reduce the position of another person. The point here is that the situation must be restated to meet our current economic realities in terms which are appropriate for our modern economy.

Hence, the concept of "economic man" requires a new formulation, one appropriate to contemporary economic reality. This is necessary for two reasons. One reason is that in the *esprit* of economics, the argument to be presented here will begin with the individual *qua* individual and then as a member of a sector or sectors, and how, in both instances the individual performs in the economy. The second reason is that as the individual is the basic "unit," as it were, of economic activity, the individual acting on what is best for himself or herself, still holds, but is expanded to relate to information systems and his or her position with respect to these systems. It is on the basis of these relevant systems that the individual decides and acts.

In our contemporary situation the individual acting in the economic sphere is not the "economic man" in the neoclassical sense. As a member of contemporary society, his or her economic decision making must necessarily be influenced by his or her standard of living, occupation and family size, and expectations from decisions taken. Therefore, instead of using the term "economic man" with its neoclassical connotations, the term "contemporary individual" will be used in this discussion.

The contemporary individual as economic decision-maker is rational, operating in all economic circumstances in a manner that, given the unique conditions and the knowledge available, seeks optimum utility according to his or her understanding and liquidity positions. The contemporary individual thus deals with information, which may be scanty—in which case the choice may be to avoid decisions—or detailed—in which case the decision to relate to the information or avoid it will be made with a degree of assurance corresponding to the levels of information.

Thus, information comes in three forms. It may be informal and loose, scanty and far from complete, in which case it will most likely be set aside and avoided in the decision-making process. Information may be detailed and systematic and therefore available to the individual as an information system that can be analyzed, evaluated with respect to alternatives, and from which conclusions can be drawn. Or, thirdly, it may be gathered by the contemporary individual from sources which seem unrelated but that are put together by the individual for his or her own use and acted upon, by either avoiding it or by accepting it within the decision-making process.

What is certain is that whichever form the information takes, it must relate to the contemporary individual as decision maker. For this to be the case, two types of information systems must be considered: the closed and the open system. It must be stated here that a system closed in time t may be open in time $t+1$, but this is not a reflexive relationship, for an open system will always remain so until it ceases to function. This is because, by its very openness, its information is dynamic and altering, according to the situation to which it relates.

## ON UTILITY AND ENTROPY

The economic information available to the contemporary individual, be it in an open, closed, or informal system, depends on the objective conditions of the economic area to which it relates. The utility of this information, however, depends on the quality and content of the information, *and* the individual's subjective interpretation of the information. The individual's interpretation may be affected by his or her peers, or by his or her economic aspirations. As the contemporary individual is the basic economic "unit," because of his or her decisions, taken in summation of the total decisions and their effects on the economy, policies are made on both sectorial and political levels.

As the information's utility depends on on objective information and its subjective interpretation, information—even in the most rigidly closed systems— has different utility schedules for $n>1$ persons. This, of course, leads to the ordering of utility schedules for the individuals involved. These schedules are expressions of preference for the various information systems and indicate their utilities and entropies respectively. However, just as information is both objectively and subjectively interpreted, so then are utility and entropy to be considered.

A closed information system is one that is bounded by a time signature and is isolated from the influence of data which could otherwise alter its contents. Any further data added to the closed systems are therefore redundant and unnecessary and the system is consistent and thus without ambiguities. For example, on a certain day a transaction occurs in which a specific sum of money is exchanged between two identified individuals each representing a firm, with the money exchanged concluding a production and manufacturing merger. Investors who have access to the information on the merger can determine the utility of investing in the new firm. This information is closed in the sense that the merger is completed with the strategies of cooperation and continuation having been formulated prior to the merger being completed. At the time of closure any further information is redundant and of no value in the decision-making processes for investors.

With the closed information system being time-signature-bound and isolated from data which could otherwise alter its contents, the system's utility, nevertheless, varies from one contemporary individual to another. Utility depends on the system's objective probability and the individual's subjective probability. For the information system $\underline{S}_t = [s_1, s_2, \ldots s_n]_t$ where $\underline{S}_t$ is the system *in toto* in time *t*, and $s_1, s_2, \ldots, s_n$ are the individual statements composing the system.

The system's objective utility is assessed by setting each of its statements in turn within the maximum and minimum boundaries of utility and entropy respectively so that for statement $s_1$, $0 < s_1 < 1$, meaning that the information statement in question lies between the utility and entropy boundaries and its position with respect to each of these limits determines its viability within the system in general. Thus, for the system, $0 < \underline{S}_t < 1$ is valid for all closed information systems for the duration of the time signature stated.

According to the neoclassical theories already discussed in this work, the assessment of utility depends on economic man's preferences as measured by his indifference curves (Edgeworth), or his comparative welfare position (Pareto), or by his ability to employ the substitution effect (Slutsky). For our contemporary individual, however, the emphasis is placed on both individual preferences— shared with the neoclassical school *and* the system's internal utility as determined by the probabilities of its statements. From the individual's position, such an information system must not only have high internal probability, but must also relate to his or her own preferences. In the example above, for instance, the decision-making individual may be acquainted with the people involved in the merger and the type of product which will result from the agreement. Although this individual does not doubt the information systems' content, he or she may be skeptical concerning the merger yielding a marketably viable product, this skepticism based on the background knowledge of the firms and their representatives. The individual may therefore assign a low subjective probability rating to the information statements, indicating that in his or her opinion the transaction will not be profitable when production and marketing begin. Another person may have a different opinion, while possessing the same background information about the people and the firms, and may assign a high subjective probability rating *in toto* and place his or her liquidity at the disposal of the newly formed company.

An incomplete system, that is, an open system, is one in which one or both types of conditions occur. Either the system has been "infiltrated" by information elements or other systems, or there is a lack of sufficient data within the system to either reduce or eliminate the uncertainty concerning the validity and utility of the information necessary to make certain specific decisions. Since the system is open, it is by definition a system that is incomplete and thus not subject to a bounding time-signature. Should a time-signature be placed on the system, it is merely for clarification of the specific time under consideration.

For example, consider the system $A$ in which are incorporated the elements $a_1$, $a_2$, ..., $a_n$.,.$b_1$, $b_2$, $c_3$, $c_4$ of information systems $B$ and $C$ (it makes no difference if $B$ and $C$ are closed or open). Such an information system exists for a firm prior to the finance minister's announcement of the proposed annual budget, when the investor's decision to place his or her money at the firm's disposal must take into account not only the firm's present condition but also the possible effects the budget may have after its presentation. This information contains the firm's position, information from other systems, and because it is open and the time is prior to the budget, also included are projections into the future based on expected budgetary considerations. An open information system is subject to conflicting information statements and therefore to contradictions. Both the firm's managers and investors are confronted with an open-ended information system that contains a degree of uncertainty determined by the utilities of the known information statements as they are evaluated, and by the uncertainty of those that will enter the system at a future date.

For the closed system, the contemporary individual relates to this system with respect to the system's probability *in toto*. This is because while each statement in the system is unique in that it expresses a specific point, and as there are no inconsistencies nor contradictions within the system, each statement depends on the other for meaning. The system's probability depends on the probability of each of its statements (i.e., elements). As there are two probability considerations—one objective, one subjective—the objective probability refers to facts, the information as presented, and is available for examination by those to whom it is directed. The subjective probability of the contemporary individual is just as important, because this pertains to the understanding of the information's viability concerning his or her own specific requirements for the duration of the information's pertinence. Thus, a closed information system may be of utility for some people and be of little or no utility for others in the same sector or peer group to which the information is directed. For some, the information may be of utility; for others, it may be entropic, even though its objective probability approaches maximum utility. It is on the basis of the subjective probability that contemporary individuals order their utilities.

For the open-ended information system, the individual's situation is more complicated. Not all information is available, and the openness prevents it from being accumulated sufficiently. Moreover, the amount of information possessed by one person may not be the same that is understood by another. Contradictions cannot be ruled out and information considered to be subjectively relevant may be objectively entropic. This difficulty is compounded by the situation of the lack of information available to some but considered by others, thereby providing different objective interpretations and subjective utilities.

Hence, the difficulty arises when the statements an individual does possess stand in contradiction with those he or she has sanctioned within the system. Another individual may possess the same statements as the first individual and be in possession of additional statements that allow the discarding of the first set of statements as being untenable; yet, these are the very statements the first person accepted as viable and of utility. Also, probabilities are often assigned to combinations of statements, for they provide fuller expression of expectations. Taken in combination, these statements may be accepted by some while rejected by others because their recombinations with still different statements provide contradictions.

Nevertheless, on the basis of available information, the contemporary individual must make choices and assign subjective utility schedules. The purpose of this assignment is to relate the information presented to the reality as it is understood, thereby bringing the subjective interpretation as close as possible to the objective probability so that judgment based on the information, is made.

The difficulties of subjective assessment can be minimized by assigning boundaries of verisimilitude according to expectations and to allow these boundaries to represent the utilities and entropies on which choices are made. With the upper boundary designated by 1 and the lower boundary by 0, these are limits that can never be reached, but can be approached. In the extreme, the upper boundary signifies the complete verisimilitude between the information system as understood and available (that is, either closed and complete, or open and incomplete) as a linguistic or symbolic structure describing the situation, so that this language corresponds as best as possible to reality. The lower limit signifies that no relationship exists whatsoever between the information system's language and the reality it purports to describe. For each decision maker, each information system lies between these boundaries and may be either stationary or fluctuating; the system's position within these limits determines its state of utility or entropy. By analyzing the system within these limits, the decision maker combines the highly subjective interpretation and its strong influence of personal expectations, with the analysis of reality and the system's language.

For the closed system, the determination of an information system's utility or entropy is an uncomplicated process. Because of the system's closure, the individual confronts a situation in which the information system either describes its reality accurately or fails to do so. Because the system's time-signature states the period of the system's presumed validity, this can be assessed with respect to the domain of reality to which the system relates. Because each of the system's statements can be broken down into its components, it can be matched with the specific aspect of reality to which it relates. On this basis each statement is subjected to the utility or entropy measurements, to determine the statement's relation to reality. After deriving a conclusion regarding the validity of each statement—and because there are ambiguous or contradictory statements—the system can be taken *in toto* to be placed between the limits of 0 and 1. While this rating determines its objective status, the contemporary individual has to assess his or her utility with respect to this rating. His or her expectations may have presented attitudes not allowed for by the information system, so that the system's rating may allow for revised attitudes, or expectations may have been reinforced and placed on firmer ground than before. In any case, the information system's position has been established with respect to utility or entropy as well as with respect to the reality to which its language intends to describe. The individual must then act on the basis of this knowledge.

The open-ended information system is more complicated that the closed system because contradictory statements may exist and the information of other systems, not necessarily relevant, may intrude. The time-signature placed on this system takes on added significance because it isolates a dynamic system, thereby allowing some control over it. The system $\underline{S}$ in time t may or may not be equal in the quantity and quality of statements and the import of their content to $\underline{S}_{t_2}$; this can be determined only by analysis, given the dynamic nature of the system. The situation is complicated further because a statement existing in both $t_1$ and $t_2$ may or may not have the same meaning because new statements in the system may have altered its nuances. Because of the influence of new statements, those in the original $\underline{S}$ may in $\underline{S}_{t_2}$ be found to be contradictory, These conditions require that the system be broken down and analyzed to assess which statements are necessary for the system and which are superfluous and can therefore be eliminated without affecting the system's objective utility—a process that may entail breaking down specific statements and reformulating them so that the troublesome parts are removed.

As for both closed and open information systems, objective utility determines the extent to which a system provides an accurate description of reality. This requires assessing the system's probability for its relationship to reality. Probability depends on the system's information content and is represented by the letter $\bar{I}$; with the expression $\bar{I}/_{st}$ representing the probability rating of $\underline{S}$ at the stated time $t$. $\bar{I}/\underline{S}_t$ is the general expression of the probability $\underline{S}\bar{i}_s = P(S_t)$, where $\underline{S}_s$ means the probability of $\underline{S}$ and where $P(S_t)$ represents the probabilities $s_1$, $s_2$, . . . ,$s_n$ statements of the information system. $\underline{S}_t$'s utility is thus assessed by focusing on each statement and determining its relationship to the reality for which it was formulated. The information system—and its utility rating between the limits of 0 and 1—is thus at the disposal of the contemporary individual as an objective perspective for consideration.

The probability of an open-ended information system's statements tends to vary over time with $\underline{S}_{t_2}$ being equal or not equal to $\underline{S}_{t2}$, in both information content and objective utility. Hence, $\underline{S}$'s utility must be revalued when acting on its information at different times. Moreover, because there is a tendency for the open-ended system to vary over time, there is a chance that the decision taken at one time will yield effects not considered at that time.

Such is the situation when the individual invests in shares. A firm presents itself as a dynamic organization bringing diversified products into the market, adjusting its product lines according to the market's needs and using its excess capital for retooling and engaging in innovative and imitative projects.[3] When becoming acquainted with the firm's internal situation, as stated in its prospectus, this, together with the information concerning the firm's performance on the stock exchange, enables the individual to decide if investing in the firm is sound. As the firm is bound by the time-signature set down by the prospectus the firm's future share prices and future profit-taking are not set in the prospectus and cannot be determined. This is complicated further by the possibility of a new government policy that will bear on the firm's activities and the status of its shares. Or, internal difficulties may seriously affect the share values. The bound information is complete at the time, but the firm's total picture is incomplete, and it is the system on which the individual has to act. As the system changes, the individual's calculations must be revised, with each calculation taken as if the system is bound even though its content fluctuates. The time signature is placed by the individual on the basis of the information at his or her disposal, while the reality is in fluctuation.

Two individuals confronted with a closed information system may choose to act on the system, thereby contributing to the dynamics that the system generates. The system may also be rejected as decisions in favor of another or other systems are made. The degree of objective uncertainty is greater in the open system than with the closed system, for the closed system is static while the open system is dynamic and fluid. Thus, the individual treats both systems as closed in order to study their probabilities to assess their objective utilities. Both systems have time-signatures when the decision is made, so that when assessing their probabilities, the individual takes into account his or her objective utility and makes the choice with regard to the desired consequences.

In the sense that the future consequences appear to be those which the individual seeks, subjective utility reflects the projected results that the individual desires. Basing the consideration of the present against the projected future, the degrees of uncertainty are related directly to the extent determined by the objective utility. Subjective utility is derived from and determines the individual's ordering preferences—but more on this in chapter 7. It can be stated here that personal preference ordering derives from the information system, which is judged with respect to alternative systems, with the consequence of the future uncertainty very important.

At this point, it must be stated that the ordering of preferences requires that each alternative system under consideration be ranked, first with regard to its objective utility and then in terms of personal subjective utility. The significance of this ordering for welfare economics is that government programs and business operations are information systems, the objective utility of which can be determined within the time-signatures prevalent for their durations and with current economic issues considered. Their subjective rankings, however, present a different set of difficulties because government planners and businesses cannot undertake the subjective assessments of the individuals involved; nor can they delineate with any degree of exactitude the extent to which populations will be affected. There are other ways for determining the influences of these programs and these will be discussed in chapters 8 through 11.

It must be noted here, however, that there is a relationship between the subjective utility as determined by the individual and the objective utility as determined by the assessment of the system's probability. Should the individual act in favor of the system, then for this person the relationship is positive; a rejection of the system means that the individual finds the relationship negative. Economic activity is generated by the quantity of positive relationships among individuals and information systems, for by utilizing these systems, individuals give life to programs, money is invested, and purchases are made. Those information systems which are inactive soon succumb to entropy.

The positive or negative relationship depends on the individual's objectives and the system's content. Should the person have an established goal and the information system fails to provide sufficient inducement toward the satisfaction of this goal, then the person will avoid the system. However, the person most likely will have established modified goals in case his or her best goal proves unrealistic with regard to the available information systems. Again, this requires an ordering of preferences on the basis of utility and the person will act on that system that provides the best future situation as determined by goal modification, with this revised goal becoming the best case.

Schematically, the objective-subjective relationship can be stated thus: $EuS_t = F(P,\underline{S})$, that is, the expected or subjective utility of information $\underline{S}_t$ is a function of $\underline{S}$ with regard to its objective probability. With $\underline{S}_t$'s objective utility approaching the maximum limit of 1, there is no necessary bearing on $EuS_t$, on the expected utility of $\underline{S}_t$, because expectation is strictly subjective and the objective $\underline{S}_t$ may yield consequences unwanted or considered irrelevant by the contemporary individual. Hence, for one individual concerned with the specific information system, $E_u\underline{S}_t = [F(P,\underline{S})_{t+1}]$ 1, while for another person concerned with the same person concerned with the same system, $E_u\underline{S}_t = [F(P,S)t] \rightarrow_{1cb} 0$, with the subscript "$t+1$" referring to the next time period which would occur when the investment would be made. Nor are these subjective assessments permanent over time, for they are often altered over time with the acquisition of greater understanding and/or shifts in subjective preferences. While $\underline{S}_t$ may have been rejected in $t_1$ because of low subjective utility, in a different time period $t_n$ ($n > 1$), the subjective reordering and possible shifts in $\underline{S}_t$'s information content where $\underline{S}$ is open-ended may result in the system's receiving a very high subjective ordering position.

With regard to the decisions based on objective and subjective utility, the sum total of these decisions at any one time can be considered the sum total of economic activity for that time. Moreover, the difficulties of the open-ended information systems over time result in the reduction of their utilities, as they are eventually reduced by the impacts on them by decision making for other individuals. Acting on a system brings about changes in its information content as, for example, investing in shares drives up their prices or entering into a highly competitive market reduces the profits of other businesses in the market. This reduction of utility is entropy.[4]

In its objective sense, entropy is the measurement of disinformation in an information system. It illustrates the extent to which the system's elements, its statements, do not relate to their objective realities, thereby providing a basis for subjective discrimination and choice. Symbolized by the letter "H" the entropy of a system $\underline{S}$ indicates the extent to which some or all of $\underline{S}$'s statements no longer correspond to the realities for which they were designed and intended. Just as utility is measured between the upper and lower boundaries, so is entropy, and thus it is the negation of utility. Where the utility of $\underline{S} \rightarrow 1$, the entropy of $\underline{S} \rightarrow 0$ and *vice versa*.

As the closed system designates a reality relevant only for the period of time stated by its time signature, the only way this system can be threatened with entropy is if it is revised and its reality therefore altered. For example, the system that states facts 1, 2, . . . , n, is bound by a certain future date. If one or more of its statements (elements) is altered to correspond to the assigned future date, this system can become entropic. If one of its factual statements is altered because of a change in the reality it describes, the entire system is brought into a decline in objective utility rating; this, however, can be rectified by a reformulation of the statement in light of the changed reality. This is a technical adjustment, for the system has become objectively entropic because of the shift in reality making it irrelevant.

On course, it is possible that such a shift in reality could be so serious and extreme that the information system *per se* would no longer have any utility and would have to be abandoned completely. In the merger example cited earlier, should one of the managers suddenly pass away, bringing instability to the firm, the merger and the plans for joint production would most likely be placed on hold and may even be terminated at least until the managerial board could instate an acceptable replacement and redraft the merger plans to the other firm's satisfaction. There is no time signature attached here and objective entropy has replaced utility, thereby breaking down the information system entirely.

For the open information system, objective analysis must pertain to $\underline{S}$'s utility being dependent on the probability of its statements relating to reality so that the information $\bar{I}$ of $\underline{S}$ equals the probability of $\underline{S}$ being relevant, that is, $\bar{I}/\underline{S}t_1$ $= P/\underline{S}_{t_1}$ , with $\underline{S}$ at $t_1$ containing a set number of statements as determined by its time signature. If the probability assessment indicates that there is absolutely no relationship between the set of statements and their precribed realities, then $\bar{I} = H$, and the entire system is devoid of utility. Of course, should the probabilities of the system's elements correspond totally to their realities during the period of time, then $\bar{I} = -H$ and the system enjoys full objective utility.

The either-or situation in which either utility or entropy exists, is the best of all possible worlds and thus is difficult, if not most times impossible, to achieve. As information systems are formulated to correspond to their specific realities, it is unlikely that they will be either totally irrelevant or absolutely perfect, even after a reasonable period of usage over time. More than likely, some degree of entropy will set into the system because of slight shifts in reality, even though the system is stated carefully before a time signature is placed on it. Such is the case when statements no longer define their realities.

However, while absolute utility is almost impossible to achieve for a bound system, absolute entropy for the duration of its time limit is equally difficult. It is only when a majority of a system's statements show an unexpected lack of relevance that the system should be considered sufficiently entropic and abandoned and an alternative system (or systems) should be sought.

Objective determination of an open system's level of entropy is achieved by assessing the probability of a system's statements with respect to the reality for which they were formulated. For example, $\underline{S}_{t_1}$ has utility approaching the maximum limit when stated—were this not the case the system would not have been formulated as is—and over time periods 1 and 2, changes occur in either the reality, or in $\underline{S}$'s content, or perhaps in both. As the assessment of $\underline{S}$ for utility or entropy requires the evaluation of its statements, it may be found that these statements contain glaring inadequacies which can be corrected within the system or cast out forthright. It is likely that these inadequacies are due to the incorporation of statements over $t_1 - t_2$ that have better definitive relationships to their realities; these provide little difficulty and once removed or corrected, $\underline{S}$'s utility will be strengthened.

The difficulties arise with those statements whose subtle discrepencies affect seriously $\underline{S}$'s utility and are not yet subject to alteration because any alteration would result in $\underline{S}$'s being drastically changed, perhaps to the extent of bringing the entire information system to a state of serious entropy, with the possibility of dissolution. This is due to the culminating influence of shifting statements and/or changing realities, rendering $\underline{S}$ as such of little utility. For example, a firm may set out to undertake a production project and thus establish its information system to attract investors and encourage consumption of the product. There may exist discrepancies between the production plans and the production processes, because of either human inadequacies or mechanical failures. The consequence is that production projects are not quite met and the planned economics of production not realized. These discrepancies will not be noticed until the feedback from production and consumption is analyzed. The result is that the information system moves into an entropic condition with its utility declining. If caught in time, such a movement to entropy will not be serious and $\underline{S}$ can be revised to cope with the actual conditions prevailing in the production processes and the markets. The information system can therefore be revised with the entropy temporarily removed so that $\underline{S}_{t_1} \neq \underline{S}_{t_2}$, with $\underline{S}_{t_2} \rightarrow 1$.

The dynamics of production and marketing are such, however, that new discrepancies will arise that are not accounted for by $\underline{S}t_2$, so that over time, this system too will be rendered entropic. The reconstruction process continues until a point in time is reached that the entropic condition that finally evolves will render the entire system of utility not worth the effort or economy to reconstruct still further. For example, increasing competition may lower the firm's profit-cost ratio to the extent that any "new" changes in the product's composition would not offset the costs involved due to declining sales. Market saturation may be then so extensive that the product line can be maintained only at break-even costs and profits or at worst case, at a loss, no matter what the possible alterations that can be made on the product with the intention of gaining a competitive edge. The decision must be made then whether to keep the product at its current profit-cost ratio, maintain advertising at a level sufficient to hold sales in light of the strenuous competition, or to close down production and allocate the resources otherwise. Should the choice be to maintain the product, then $\underline{S}$ is acted upon to remain stable within its utility boundaries at worst case, and to move it toward maximum utility at best-case. Should the product be abandoned, then entropy is immediately *introduced* and the system is intentionally rendered beyond reconstruction. The latter decision is final, while the former still preserves the product's dynamic which will remain active until either a decision is taken to phase it out, or until consumer demand and the economy's general dynamics no longer provide support for the product but direct resources to other enterprises.

Discrepancies exist also as a direct result of the information system. For example, revised production plans, no matter how slight the revision, result in difficulties not considered previously by the system. Different production techniques instituted to gain economics of cost will incur such difficulties as bottlenecks in moving the product in its directed markets. This is because of the conflict between the original plans and the revised version which takes time to work out. Another difficulty is the reallocation of resources required for the revised version, together with their redistribution according to previous and future priorities. A further difficulty, especially in highly competitive markets but also existing in new markets, is that usually the revision results in cost reductions which are passed on to the consumer, reductions which the markets are unable to absorb nevertheless because of already committed consumer liquidity. Further, as prices are reduced to move stock, aggregate demand may be scheduled so that profits are reduced more than planned (entropy) so that the viability of the project becomes questionable. While lower production costs for the same quantity yield result in lower costs to the consumer, the aggregate demand must warrant a reasonable profit; otherwise, the project will be abandoned. In this case, output advantages and cost reductions are restricted. Should the change be implemented and the difficulties be overcome, this would generate similar changes in close competitors' projects and initiate entropy into their programs when hitherto they were successful, even to the extent of taking competition into account.

Even though open-ended information systems are fixed temporarily by their time signatures, they may be subjected to entropy at various levels of intensity at all times. This is because the realities of their situations as defined by the systems change resulting in *de facto* probability measurements or the system's statements and the areas to which they relate requiring alteration. While the time signatures indicate the system's durations, as well as allowing for the indication of their positions with respect to utility and entropy, as time changes, so do these positions, but with respect to the events that occur. Only through analysis can the extent of these changes be understood, and the reasons for them comprehended. The measurements of the systems' positions is taken periodically, especially when there is reason to suspect that disinformation has entered the systems. Nevertheless, their objective positions are changing as a result in the alterations in their defined areas, alterations that can be detected only by proper assessment.

Unlike objective entropy, subjective entropy is not necessarily reflexive, that is, not in response to real changes in the area of internal structuring. For example, an information system may be approaching maximum objective utility, yet be considered entropic by an individual with a different ordering for the area that the system defines; the individual may choose to work with an alternative system that has a lower utility rating and thus a higher risk, rather than a system with a higher rating, providing that the lower rated system is not in serious trouble. As the contemporary individual is considered rational economically in his or her preference ordering, and although his or her reasons may not be understood by others for this ordering, his or her choice will not be for a system whose entropy is threatening the system's intergrity. There are cases where, subjectively, the individual may prefer not to act at all, to wait and see what happens over a self-set time span, in which case his or her behavior is as if all other systems are entropic even though their objective ratings indicate otherwise. The latter case is both personal and rational and depends on the individual's liquidity position and his or her understanding of the possibilities in the time he or she considers significant for waiting and for acting.

Subjective entropy is therefore due to personal assessment and depends on the ordering of preferences with respect to the psychological aspect of expectation. Expectation is related to reality by the understanding of current events and how these events may influence the future, so that preferences to work with an information system or opting not to are reality-based to the individual's best understanding. Hence, there is no contradiction in the situation where $\underline{S}_{o} \to 1$ and $\underline{S}_{s} \to 1$, (the subscripts O and S meaning objective and subjective). Furthermore, $\underline{S}_{s_{tn}}$ may have a very high utility rating, with $t_n$ being a time in the assigned future, beyond the present time.

Unlike their objective counterparts, subjective utility and entropy cannot be analyzed with respect to the probabilities of various information statements as they relate to their respective areas. Entropy in its subjective form may be due to personal whims or values and tastes, or improper or incomplete understanding of the information, or an assigned period of waiting for alternative systems that are expected to be of greater utility but will not materialize when the future is finally reached. As there is no real accounting objectively for personal tastes and preferences information systems provide expression for these idiosyncrasies that economic activity seeks to control and channel, by focusing on consumer products, on investment opportunities and production projects.

Subjective entropy, nevertheless, also has its impact on the direction economic activity takes. Since the decision to operate within one information system is taken at the expense of using other possible systems—the decision restricted by personal and/or corporate liquidity—the impact made by working with a system influences the system's statements and altering their relationships to the area realities. Rejecting a system because of its subjective entropy will affect the system objectively in a negative manner. For the closed system, this rejection inhibits the realization of the system's dynamics, which would certainly be that much more activated by the influences of the individual's participation. The closed system, defining a specific set of circumstances that are valid for the period indicated by the time signature, will undergo a decline in objective utility if ignored because of subjective entropy by the populace to whom it is directed. This case is usually extreme but the extent of objective entropy as far as the system's relevance is concerned to its populace will be determined by the extent of response of those willing to opt for the system. A system without sufficient takers, no matter how efficient it is internally, will collapse.

The open system is in a different situation, because it is formulated to relate to an area which cannot be closed by the system's statements for a specific period of time. Dynamics within the delineated area require the system's statements to be revised or discarded as need be. New statements will also have to be formulated, and the existing statements of utility as well as the reformulated statements will be retained as long as they conform to the general probability rating of the system, thereby maintaining the system's overall utility. In this sense, the system's dynamics depend on the populace that works with it. For example, consider the extreme case of an open-ended system without anyone working with it; the system will soon collapse because of the objective entropy generated by the changing area for which it was formulated. Subjective entropy, the preference ordering that allows the populace to avoid the system, will therefore bring about objective entropy and the system's dissolution. The extreme case is unlikely in both situations because managers and business directors are realistic people who are not likely to formulate systems that they think will not attract. These examples do show, however, that the extent of objective entropy is dependent to a large degree on subjective entropy, as the system is unused.

The qualifier, "in this sense," is important, for it indicates one way that subjective entropy influences objective entropy. In the closed information system, subjective entropy influences objective entropy by also acting on the system before its time signature expires, thereby disrupting its objective utility. For example, a system states that on a certain date, conditions $x$, $y$, and $z$, will occur. A disagreement ensues over the accepted system's terminology and statements, after it has been formulated. One individual decides to act to render the system entropic before the other people involved realize this action; the dissenting person acts to prevent one of the system's conditions—say $y$—from being fulfilled. Since the closed system is so constructed that all its statements have to hold together and relate to their realities exactly as expressed, altering the $y$-statement will bring down the entire system. Subjective entropy can thus inspire action that generates objective entropy and brings about the program's collapse, the cancellation of the deal, or whatever the situation may be.

For the open information system, the situation is different. Assuming that the open system is at maximum utility so that no objective entropy has entered the system, an individual may disagree with the specific relationship between a statement and its reality, resulting in his or her changing the statement without the proper consideration of the new statement's probability function. This will bring the statement farther away from its previously existing probability rating. Over time, enough dynamics will be generated to require changes in the statements—a process which, as it continues, will bring the system into an entropic condition and its natural decline. But tampering with a statement in a system of high utility, to suit the individual's personal preferences, brings the system down faster than the natural decline by generating entropy prematurely.

It is assumed that the contemporary individual participating in economic activity, whether on the production side or the consumption side or in the auxiliary businesses that support productive industries and supply consumers, acts rationally according to his or her preference ordering. On the production side, the profit motivation and the search for alternative projects is rational and the individual relates to economic events and acts on them according to his or her own best interests. As those people in the auxiliary businesses rely on prime producers and manufacturers, they must also provide the best services at competitive prices while maintaining efficient operations to keep their customers and continue to maintain profit levels. The consumers, often considered irrational are approached with subliminal advertising and/or sheep-like behavior initiated by others in higher socioeconomic groups, purchase according to their wants, needs, and liquidity schedules. The consumers are, in fact, the very manufacturers, business people and employees and their families who live and act according to their budgets imposed by the heads of their respective households.

Rational individuals of course have their preferences and subjective utilities and entropies, and influence, and in turn are influenced, by their understandings of their information systems and their realities as they are defined. The economist must deal with decision making, be it based on subjective, objective, or combined considerations. However, just as their personal realities change, their information systems must also be altered; on the basis of these systems, choices are ordered and decisions are made.

## THE DYNAMICS OF THE INFORMATION SYSTEM

It is necessary to consider further the closed and open information systems with respect to their required alterations because of the impact of entropy. It is impossible to discuss the utility option without taking into account entropy as the dissolution of utility and without examining the methods of repair. These alterations serve to maintain systems' integrities until they are beyond repair and abandoned or until they are replaced by systems lacking in entropy and capable of performing as stated.

The elements in both the closed and open systems define and delineate the realities to which they refer; these elements are therefore information statements about the realities for which they are constructed and, because of the definition and delineation, they also tell what these realities do not contain. These information statements, or elements, are isomorphic, with each element referring to only that aspect in the area pertaining to its reality, the scope of which is contained only within the element. This is a reflexive relationship in the sense that as each element relates to only its specific particle of reality, the particle relates only to its unique element. When first established, these systems lack the difficulties of ambiguity and of metalanguages and metainformation system relationships that usually from through use.

System $\underline{S}$ therefore contains the information elements and the reality elements for which these information elements are constructed. Stated another way, $\underline{S}$ if and only if R, with "R" being the defined reality. Hence, $\underline{S}_{to} = [\underline{S},R]_{to}$ with $t_o$ being the time of origin and with the elements of $\underline{S}$ corresponding isomorphically and reflexively with the particles in R.

In the closed information system, entropy sets in only when the reality is altered and the elements no longer retain their isomorphism, so that the reflexitivity is destroyed. For example, the city government floats a municipal bond to finance a specific project that it defines and for which a specific recipient class of people is targeted. The project is explained, with all the costing and intended benefits expressed. This occurs in time $t_1$. The difficulty is that no matter how much control may exist over the costing processes and the recipient class in advertising, the factor of uncertainty during the time-span may be low but never eliminated. In $t_2$ during the time period from $t_1$ to $t_n$ $(n>1)$, the costing may be found to be underestimated or there may be external conditions, such as a sharp fall in the stock and commodities markets resulting in reduced liquidity, resulting in external objective entropy over which the project designers have no control and which render the project entropic. Or, in light of the prospectus, other projects by competitors are formulated with the result that the targeted populace places its liquidity among the competitors instead of with the original project exclusively. Should the project be continued, in view of these and other such circumstances beyond the city's control, the information presented must be restructured to relate to the new realities. The sources of this information change is not important here; what is relevant is to note how the change is made.

Stating R' as the new reality, system $\underline{S}$ must also be altered. Consider the relationship $s_d r$, that is, information element $\underline{s}$ defines and delineates the reality r. When r is altered to become r' its defining element must also be altered to become $\underline{s}'$, because the shift from r to r' renders $\underline{s}$ inadequate, thereby rendering the relationship entropic. Entropy can be reversed by combining $\underline{s}$ with relevant information and by casting out that part of $\underline{s}$ no longer adequate without destroying the general import of the defining element. Hence, with $\underline{s}$ altered to $\underline{s}'$ and with the general import still intact, r' is covered and the relationship still retains its viability.

What has been considered here is a slight shift in R with only a single r element affected. Should there be a radical shift in the reality for a closed system so that the majority of the elements are affected either $\underline{S}$ will be abandoned leaving the entire system entropic, or a new relationship between $\underline{S}$ and R will be constructed in which those parts of the previous system whose viability was not affected being maintained while constructing relationships to correspond to the changed reality. However, should such a reconstruction be considered not worthwhile because of uncertainty, then further research and planning which are unprofitable with respect to the project will be abandoned and no attempt at reconstruction will be undertaken.

While in the closed system only the reality is subject to alteration, in the open system both the defining elements and their realities can alter. Because of the system's openness, the likelihood for entropy at any given moment is greater than in the closed system. When entropy does attack the open system, however, it is usually not as devastating as it is with with the closed system, because its openness gives it the ability to expand and thus it has a greater ability to salvage itself than has its closed counterpart.

Three reasons for entropy must be considered, First, there may be a change in the reality of the situation defined by the r-elements. As $\underline{S}$ contains the elements of $\underline{S}$ and R so that $R = [\underline{S}/\underline{S}_d R_t]$. As both $\underline{S}$ and R are open-ended, the definitive relationship holds only for those elements bound by the time signature. At time $t_o$, $n$ relationships exist and at time $t_1$ the e-th particle in n is altered due to the reality shift of this particle, which alters $e$ but not to the extent that $e$'s identity is totally destroyed. Because of this alteration, the defining element must also be altered, but with the open ended system, care must be taken not to interfere with the other relationships. This situation is similar to, but not identical with, the changes that occur in the closed system. The difference here is one of nuances, but it is significant because changes in the reality of the particle in question can come about from changes in other relationships in the system. This change may be due to improved information in the reality that may threaten the entire relationship. It may be due to a deterioration in a particle aspect of reality and this requires a better definitive element. It may also be due to the merger of two or more reality particles due to information that eliminates the nuances responsible for the necessity of separating elements for definition and demarcation. The specific instances of change must be met with the appropriate alterations in the defining elements and their corresponding realities if the information system's viability is to be is to be maintained and entropy eliminated.

An example of this is a country that has a national insurance, that is, social security, scheme initiated by the government and distributed by its welfare agency. The terms for receiving social security are well defined and the rates of payments are clearly delineated according to salary, the amount paid into the fund during a person's working years, and the years of retirement. The isomorphic and reflexive definitive reality-statements are clearly stated and delineated, with government policy bearing de facto on this system. Where the system is subject to alteration due to cyclic changes and resulting unemployment which diminishes security payments, either the terms of the system are affected, or alternative systems—such as unemployment insurance—are activated to maintain the system as best as possible until employment is reinstated and payments into social security can continue. The system is maintained due to alterations in the reality that are compensated for by other schemes. Also, the government can invest in this system even though payments are reduced by the public, thereby altering the system's reality to correspond to the conditions while maintaining its viability.

The second reason for entropy in the open information system is the improvement in the quality of the defining elements and the manner in which this improvement brings about a break in the isomorphic and reflexive relationships,

The consequence is that a statement $s_d r$, that is, that $\underline{s}$ defines $r$ if and only if $r$ is defined by $\underline{s}$, so that changes in the defining element, no matter how small, must be met by changes in the reality particle, if the isomorphic and reflexive relationships are to be maintained. Due to a greater understanding of the problem over the the time period, $\underline{s}$ may change, while the reality particle remains stable. The defining language, being sharpened, opens new vistas for dealing with reality. When the proposals for establishing national insurance were considered, the ramifications of the social security system may not have been throughly explored or understood. As the dynamics of the system are worked out in reality, further understanding of the situation requires some redefinition of the problem; differences in the nuances in the system's operation, such as the further classifications and changes in levying payments into the system and the distinctions of retirement age to gain the benefits, have to be revised, while the reality for which the system was constructed remains unchanged.

The third reason for entropy in the open information system is that changes occur in the defining elements, due to a refinement of information *and* in the realities, independent of, and not corresponding to, changes in the defining elements. For this condition, appropriate adjustments have to be made on both sides of the definition if the relationships in question, and ultimately the system, is to be maintained. An innovative policy for dealing with unemployment captures the imaginations of the citizenry, for example, and thereby defines the problem of unemployment in all its nuances. Claims made for the policy's success are substantiated by the rate of unemployment being reduced fairly substantially. A refinement of the policy in light of its success leads to a further refinement in the conditions for which the policy was formulated. The reality has been altered by the policy, and for the policy to remain operable it must also undergo sufficient alteration to cope with the new reality. As such changes in reality are not radical— with unemployment changing in form and in classification, so that some types of unemployment can be employed through training and inspired with motivation—the system's funding and restructuring are to be undertaken to correspond to the new reality. The system is preserved and the reality changed, with entropy on both sides of the definition removed.

In both the closed and open systems, entropy is at its most destructive when these systems are unable to handle changes in their defined realities through the reconstruction of their terms and statements. In the long run, the consequences of entropy are either the reconstruction of a system until its original intention and purpose no longer remains, or the retention of the system with as much modification as necessary until a better system is formulated. Social security systems are in need of reconstruction when living standards no longer correspond to the conditions for which the security system was originated; our economy is built to have cyclical fluctuations, but the conditions similar to those of the Great Depression will never exist. One possibility for dealing with this is to reconstruct the system to adjust to differences over time in living standard; another possibility is to maintain ad hoc adjustments until a revised system, one dealing with contemporary economic problems such as shifts in production orientation because of foreign competition, and inflation and its effects on market orientation and employment, can be formulated.

The point is that for every information system $\underline{S}$, given a change in either $\underline{s}$ or $r$—and in the case of the open system only, in both—validity is maintained as long as alterations are made in the changed elements and the system's utility is kept intact as a total information system. Should these alterations be neglected, the system begins to become entropic at an increasing rate, bringing about the system's decline. Economic activity requires that such alterations be made when entropy is present, otherwise the necessity of profit-maximizing in private business and government decision making will establish conditions by which the projects in question will be abandoned and replaced, eventually enforcing on the economy criteria for recognizing and dealing with entropy.

## THE UTILITY OPTION: MAXIMIZING AND SATISFICING

The basic tenet of neoclassical reasoning, that the individual knows his or her best interests, holds for this discussion. The psychology of personal interests is important in economics only when the psychology is given expression as to purchasing and as to the influences of commercial and/or private advertising, such as the recommendations for consumption by peer groups and vested interests. This basic premise becomes significant, therefore, when the expression of personal interests is given economic meaning as people distribute their liquidity among competing ends. The utility option is the manifestation of this activity as people seek to gain the most from their purchases, even when close substitutes have to be made due to reduced liquidity resulting from wage increases lagging behind price increases.

The utility option thus takes on the semblance of decision making. The question to be addressed here, is whether the argument from the specific individual to the general decision making by governments with respect to the citizens' welfare, is a valid leap, or an error of logic, arguing that the utility option is valid for the general economy *because* it is valid for the individual in the economic system.

One aspect of this argument has already been stated in the previous section, in the discussion of information systems and utility and entropy. Information systems are constructed for individuals, acting alone or in groups, with respect to the available options. The example of social security demonstrated that the options formulated by the governments to deal with the problems of financial security and the obligation to their citizenry depend on the specific conditions within each country in which the principle of national insurance is operative. While these different systems have much in common because their problems are similar, their differences take into account the specific conditions within each country. Hence, economic classes as well as specific individuals are covered by the systems and, in this case, the systems are both specific and general. The encompassing of both the specific individual and the general economic groupings is the basis for economic welfare reasoning.

According to neoclassical economic reasoning, maximizing, whether it be for profit taking, or for the satisfaction in consumption, is the main objective in economic activity. For Edgeworth, such maximizing is achieved when further indifference curve movement is impossible, given the conditions for bargaining. Each participant has achieved the maximum position and can move no further to benefit from the other's situation. Pareto argued that maximum utility is reached in the economy when compensation for one sector cannot be made without hurting another or another sectors. Slutsky weakened the argument by advocating substitutes, when because of liquidity the original preferences cannot be purchased. This situation extended to the macro economy is for Slutsky a maximum utility position, given the realities of restricted liquidity. But as was argued earlier in Chapter 4, Slutsky's reasoning represents the neoclassical transition.

Hence, given individual liquidity with respect to the money supply and the available options, choices have to be made for the distribution of personal income among competing ends, one of these ends being saving. Since the post-Keynesian economics of managerial capitalism, some economists claim that the optimum, together with the time-revered concept of the profit motive, cannot be attained. The complexities of contemporary markets, coupled with the intense competition and the existence of so many close substitutes that the optimum has lost its significance, have eliminated the neoclassical requirement of the optimum, replacing it with satisficing.

According to Robin Marris, for example, satisficing is the behavior

in which the subject, faced with a difficult problem to solve, prefers to sacrifice some of the rewards of the optimum solution in order to reduce the pains incurred in searching for it. Rather than maximize, he chooses to "satisfice," i.e., to accept some solution which is "good enough" in relation to various criteria such as survival, aspiration, or avoidance of pain.[5]

Satisficing is, therefore, consistent with Slutsky's substitution effect, although it is doubtful that Slutsky would accept the aspect of psychological reasoning expressed by Marris.

H.A. Simon, however, did accept the psychological aspect. Indeed, as one of the pioneers of satisficing in economics, Simon argued that models of satisficing behavior are richer than models of maximizing behavior, because they deal not only with equilibrium, but also with methods for achieving equilibrium. In these satisficing models, the individual's aspiration level defines a natural zero-point on the utility scale, compared to the maximizing models for profit and utility in which, according to Simon, the aspiration level is arbitrary. The individual as decision maker, whether as consumer or as the entrepreneur of a firm, limits his or her goals by seeking the maximum utility. Opting for the satisficing position allows the person to develop consumption or entrepreneurial strategies that allow for optimum positions instead of seeking only the maximum, which is unattainable. Neoclassical reasoning stresses only consumer and profit maximization while proponents of managerial post-Keynesian equilibrium reasoning maintain that the maximum is an abstract goal that can never be reached and must be replaced by optimal conditions. According to Simon,

When the firm has alternatives open to it that are at or above its aspiration level, the theory predicts that it will choose the best of those known to be available. When none of the available alternatives satisfies current aspirations, the theory predicts qualitatively different behavior: In the short run, search behavior and the revision of targets; in the longer run, what we have called above emotional behavior and what the psychologist would be inclined to call neurosis.[6]

Psychoses and neuroses aside, Marris describes one way in which a firm satisfices: this is when a firm maintains a substantial but non-optimal growth rate by deliberately setting an above-optimum retention ratio—that is, the ratio between retained earnings and gross earnings—thereby providing its maximum sustainable growth rate at its satisficing level, that is, by setting the growth rate at a level lower than that which can be achieved and thus increasing the ratio of the firm's market value to net assets operating within this value constrained. This ratio can be passed on in the future in the form of higher prices demanded for new share issues, allowing for the increase in the ratio of liabilities to assets and the gearing ratio (i.e., the ratio between money borrowed and money reinvested in capital structure, and according to the market demand for the firm's shared).

Simon argued that the satisficing models are the only models valid for describing the contemporary firm's operations. Such practices as those Marris mentioned are indeed valid and legitimate and operable in corporate decision making. Moreover, the theory of the managerial firm is important in welfare economics to determine under what circumstances the firm's behavior will lead to an efficient allocation of resources. From this, Simon commented that

the satisficing model vitiates all the conclusions about resource allocation and are derivable from the maximizing model when perfect competition is assumed. Similarly, a dynamic theory of firm sizes, . . . has quite different implications for public policies dealing with concentration than a theory that assumes firms to be in static equilibrium.[7]

In this comment Simon identified the problem with satisficing—that it is effective only when dynamic equilibrium prevails, for in such a setting firms of different sizes compete and equilibrium is maintained in spite of each firm's ability to control its resource potential and its share of the market. Thus, it is important to note that by maintaining that welfare economics is a static branch of the discipline, he implied that the allocation of resources for welfare recipients is affected by those conditions in the equilibrium economic state that bring about change. According to this framework of dynamic equilibrium, the necessity for resource allocation exists and is controlled by the the dynamic condition necessary for maintaining growth and stability and is underwritten by government monetary and fiscal policies.

Yet, the question here is not one of dynamics or statics for those firms whose policies have necessarily implications for the welfare distribution as well as for the accumulation of profits and the national wealth, the composition and level of aggregate employment, and the structure and distribution of productive liquidity and capital. The post–World War II use of statics has been only for the analysis and neither for micro or macro policy formulations. Moreover, the use of dynamic equilibrium theory has been for the building of models to demonstrate how the economy could operate in the ideal world of an economy that produces the same goods and services and requires the same resources in permanently fixed ratios. The de facto dynamics, those operating in the economy and considered by business people in the large firms and to some extent those managers in auxiliary businesses, are the dynamics of disequilibrium. Unfortunately, welfare considerations should change accordingly, but this branch of economic thinking has lagged seriously far behind. The difficulty with the satisficing approach in contemporary decision making is accepting that since the advent of post-Keynesian managerial economics the areas of concern for managers are the generation of market dynamics for new products, the maintaining of those products that retain an accepted profit-cost ratio, and the phasing out of those products for which the profit-cost ratio is unacceptable. Hence, the derivation of satisficing conditions from maximizing models where perfect competition is assumed is, again, a technique for analysis that is important, perhaps, for the formulation of policy alternatives, but no more than that. Releasing the perfect-competition restraint brings the model that much closer to reality, although it reduces the control on it; it also allows for greater flexibility between maximizing and satisficing. The point is, however, that the closer the model approaches the real situation of the economy, the closer maximizing and satisficing become.

In other words, when plans are drawn up with a realistic appraisal of the economy in the restricted area for which the plans are formulated, maximizing and satisficing become unity and at that point the utility optimum is reached. This does not, of course, mean that there are no best-case and worst-case scenarios, strategies planned for exploiting the most advantageous situations and possible difficulties. These strategies are valid as part of the planning, although they often do not take into account all the possibilities in the worst-and best-case scenarios because these situations develop while the program is being implemented. Strategies are not, however, goals, and the goal to be achieved for any economic program is the optimum results and benefits accorded by the reality of the situation as understood by the planners and decision makers. This optimum is determined by the utility of the plan or program, that is, how its information relates to the reality to which it defines and delineates. While the program is still "on paper," proposed as a project and even accepted and acted upon within the firm or in the case of welfare, in the respective government circles, the program can be faulted for consistency and relevance with respect to its defining and defined terms. At this stage, the probability criteria are defined and the relationship between probability and information stated. The time signature is then placed on the program, so that the closed information system's validity is stated with respect to its assigned duration and the open system's validity is stated with respect to its changing time-periods.

If no inconsistencies or other difficulties are exposed during this stage, then the program is set into motion and relates to its assigned reality. As was discussed above, the closed system is terminated when its time signature ends, that is, when the duration of its specified time has expired. The open system continues and is revised according to the extent of the entropy that invades the system. For the closed system, the utility optimum is stated and is either achieved or is not; for the open system, the utility optimum is maintained only by making the corrections necessary to insure the system's continued viability, without the system's original identity and purpose being destroyed as a result of the changes made. As long as the system's utility is maintained and entropy kept at bay, the system is at its maximum and maximizing and satisficing are equated and identical with utility. Should entropy become too pervasive so that the system can no longer be corrected without its identity being destroyed, there can be no maximizing, nor satisficing, for the system no longer exists. This is the eventuality that confronts all open information systems, and results in programs that were once successful to be phased out and other programs formulated in their places, only to run their courses and meet the same fate.

This situation poses difficulties for welfare projects that the firms do not have to confront. The firm's actions, their plans and projects, and their resource allocations to realize these plans, can be altered when profits decline because of strong competition and/or because their consumers choose to place their funds in other patterns of consumption. Because businesses are profit-motivated, they have the flexibility to shift production and consequent market orientation, to rid themselves of non-profitable projects and to enter into markets that their decision makers consider to offer potential profits—this, to be tested in the markets. Governments, however, cannot adopt such flexibility, for the problems for which they devise welfare projects will not go away; they are not profit-cum-consumer oriented, but are difficulties within the socioeconomic structure. The programs may become entropic and must therefore be revised—if possible, without losing their identities over time. Governments thus confront situations unlike those of businessess, but operate in a business-oriented socioeconomic situation. Their goals are also based on the utility optimum but because there is no profit mo- tivation, they must be approached differently. Moreover, the difficulties of wel- fare economics are compounded still further by the fact that they must assist business in maintaining their vaiabilities, providing them with the proper climates for continuing business operations. This does not mean that businesses should be subsidized or compensated in any way for failures in judgment or the inability to compete successfully, especially when foreign businesses offer close substitutions at lower prices. It does mean, however, that cyclical fluctuations, so much a part of economic activity and certainly not prevented by post-Keynesian managerial economics, should be countered to the extent that the benefits of these functions are not restricted, but their negative social consequences—such as unemployment and higher welfare payments—be kept at low levels relative to the situation. The problem for economists dealing with welfare is that while the general body of economic theory has developed and expanded since the neoclassical Marshallian theory, moving to the Keynesian resolution of the Great Depression and into the post–World War II theories of managerial economics, welfare theory has advanced little since Pareto's theory and A.C. Pigou's treatment of welfare and full employment.[8]

The problems that welfare theory deals with are indigenous to economics, and the difficulty in handling them is due to the governments' lack of flexibility in policy formation—a difficulty that is not problematic for profit-motivated businesses. This is no reason, however, for policies to be based on outdated theories of neoclassical economics, important and significant as they were then.

It is argued here that a theory of contemporary welfare economics must be based on the utility optimum, although this optimum serves different goals for businesses and governments. However, because both the governments and businesses operate in the same socioeconomic ambience, there must be cooperation between them to rid the business cycles of their extremes, so that businesses and the citizenry in general can benefit from the product of economic activity. Without a unifying approach taken by governments and businesses, economic chaos will continue, with those most badly affected being those relying on welfare. In our contemporary situation, there is no valid economic reason for the lack of housing, for poverty and unemployment. These should remain the relics of a past age, for we now have the socioeconomic infrastructure to resolve these issues once and for all. We need the economic theory, that body of knowledge that gathers all these factors into a single well-defined expression, that will allow us to tackle these problems.

# 7

# The Economy in Disequilibrium

## COMMENTS ON EQUILIBRIUM

"Stated in very general terms," wrote Emmanuel Farjoun and Moshe Machover, "a system is in a state of equilibrium when all its internal forces neutralize each other, so that if left to its own devices the system will continue in the same state, and will be perturbed away from it only under the influence of external forces."[1] They maintain that if the equilibrium state is stable, with the system subjected to small perturbations by external forces, the system's internal forces generate a negative feedback, an effect that pulls the system back toward equilibrium, so that the system will either converge on that equilibrium condition or oscillate around it. They provide an example of the pendulum, oscillating around a fixed point, moving by the continuing forces of planetary motion. The pendulum will continue its path, moving in an equilibrium state, to be disturbed only by an outside force acting on it to disrupt its pattern. The applications of equilibrium for economics are clear with respect to the concept of perfect competition.

The perfect competition model is useful for explaining economics to the first-year student. The model contains many firms and many consumers and a rate of production and consumption that are equal. Should there be an abnormality, in the sense of a producer's overmanufacturing and lowering prices to sell more, other firms will quickly follow suit and the edge held by the first firm will be removed with great rapidity. Should a firm raise its prices, consumers will shop more at its competitors, thereby bringing about a rapid lowering of the prices in line with those of the other firms. Should consumers prefer one firm over the others, they will lower their prices making it worth the consumers' while to return to them. All changes occur around the equilibrium position and the purpose of this model is to instruct students on the beginnings of economics, to demonstrate how only supply and demand are regulated by consumption and production, and how all movement in the nonexistent world of perfect competition returns to an equilibrium position where aggregate supply and aggregate demand equal.

This nonexistent world, however, played an important conceptual role in the development of economic theory. Not in its textbook form, of course, but as it is found in the highly sophisticated arguments of John Locke, David Hume, and Adam Smith, refined by the Frenchman J.-B. Say and given its most famous expression as Say's Law of Markets. It states that production generates consumption, so that all that is produced will be consumed. This economic law is based on Adam Smith's "invisible hand," which regulates the markets by clearing them and maintaining competition. This law was criticized by Thomas Malthus and later by J.M. Keynes who brought the Law of Markets into question and demonstrated in his critique of Pigou's work that full employment, necessary to maintain consumption, does not hold, as the real world of the Great Depression so sharply revealed.[2]

There is another aspect of economics that brings the Law of Markets into question, that being the role of government. In the early years of the Industrial Revolution, governments out of necessity had to become active in economic development. The printing of currency had to be a government affair, so that a unit of currency could be standardized, providing a monetary basis for economic development. This was an open act into socioeconomic infrastructure that expanded into the area of public domain in the building of roads, in underwriting transportation projects when private investors could not be found, for maintaining a military service—a form of employment, especially when conscription was not enforced—and for regulating the economy when cyclical fluctuations became too extreme. This last point was taken with great restraint in the industrializing countries because of the doctrine of *laissez-faire* established by Smith (and Thomas Jefferson, who advocated minimal government).[3] Left to their own, with government intervention only when necessary, the cycle will reverse itself and move upward after a depression and turn downward after prosperity. This was nature; this was the mechanism of economic activity. The government would be required to intervene only if the upward movement was too sluggish, and then the printing of money or the development of new territories—this was especially the case in the United States—would spur activity once again.

The point is that equilibrium would be maintained. Albeit, this is not the equilibrium described in the textbooks, in the neoclassical theories that gained great refinement and sophistication with the works of J.S. Mill, Alfred Marshall, Wesley Mitchell, Pigou, and many others. The basic premise of these arguments, however, was the same: equilibrium is maintained, with the fluctuations moving around it in cyclical fashion. Short-run disturbances will be cancelled-out in the long run as the cycle runs its course and equilibrium is reinstated.

The textbook discussion on perfect competition is economics in static equilibrium. In this perfect situation there are no new markets, no new businesses, and no new consumers. The consumer/business ratio is given and fixed; the purpose of this model is strictly descriptive and explanatory. The static equilibrium model describes a situation that is nonexistent but useful for the clarification of concepts of economics for the novice and the beginner; it is explanatory because it analyzes the rudiments of the market economy—rudiments that were accepted as valid to a certain extent even in the most sophisticated of neoclassical theories.

That this is so is demonstrated in the complex body of theory of economics that was developed by Alfred Marshall and expanded by the macroeconomists such as Joseph Schumpeter[4] into highly refined and intricate systems involving the development of markets and the phasing out of competitors due to strenuous competition and market saturation.

During the Great Depression, while most economists formulated theories for explaining and resolving the economic crisis while maintaining the sacrosant basic tenet of classical-cum-neoclassical reasoning of full employment, Keynes brought this tenet into its correct position of being unrealistic. The very high unemployment during the depression was surely a point that could not be overlooked, and it was blamed on such strawmen as the unions preventing the market forces to operate, or too much government intervention that restricted market functions. But in spite of Keynes's criticism of the full-employment tenet, his theory also posited equilibrium, dynamic as it is, thereby maintaining employment and production.

Say's Law of Markets can be derived from Keynes's argument, even though he argued against it, thus: Let Z be the aggregate supply price of output whose production requires N employees, with the relationship between Z and N being $Z = \phi(N)$, which is the aggregate supply function. Similarly, let D be the proceeds entrepreneurs expect from N employees, so that $D = f(N)$, which is the aggregate supply function. For a given value of N if the expected proceeds are greater than the aggregate supply price, that is, if D is greater than Z, there will be an incentive to increase employment beyond N and if necessary to raise costs by competing for the factors up to the value of N for which Z becomes equal to D. At this point of intersection between the aggregate supply and demand functions the amount of employment is fixed. Keynes said that at this point the entrepreneur's expectation of profits (but not necessarily the profits themselves) will be maximized.

Keynes challenged this classical argument: Say's Law, stating that supply creates its own demand, involves a special assumption about the aggregate supply and demand functions, that being that $f(N)$ and $\phi(N)$ are equal for all values of N and that therefore an increase of $Z = \phi(N)$ corresponding to an increase in N necessitates an increase in $D = f(N)$ by the same amount as Z. Thus, instead of having a unique equilibrium value, effective demand is at an infinite range of values, each admissible as equilibrium points. Furthermore, should this condition persist, competition would always result in the expansion of employment, which amounts to the same thing as continuous full employment. Malthus commented that Say's Law is not in accordance with economic reasoning; this comment rings true, for the Law of Markets as analyzed by Keynes most certainly did not hold for the Great Depression.[5]

However, according to Keynes's theory, where $Z = D$ for each product, then there is equilibrium; when the aggregate supply and demand functions meet, then aggregate equilibrium is achieved. From the vantage of historical reasoning, three points can be made. First, to reach aggregate equilibrium, supply and demand must be for each product. Second, although these schedules are not infinite, they are as many and as diversified as the products. Third, according to Keynes's comments, for Say's equilibrium to be reached for the aggregate supply and demand schedules, the amount of labor must be infinite to account for increased production and increased demand. However, Keynes failed to account for a fixed or slowly increasing labor force, supplemented by increasingly sophisticated technology for increased production and diversified goods and services, thereby allowing the greater portion of consumer liquidity to be directed toward demand. No necessary correlation exists between increased production and diversity requirements, for these can be, and very often are, offset by technology.

Moreover, in the contemporary post-industrial economies, aggregate equilibrium cannot exist. It is ruled out by increasingly changing markets with some markets being introduced and others being phased out, while others still are expanding. Also, supply and demand schedules are not for single products from a macro perspective, but for similiar (imitative Slutskian) products, based on a single theme. Here, infinite production for a single product is prohibited by the consumption of close substitutes and by the allocation of resources for other product lines.

Furthermore, to say that $Z = D$ in aggregate equilibrium means that for every market m, $Z^m_i = D^m_i$ for the manifold products and markets. At each point of juncture for Z and D in each specific market $m$, supply and demand are equal and employment is of sufficient level to maintain this equality. Hence, even considering technology's impact on the labor market and on production, the labor force must consume only what is produced, with the products marketed *in toto*. Here, therefore, is a case of supply generating its own demand as consumption must relate to production for each $m$ and for aggregate equilibrium. The situation is that Say's Law, criticized by Keynes, has indeed been reinstated by Keynes in the guise of equilibrium reasoning.

Assuming a degree of realism, the perfect competition situation is impossible because the impact of technology cannot allow for the static economic condition necessary for the perfect competition model. Technology brings about change in the economic composition: in the manner in which goods are produced and services performed, and in the methods of transportation and distribution. This model is merely a textbook description to provide the basis for understanding the more complicated dynamics of competition and market development.

With respect to the perfect competition model, the Keynesian model of dynamic equilibrium is certainly more realistic. For Keynes, markets can change, production plans can be altered. But production is geared for targeted demand and this demand is generated by the supply of the goods and services; therefore Say's Law holds for Keynes's theory.

Dynamic equilibrium necessarily implies a Say-like situation, for equilibrium is what Say posited and even the most sophisticated dynamic equilibrium systems have the Say-like aspect. For equilibrium to exist—be it static or dynamic—supply must generate its own demand and there must be equality in the long run between supply and demand. This entails a labor force that is either expanding with respect to the increased production, or a labor force whose earnings are increasing commensurate with increased production, or perhaps a mixed labor force expansion–purchasing power increase to correspond to production increases. This is necessary in order to move the goods and services, so that equilibrium can be maintained. Furthermore, with the labor force–wage situation in this system, there can be no cyclical downturn, for there would be no reason to reduce inventories as all production will be sold. There would be no wage cuts, no reduction in the labor force, because people would continue purchasing. There can, in the system of dynamic equilibrium, be only increased production and the introduction of new products to stimulate further consumption and the diversification of consumption patterns. For those products in which there are declines in consumption due to the diversification of products, their prices would be lowered and they too will be moved. No inventories remaining in the long run would mean a continuation of production and diversification, and the system would be maintained on a dynamic equilibrium growth pattern, such in the macro economy in the Harrod–Domar model, and for the economy of the firm in Robin Marris's model.[6]

The models of dynamic equilibrium are important because they remove the restrictions on reality placed by the perfect competition equilibrium model. They demonstrate how an economy relates to changes and how new products are brought into the markets while those products whose profitability has declined sufficiently are phased out. These models also demonstrate how governments can act to maintain the equilibrium by regulating the money supply through taxation and open market activities so that equilibrium is maintained. For example, should the money supply in the aggregate outstrip aggregate demand, tax increases can be levied to the extent of the difference to maintain the equilibrium and keep the economy on an even upward growth pattern. Open market operations, such as increasing the discount rates that banks must hold, reduce the money supply for financing new projects when current revenue from sales is insufficient.

Dynamic disequilibrium is far more realistic than the static equilibrium of the perfect competition model and is certainly more informative as it demonstrates the operations of firms and of governments in the economy. But this is where the value of this model ends, for it does not allow for cyclical downturns, nor for unemployment other than frictional that is, in any case, balanced out in the long run in dynamic equilibrium.

Monetary phenomena, such as inflation or deflation, can exist in this model because the government automatically steps in to regulate the currency with respect to supply and demand for consumer products. However, no automatic guidelines are established for printing money annually, no procedures for taking money out of the economy are provided, and all such operations proceed in fact ad hoc, according to the circumstances prevailing at the time. Therefore, while the dynamic equilibrium model may be the ideal situation and most certainly one closer to the reality of our world, it still leaves much to be desired.

The model that resembles reality the closest is that of the economy in dynamic disequilibrium. The image of business operations moving in cyclical fashion, with the peaks and troughs of the cycle, is inaccurate for this model. Although periods of high and low economic activity do occur, through the bringing of new products into the markets and the imitation of close substitutes (Slutsky) and the phasing out of business activity due to the stringent competition that reduces profits and prevents the entry of new firms, the cycle must be viewed as moving with height, depth, and width. This third dimension takes into account the economic expansion generated during the previous period of intense activity of new products being introduced into the markets, and the imitative activity of close substitutes competing with those products that prove commercially successful.

As consumer liquidity is fixed, however, that part of aggregate liquidity channeled to new products and the close substitutions which follow, have to be taken from other consumption sources, in which case, the firms producing those products which were consumed previously will suffer losses for these products, even though they may be the very same firms producing the new and/or substitute products. Liquidity may also be obtained from savings, thereby affecting adversely the liquidity positions of those institutions that rely on savings for their revenues. In either case, these firms whose profits are marginal for their competitive products may decide to withdraw these products and channel their resources into the newer and more demanded production. In the case of the savings institutions, those that hold marginal positions will fold under the pressures of withdrawal, while others may receive government assistance in the form of reduced discount rates and/or the opportunities for opening new savings schemes that compete for consumer liquidity with consumption.

In his chapter on prices, Keynes formulated a Velocity Theory of Money from which the price elasticities, output, wages, and employment can be determined, but this resulted in a dichotomy in his treatment.[7] These terms are not loosely associated, but are a process that allows for derivation. His formula is MV = D, where M is the quantity of money, V is the income-velocity of money, the value of which is dependent on the institutional factors of banking, of social habits, on the social income distribution, and on the effective cost of holding personal cash as opposed to investing—itself-determined by the available personal holdings and by the interest rate. Keynes had defined money as consisting of two parts: $M_1$ for precautionary holdings and transactions; $M_2$ for the amount held for speculative uses. Hence, $(M_1 + M_2)V = D$. D is the effective demand for money as determined by these components of money and its income-velocity, which is a social-institutional component of the equation.

Further, $M = L_1(Y) - L_2(r)$, with L being the liquidity function so that $L_1(Y)$ is the income function and $L_2(r)$ is the interest-rate function. Substituting L for M in the Velocity Theory shows that the velocity at which money circulates is equal to the effective demand for goods and services, both of which are functions of income and the interest rate.

From his formula, Keynes derives the elasticities of employment, wages, output, and demand, keeping true to his claim that he united a quantity theory of money to elasticity. He did so by differentiating each factor with respect to the standard elasticity equation, so that elasticity $e = Ddp/pdD$, and so forth. The dichotomy in his approach is that elasticity is a microconcept while the velocity of money is a macroconcept. He could not remove this dichotomy because, as he maintained, money is the economic connection between the past and present; elasticities show only short-run movement while the effects of the money supply and its velocity in circulation are long-run and concern investment and liquidity that cannot be measured by elasticity but must be considered from a different view.

This dichotomy can be resolved, however, by the formula $M = Y$, that is, by equating money in the economy to the national income. Y is broken down into three components: $Y = Y_p + Y_g + Y_f$. $Y_p$ corresponds to Keynes's $M_1$ and $M_2$—that is, it is money for personal transactions and precautions such as sound investments and savings in the form of government bonds and blue-chip shares, as these are programs that contain only marginal risks with dividends paid according to the demand for money for these investments and savings, and in relation to other savings and investment programs. Speculation is included in this classification, in which both the risks and remuneration on investments are high. $Y_p$ (personal income) is derived from wages, profits on investments, inheritance, and other money sources at the individual's disposal. $Y_g$ is income generated by the government and is that income at the government's disposal as a result of tax collection, payments on loans and interest by foreign countries, gains from bond purchases, and grants from foreign countries and international bodies—a factor that is significant for the lesser-developed countries. $Y_f$, the firm's income, is the net profits from the firm's business transactions, monies from government and institutional grants and loans, monies from stock and bond issues, and liquidity gained from mergers.

As $M = Y$, the $M_p = Y_p$, $M_g = Y_g$, and $M_f = Y_f$. The importance of this formulation is that it leads very easily to a value theory relating the micro aspects of price changes to the macro aspect of the velocity of money. This occurs because the theory of value is based on utility and entropy. This must be considered because a difficulty in determining value—that has persisted in economics—is due to economists maintaining that their discipline is a science, with analytic, descriptive, and predictive powers normally attributed to the physical sciences. The concepts of utility and entropy—defined and described in this work—form a theory of value that meets the scientific requirement of being derived from reality and being used to explain it. Utility is both subjective and objective. In its subjective state it affects the economy only when individuals act; objective utility is thus influenced through this economic action. The same holds for entropy: It is manifested subjectively through choosing alternatives, but its objective manifestations are noted through the decline of the forces previously held and considered viable.

Hence, the concepts of utility and entropy form a theory of value in their expression of satisficing and maximizing. People impute value according to their understanding of utility and entropy, which explains why there is no necessity for two contemporary individuals to have the same value schedule—a consideration of great importance for welfare economics. Acting to maximize under the restrictive conditions of satisficing, individuals choose their purchases and make their decisions according to their personal utility-entropy scales. Because these are related to the economy in the aggregate, they provide a picture of total value, which may, in turn, influence the decisions of other contemporary individuals. It is in the aggregate that value becomes objective and is manifested in forms of commerce and decision making and the formulation of government policy concerning welfare. Hence, the requirement of deriving a theory from reality and applying it to its defined reality is accomplished. Indeed, objective value is the total of the utility and entropy schedules as maximizing is undertaken by all contemporary individuals subject to the satisficing constraints. This, then, is the impact that these total utility and entropy schedules have on the economy as people seek the economic maximum, constrained by satisficing.

In Keynes's $MV = D$ equation, if the velocity of money is constant, changes in price will be proportional to changes in the money supply, providing that the change with respect to demand is unity. The notion of elasticity explains the situation after the price changes, and provides no guidance concerning the dynamics of such changes. However, for the $M = Y$ equation, part of the money in the economy—part of the $Y$ component—will be held as liquid assets. This is liquidity not in circulation, so that the equation can be written $M = Y_c + Y_d$, with $Y_c$ being money that is in circulation and $Y_d$ being the money withheld from circulation. $Y_d$ is the liquidity element for both personal disposable income and that income held by firms and the government that is not used nor has been earmarked for investment. It is to this liquidity that the value theory must relate and apply.

This is because all changes in prices, wages, output, and employment affect the liquidity preference. Upward price changes result in a lower disposable national income and hence a reduced short-term liquidity expressed first in altered and then in adjusted and fairly stable demand. Price rises have a short-term affect on wages, output, and employment, that is realized in the medium and long run when disposable income is still further reduced and the liquidity preference altered still further by the multiplying effects of inflation. Unless wages are adjusted upward so that the value of expected utility has the same weight as before—given the current basket of goods and services with respect to those of the earlier period—output, and the economy in general, will be affected by labor unrest and the losses of renevues due to strikes and sanctions, resulting in the cut-back of production as unions and management seek to maintain the present wage levels so as not to inflame the situation still further. Should the existing wage structure or even an increased wage structure for employment be maintained, unemployment, being larger in its seasonal and frictional levels, will increase inflation because of competing consumer disposable income for the same goods and services. This is offset, however, when consumer spending encourages greater manufacturing turnover, so that in order to move the goods and services, prices are reduced in competition. As prices rise, however, the value of disposable income will then decline as a greater proportion of liquidity must be sacrificed for consumption. Following this will be a decline of the quantity of goods and services in the various markets because of unemployment and the reduced levels of innovative and imitative programs brought about by businesses' cautious outlook.

In contrast, even with fixed incomes, an overall decrease in the general price level will result in the increase in the value of disposable and saved income, with businesses becoming more indulgent correspondingly by engaging in more production to increase their profit levels. Either investment will remain steady in this situation, or it will increase according to the expectations of the public with regards to the general optimism in the economy, with this influencing borrowers' interest rates. Aggregate price reductions are due, in part, to greater competition which increases consumer liquidity. Lower prices with high rates of disposable income increase liquidity. This liquidity can be channeled into either investment or increased consumption; in either situation increased liquidity is short-lived as its value is eroded because of increased production and investment opportunities that eventually cease to be attractive as consumer products due to their inability for further accomodation. Production will cease or be maintained at levels that will not allow further liquidity advantages as competition no longer has weight in attracting consumers due to committed purchasing patterns. Investment programs will become saturated, so that they discourage consumers—an example of this is a paper transaction that becomes closed to future buyers. The rate of $Y_d$'s being brought into circulation, therefore, depends on the levels of competition for $Y_c$. Where this competition is strong, $Y_d$ retains its value as disposable income not yet brought into circulation; when competition tapers off and prices rise, $Y_d$ is transferred into $Y_c$ at rates corresponding to the decline. As the transfer from $Y_d$ to $Y_c$ continues, liquidity declines accordingly and with this decline is also the decline in the propensity to save. The markets move toward stabilization in an equilibrium position, but this is temporary as further liquidity is transferred into consumption. Production declines as revenues from sales are transferred into meeting fixed costs and maintaining a reasonable level of profits in light of the situation. Because of the declining production rates, unemployment sets in and the entire economy heads for a downward turn. Prices remain fairly constant and subjectively high, given these conditions, but they too will decline, given a sufficient time lag. Markets will shift, so that certain geographical locations can provide the better sales terms because of their relatively low fixed costs while the more expensive products will maintain a certain percentage of their clinetele who are unaffected by these economic events. Greater unemployment requires, however, a welfare system that is sufficiently prepared and capable of handling this influx. This system also has to be flexible enough to account for the reduction of recipients as $Y_c$ is transferred into $Y_d$ once the cycle turns upward.

## COMMENTS ON THE BUSINESS CYCLE

That markets are interrelated can be seen in the crash of 1929 and more recently in the fall of the world's great stock exchanges on October 19, 1987. The first crash, and certainly the more famous of the two, brought about a severe world depression, the results of which are still being felt. Indeed, every economic ripple since then has conjured up memories of that Great Depression, and it is no wonder that the October crash had lead to comparisions of depth and intensity, and to projections about the immediate and long-run future of capitalist systems.

While the world's economic systems have become so interrelated that events in one country affect those in the others, the term *trade cycle,* or *business cycle* as it is alternatively called, dates back to the early days of the Industrial Revolution, when industry and business merged to make production more efficient and to increase output at lower costs, which allowed the openings of new markets, thereby bringing a greater proportion of the countries' populations—once primarily agrarian in orientation—into the production and consumption processes. The term *cycle* is derived from the Latin *cyclus,* which is based on the Greek *kyklos,* meaning a circle or ring. The image that the term conveys is that the beginning gives rise to the ending and the ending brings about the beginning. This image is intended in the word's usage in economics, so that in the neo-classical argument, an economy in a period of recovery reaches a point of overheating and results in unemployment and reduced production; this leads to recession and eventual depression, with most of the productive stocks and equimpment, together with a goodly portion of the labor force, lying idle.

Prior to the Great Depression, cyclical downswings affected only those people whose liquidity was limited. Unemployment remained until the first motions of recovery were felt. Workers migrated back to agriculture and in the case of the newly-formed United States, they often moved into new territories to seek new lives. Established countries such as Great Britain, France, Germany, and Italy often had their people charting the seas and moving into new countries. One of the significant aspects of the Great Depression is that such migration was limited in scope. The shock of the fall of the stock markets and the failings of the banks was so profound, that only the governments could step in and intervene. It was in light of this depression that welfare systems that were an offshoot of capitalism in any case—education, for example, to know how to live and work in the newly developing industrial environment and to cope with the impact of science on society, as well as governments acting as employers in the developing of necessary socioeconomic infrastructure—became more comprehensive and sophisticated, taking the aspects of unemployment insurance and social security to buffer the worst of the depression and recession periods of the cycle's activity. In any case, prior to the Great Depression, it was assumed that the cycle's momentum does not allow for depressed periods to remain but swings the cycle upward again, bringing about prosperity and full employment in their recurring patterns.

According to this argument, the cycle works in the following manner. Recession sets in when the economy in its cyclical motion passes its peak of expansion with industries reducing their inventories. Since, after this point all further expansion is not profitable because sales will not be made at a rate comparable to production, stabilized production in the recession period allows for current inventories to be moved. Unemployment eventually sets in as stocks are cleared and increased production is unprofitable, so that businesses cannot maintain their employment levels. The consequence is that reduced employment means reduced liquidity (that is $Y_d$) that translates into reduced aggregate sales because the work force has less purchasing power. This downward cyclic trend continues until current inventories are sufficiently depleted and the economy declines still further to its lowest level of depression.

When this level is reached, managers realize that in order for fixed costs to be met and an acceptable profit level to be maintained, sales must be increased. Managers begin reordering inventories and this stimulates reemployment. This process continues as people now employed begin spending their wages, and as stocks of goods and services are fully replenished. The downward swing leading to depression has its own momentum and moves upward, along the path of recovery. As the aggregate liquidity level is increased, this is partially transferred to demand; with the new optimism, as stocks are depleted this upward movement continues, with momentum of recovery commensurate with the impact of the various forms of demand as expressed in the aggregate.

The final stage in this four-part cycle is prosperity, during which the momentum of recovery expressed by the increasing levels of aggregate demand begins slowing down. During the period of prosperity there is near-full employment with a rapid turnover of inventories. The problem sets in with the anticipation of further sales resulting in overstocking of inventories with respect to sales. This brings about a greater abundance of goods and services that can be absorbed by the current levels of aggregate demand, resulting in a marginal decline in orders, which leads to reduced employment, lower demand, and declining output. The cycle has moved from its highest position and begins its downward motion into recession and depression.

The neoclassical cycle is repetitive and contains elements of the two competing interpretations of overproduction and underconsumption, which most certainly stand in contradiction to the requirements of equilibrium. Even the argument that equilibrium exists in the long run as the cycle moves around a fixed—and therefore equilibrium—point does not hold, for according to equilibrium con- siderations, economic disturbances such as recessions and depressions, as well as heating up of the economy during prosperity, can be corrected by monetary and fiscal policies, which regulate demand in the short run and which therefore exert a corresponding regulative effect on supply. Equilibrium requires stability through motion, without the sharp peaks and troughs of the business cycle; equilibrium explained within the framework of movement around a cyclical fixed point is invalid and unhelpful.

Another criticism of the neoclassical cycle is that it has the economy on approximately the same plane of development. In contrast, the neo-Keynesians have been concerned with shifts in the levels of business activity and the move- ments that bring the cycle not to its original starting position, but to a higher plane. This means that in the course of the cycle's movement greater infras- tructure and more production potential have been established. Thus, when re- covery sets in, its effects will be wider and a greater number of people will benefit. This requires higher levels of technology and therefore a trade-off be- tween standard methods of work and the applications of new technologies, which leads to shifting socioeconomic patterns. Redundancy in employment results from this trade-off, which must be absorbed by the welfare system. Labor mo- bility also results as outdated skills in one geographical location can be applied in other locations, but this is a time-based situation as the dynamics of the new technologies will catch up eventually. Hence, welfare economics cannot be detached from the business cycle; even the neo-classical and the neo-Keynesian interpretations are not exempt from this.

## FURTHER CONSIDERATIONS ON THE CYCLE

The periods of recession and depression tend to mirror inversely those periods of recovery and prosperity. But because the cycle has come to be considered a permanent fact of economic life, various proposals have been put forward to ease the disruptions and diseconomies brought about by the recession and depres- sion phases—but interestingly enough, none have been posited for the disruptions in the changeover to recovery and prosperity, as these phases are considered to be constructive and the disruptions minor when the benefits are concerned.

Keynes, for example, maintained that interest rates at levels required by the market forces would ease the slump and prolong the period of presperity. In his own words:

Thus the remedy for a boom is not a higher rate of interest but a lower rate of interest: For that may enable the so-called boom to last. The right remedy for the trade cycle is not to be found in abolishing booms and thus keeping us permanently in a semi-slump; but in abolishing slumps and keeping us permanently in a quasi-boom.[8]

Consider the implications of this argument: If market forces require higher interest rates to reduce borrowing and thus deflate the economy by reducing the money supply, by following Keynes's advice the authorities maintain artificailly low interest rates through banking operations. By increasing the money supply, productivity will certainly increase, but at a rate lower than aggregate demand. This will bring about aggregate price rises with demand increasing more than supply and with prices rising increasingly to offset the demand. This is a highly inflationary state of affairs resulting in upward-spiraling prices and costs with little incentive to increase supply accordingly. The quasi-boom this policy sets out to maintain will result in inflationary chaos eliminated or eased only by economic authorities acting swiftly in the opposite direction; if not, the diseconomies for industrialized countries would certainly be considerable.

Another approach is that of taxation. The government may level high taxes as the cycle moves to the peak of prosperity: reducing these taxes as well as providing other monetary incentives, such as reducing interest rates and using other open market procedures as the economy moves from the phase of recession to depression. The reasoning is that if the upswing is blunted before reaching its peak, the downturn will not be severe. The objective is to flatten out the cycle as much as possible while retaining a higher upward turn and a minimum downward turn. However, there is no guarantee that a blunted upward motion will result in an easier downswing. Moreover, no matter how much control is exerted over the economy and no matter how skillfully econometric models are constructed, the results of taxation policies cannot be determined with great accuracy. The possibility exists, for example, that the effects of higher taxation will bring about an overreaction on the part of investors and business people retracting investments and closing businesses, bringing about the downward swing before its natural time and causing it to move with greater intensity. The consequence is the postponement of projects and unemployment resulting from the decline in industrial liquidity and the uncertain economic situation. From the policies of taxation there is the possibility of a weakened industrial and labor base, which may be felt severely in the arena of international competition.

Nor are there lacking doctrinal remedies to the problems of the business cycle. A free-market economy, one in which the government's regulations are suffered as necessary evils, will, it is argued, overcome the difficulties when economic power groups act with restraint during periods of high prosperity, when the cycle shows signs of moving higher at a slower pace. This argument posits that the government should provide the legal basis for economic activity, exerting its influence over monetary and interregional (interstate, or however the country is partitioned) affairs but refrain from direct involvement in business. A relatively unrestricted economy acts according to the market forces and functions well, according to this doctrine, when its participants behave in their own best interests (the position assumed by Edgeworth, Pareto, and Slutsky, among other neo-classical economists), so that when they realize that during certain phases of the cycle specific modes of behavior are in their best interests, these behavioral patterns are acted upon, providing sufficient momentum to the cycle to carry it along its path.

The problem with this position is that in spite of its doctrinaire appeal it bears no relation to reality. For example, at the time of the Great Depression the economies of the industrialized societies were integrated both internally and externally through foreign commerce, to the extent that no cyclical momentum could lift the economies to the phase of recovery. Moreover, the Keynesian government intervention appropriate for the economics of the Great Depression was inadequate even in its post-Keynesian form, as the advent of post-World War II managerial capitalism set new approaches to economics. Furthermore, replacement of laborers with machines altered the employment situation, which neo-Keynesian economics has not adequately considered in the employment aspect of that theory. The stock market collapse in October 1987 demonstrates that the tools of the reasoning of the past era are now inadequate for contemporary economics.

The argument for more government intervention in economic affairs is just as doctrinaire. The argument maintains that people acting in their own best interests are not able to influence the complex interlocking systems in the economy that are not within their immediate spheres of activity and occupation. The government, acting with respect to its legal obligations, subjects the people to controls, even though they may not comprehend the necessity of these restrictions. Indeed, more controls should be implemented to prevent people from acting in their own best interests entirely by making these interests those of the economy in general, so that the effects of the cycle's extreme phases and the subsequent macrodiseconomies that result can be either reduced to the level of insignificance, or eliminated entirely.

The difficulty with controls is that although government officials have programs for maintaining the economy, the controls they impose to direct economic activity often have unexpected and unprepared-for results. The economy is not a mechanism but an open-ended system of information and ramifications so complicated that it cannot be expected to yield the desired results. Controls have a role in economics; they are guidelines for behavior and should not be treated as strict legal dictates. The economy, since the development of the relationship between business and technology in the Industrial Revolution, has been too complex to be so tightly regulated; moreover, the "wisdom" of those who impose restrictions and limitations may not be so perfect, nor their motives free from self-interest.

Furthermore, history bears witness to many situations in which the other situation holds, in which the lack of necessary controls leads to complete chaos, (i.e., in which a passive government in times of crisis leads to cynicism, distrust, and economic and social breakdown). But history also bears witness to the contrary: Economic regulations that are too extensive lead to vested economic interests' becoming involved with the political authorities, thereby providing a serious threat to the social fabric on which the economy is based, expands, and grows.

Thus, in spite of all attempts to eliminate its extreme peaks and troughs, the business cycle still remains an integral part of the economic system. The cycle persists over the extreme socioeconomic changes that have transpired during the development of the industrialized capitalist countries. The cycle persists and functions in spite of attempts to eliminate it in the sectors of agriculture, finance, and industrial production. Moreover, the cycle's intensity and duration are beyond prediction, with each cycle relating to the specific conditions in which it exists or that are being formed uniquely by the particular economy in question. Those who hold the reins of governmental and industrial power have progressed very little when coping with the fluctuations of the business cycle; it is deeply rooted in our economics and must be handled appropriately when crisis proportions are reached.

## THE TRADE CYCLE AND CONTEMPORARY ECONOMICS

The contemporary trade cycle differs from the neoclassical cycle in a significant way. The present economic crisis of near stagnation, together with high inflation and uncertainty in the financial markets after the October 1987 crash is unique to economies that have achieved high degrees of integration and strong infrastructures, so that all sectors are influenced in similar ways during the cycle's movement.

It is because these conditions are unique to contemporary economies that the cycle must be viewed in a manner suitable to our times and situation. What is required, therefore, is a different approach to the cycle, not within the terms of reference of the four-phased neoclassical cycle, but as a three-phased cycle with the fourth traditional phase of depression eliminated. The fact is that since World War II there has been no depression with the resulting extensive idle capital and labor. This does not necessarily mean that severe recessions will not be experienced; but it does mean that even that when such severe shocks occur as the October 1987 collapse of the markets, neither government nor industry will allow the ceasing of economic activity to the extent that depression sets in. For as integrated as these economies are, there is the impetus of economic activity, increasing as the cycle moves upward and decreasing to the extent of near paralysis as recession sets in. The October 1987 stock market crash demonstrates this. The market declined very rapidly and severely as the fall in prices devastated the psychological confidence in the buoyancy of the market. The market forces, when considered impassionately, could be seen to be fully in operation. But the specter of the Great Depression suddenly loomed over the economy and there was apprehension the stopgaps and measures instituted by governments to prevent such a vast and near-total decline from happening again would not work. The logic of the psyche replaced the logic of economics, and large firms brokering on the markets initiated unemployment, in the form of a negative "self-fulfilling prophecy" of another severe depression.

While the economies of the industrialized countries have been experiencing difficulties, especially of stagnation and inflation, it is questionable whether this, together with the fall of the stock markets, can be taken for a depression. To determine this requires a comparison of eras, which is difficult because of the extreme differences in the industrial bases between the period of 1929 and that of 1987–88. Moreover, it is difficult to measure the differences in the trade-off between labor and technology then and now, as well as managerial orientation and the differing approaches to commerce and international trade. Developing countries then, for example, presented no real challenge to the industrialized countries, while now they provide a great percentage of technological output (such as South Korea does). Moreover, the existence and importance of multi-nationals now allows for the employment in many countries and their being brought into the arena of serious competition, when in the prior period they were insignificant economic forces. The definition of depression for contemporary economic conditions must therefore differ from that of the past era, and this difference shows that depressions are no longer acceptable and allowable as a means for clearing the markets and for revamping of inventories according to the neoclassical explanation by those who exert control over the governmental and industrial aspects of the economies.

For contemporary economies, then, the bottom phase of the cycle has been eliminated but this does not mean that its upward motion will be more rapid and expansive; nor does it mean that because the cycle's bottom position has been eliminated, its upward momentum will be dampened. The manner in which the period of recovery is undertaken depends solely on the vitality with which managers and government officials respond to and act on the challenges. The areas of activity must be therefore innovative, both politically *and* economically.

For welfare economic considerations near stagnation, expressed by the term *stagflation,* in which inflation is high relative to output, exists because imitation is being emphasized over innovation of economic products during this time of uncertainty. Firms then, with available resources, enter those markets where profits—no matter how small—can still be made, while other firms unable to undertake imitation, remain somewhat dormant at the expense of their resource utilization and employee output. Unemployment results and business activity slows down to retain profits. Prices are raised and costs either held constant or reduced in order to maintain a competitive position.

Thus, the consequences are: welfare programs; unemployment insurance being paid to match the unemployment rate; government contracts for socioeconomic projects being tendered; and instruments for regulating the money supply, including manipulating the interest rates, being brought into action. These measures for easing the socioeconomic impact of the downward swing are insufficient, however, unless there is active participation by industry as well. Innovating products—beginning new markets and commensurate consumer activity—is a response to liquidity, so that when liquidity is low in the aggregate the first effect is a corresponding and considerably slowed aggregate innovation rate. The second effect is that imitation—the entering into established markets with closely competitive goods and services—also declines, but at a rate slower than innovation because the new markets have already been pioneered and have established themselves with imitation exploiting existing markets. Near-stagnation becomes established when prices in which the aggregate rise to compensate for declining sales, reaching such levels that aggregate consumer liquidity has been reduced sufficiently to restrict to a great extent changes in purchasing patterns established during the cycle's movement. This is also a criticism of Slutsky's substitution effect, because prices tend to equal out and remain fixed on their levels during this situation that substitution is significant only in individual marginal conditions. Aggregately, its meaning is lost because the substitution effect is irrelevant due to of price equalization.

The government's measures bring into the economy only marginal utility because they are substitutes for employment and economic productivity. The accepted post-Keynesian policy of the government's underwriting the economy to provide a basis to prevent the low point of the cycle's phases from being reached, is itself insufficient. Should industry remain passive, or because of government policies be encouraged to remain passive, the threat to society is evident, for the government's influence will be overwhelming, with the danger of dictatorship most certainly real. The problem is, how can government and industry act to move the cycle upward and revamp the welfare system? This is discussed in the next section.

## THE CYCLE AND DISEQUILIBRIUM

We have a situation where inflation is eroding workers' wages and savings, where interest rates are high because banks and other lending institutions seek to protect their liquidity, where businesses are becoming increasingly insolvent and the gearing ratio is used as a factor for accumulating liquidity. Keynesian and neo-Keynesian economic theory have failed to provide prescriptions for this situation. Moreover, with the fall of the stock market, the entire body of mainstream economic theory is being questioned. Comparisons are made with the

Great Depression for which Keynes's theory provided solutions, but no solution seems to be in sight for our current predicament. New thinking must be employed to deal with this situation.

Indeed, further comments on the cycle are in order. In the contemporary economic situation, the image of business moving in cyclical fashion, with activity peaking and then turning rapidly downward, is an illusion. Although periods of high and low economic activity do occur, through the dynamics of innovation and imitation the economy widens its base for which the corresponding infrastructure is established. It is important to note that when the cycle turns downward, the infrastructure remains intact, with that part which is inactive during the downturn becoming active again when the cycle begins swinging upward. Hence, the downward movement expressed by the decline of innovation and the slower decline of imitation does not affect the widened economic base, which is one reason that proper economic policy can eliminate the diseconomies of the sharp downswing.

Indeed, the image of the cycle moving upward and downward is inaccurate, for along with these fluctuations is the widening economic base in which the cycle moves and in which the infrastructure is based and is expanded. The cycle must therefore be viewed as moving with height, depth, and width, for this third dimension takes into account the economic expansion generated during the previous period of high innovation and imitation.

Assumed here is that responsible governments are in control and watchful of economic considions. For, even in our contemporary situation, if the business cycle is left to its own momentum, the depression phase will be reached; the cycle's "mechanism" has this downward trend built in, but this does not necessitate a time period when the phase of recovery will set in. Indeed, contemporary industrial economies have become so integrated and so complex that the weight of such a depression may be so heavy that the cycle's momentum may be lost and depression may last until a revolutionary political movement takes control and alters society completely.

The depression phase is therefore eliminated by a post-Great Depression commitment on the part of responsible governments to never allow such a situation to occur again. But this brings up a semantic issue. Given that responsible governments will not allow another Great Depression, how are recessions to be measured? According to the post–Great-Depression policies, depressions will never be allowed again; according to the judgment of each situation on its own standards and conditions, such as the extent of economic decline with respect to the economic levels of growth achieved during recovery and prosperity, there is no objective reason preventing the cycle's downward position, when it becomes extreme, from considered a depression. Of course, such a definition may be repugnant in the contemporary politician's lexicon. To avoid confusion, therefore, the depression phase will be considered a severe recession.

Moreover, this definition and its abolition of the term *depression* is not made to please the politicians, but is based on sound economic reasoning. Because the economic infrastructure established during the previous period of recovery is substantial, the quality and quantity of goods and services is greater than in the previous period. Combining these facts during the innovative and imitative processes and comparing them with the previous cycles, the cumulative effects of economic growth can be seen very clearly. This contemporary situation contrasts to the Great Depression, where the preceding cyclic movements offer no basis for comparison and where the economic collapse was almost complete. The cumulative effects of previous growth periods were wiped out as the banking and industrial systems collapsed and the decline of the stock exchange resulted in the elimination of many businesses and entrepreneurs. Although the current situation is severe and many people are affected. It is nothing like the Great Depression, for governing officials have learned the lesson of underwriting the economy.

Another point must be considered here. To maintain that the business cycle carries its own momentum moving in its phases as a machine in perpetual motion, is a neoclassical fiction based on economic determinism. Granted that the cycle is inherent in economic activity, but it need not operate in a consistent pattern. It is innovations and imitations, programs carried out within the context of each firm's abilities, that determine the firms positions with regard to their performance, and this performance depends to a significant extent on the cycle's position, which reflects the business attitudes. The business cycle can be considered as a force generated by the dynamics of closed-ended production cycles, in which the product is phased out because the production line is no longer profitable—as is the case with closed information systems pertaining to business operations. The cycles can also be seen as a consequence of managerial decisions based on liquidity positions formed through revenues from investment gains. With the firm's liquidity high, more risks are likely to be taken, but high liquidity is a result of good profitable turnover, which reflects consumer liquidity in consumption as the aggregate decisions are made to transfer disposable income to consumer income. As these two conditions are generated, they bring about dynamics unique to their own special circumstances—which is why no two cycles are alike, nor are the amount and quality of infrastructure generated comparable.

Managerial actions are based on the utilities of the programs, both subjective and objective. Prime importance is objective utility because this is the probabilistic interpretation and understanding of validity of the information pertaining to the programs, and it is on this basis that subjective utilities are formulated in which the decision makers and consumers order their personal preferences and choose to enact programs and to purchase the resulting goods and services respectively. From the managerial position, these programs have their effects on the economy and as they get under way, using resources and plant facilities that could have been used for alternative programs, their dynamics are generated and incorporated into the objective utility schedules of other decision-makers.

Basically, the business cycle moves in response to the expansion and contraction of innovation and imitation. The decisions to act on these projects or not to act, depend of the firms' objective utility positions, the objective ratings given to the proposed projects as best as they can be ascertained, and the managers' subjective utility preferences for the proposed projects that influence their decisions to act or not to act on these projects.

Thus, the contemporary business cycle is a combination of product cycles and liquidity positions of the many firms and industries in a society. While some product cycles tend to stabilize over time, new projects are introduced, either through innovation or imitation. This requires the commitment of funds and because of the profit motive, liquidity tends to be fully committed so that after these projects are introduced, further new production is unfeasible. It becomes feasible at a later date, when revenues are of sufficient quantity to allow for further investment. The element of competition, however, tends to make the firms' liquidity positions unstable as revenues are reduced because of the competitiveness of close substitutes.

Consider now how the cumulative effects of the various firms' product cycles bring about the aggregate business cycle, while they influence industries and the economy *in toto*. For example, the firm F in time $t_n$ has high liquidity and its production is imitatively oriented. The cycle's dynamics will be suppressed for the moment in order to isolate the firm as a working unit and to show how it generates dynamics. Since F's markets are imitative its supply and demand functions are fairly stable (the condition for the heuristic law of markets),[9] with all fluctuations that do occur being minor, requiring no serious managerial attention.

With stability and high liquidity, managerial decision making becomes oriented toward innovation. Liquidity is thus channeled into innovative production after sufficient market research has yielded a high utility rating for the proposed project. Entering the markets after sufficient advertising to generate pioneering consumption of the product in time $t_{n+m}$ (*m* being the time of marketing) generates the interests of the managers of other firms who have recognized a positive consumer response in the targeted groups. Thus, as sales increase and the consuming public continues to respond, F has initiated a market that draws imitators and initiates new growth. F's profits are then reduced according to the extent of competition; eventually a point will be reached in F's product cycle where growth will decline and a level of stability will set in once again, thereby equaling supply with demand for this particular product. The same occurs with the products of the competing firms until market saturation allows for no further competitive entry.

Thus, over time the innovative product has led to the development of a new market and economic growth increases accordingly. This in itself, however, is insufficient to generate the dynamics of the aggregate cycle. The point to be made here is that consumption is drawn toward the new product and its competitors, which means that it is drawn *from* other sources. Money for consumption may be taken from savings, in which case the liquidity positions from those institutions is reduced and their funds available for loaning and investment affected accordingly. The money may be drawn from other patterns of consumption such as in other markets, bringing about the phasing-out of those competitive firms whose profits are marginal, thereby increasing their liquidity as a result of eliminating that product, or their proclivity toward innovation, with the dynamics that innovation generates.

Still, these dynamics in themselves are inadequate to generate the aggregate business cycle, for the recirculation of money brings about a decline in one sector while raising the growth level of that sector which receives the money. Shifts in consumption patterns are not causes of cyclical motion as such, unless these shifts are very large. Innovation and imitation are effective only when they reach their target groups, these being the consumers who allocate their liquidity according to their acquired and accumulated tastes and preferences. Thus, that innovation and imitation bring about shifts in consumer spending is not sufficient to generate cyclical economic movement when undertaken on a small or moderate scale.

The cycle is, however, generated by the cumulative effects of innovation and imitation due to the establishment of consumer purchasing patterns for the duration. Again, the liquidity of the majority of firms when high is due to the preference of liquidity brought about through the phasing out of products with low utility and the costs saved from the expenditures of production. Fixed capital expenditures are written-off in taxes so that short-term payments are cancelled out by the long-run return on costs; the point is that high liquidity is a result in the decline of the firms' involvement in economic activity, which results in an increased gearing ratio and provides the basis for accumulating investments of a level sufficient to underwrite other innovative and imitative undertakings that management is unwilling or unable to undertake at that time. In other words, this indicates that for the economy in the aggregate, the trade-off between liquidity and production, with the preference to hold liquidity instead of investing in production, means that economic activity has declined to the low trough of the cycle's movement.

This trade-off will not last, however, because holding liquidity over time instead of channeling into production means that plant facilities are not being used and that liquidity is held without earning a profit. This liquidity allows for the initiation of projects not previously acted upon but that are of sufficient market utility to be acted upon when market conditions are right. During this phase production has declined generally and prices are high because consumer goods and services are in short supply compared to the earlier cyclical phase; moreover, many firms have opted for liquidity over production because their products have reached the stable stage in the particular product cycle and revenues have been reduced because of competition. This results in a scarcity sufficient to drive the aggregate price level upward. Moreover, the employment level has declined as firms seek to increase their liquidity by reducing their employment costs because of lost revenues due to competition and the ceased production. High prices, together with unemployment, bring about a psychological socioeconomic condition in which innovation is engaged in reluctantly and consumers change their purchasing patterns mainly by restricting consumption.

To resume economic activity, innovation as a trade-off against liquidity must get underway so that employment can increase and new purchasing patterns be established. The underwriting of this socioeconomic climate is the task of government—which will be discussed shortly. What is important at this phase is to understand that innovation requires reemployment to work the production lines. This in turn leads to the development of of local secondary and auxiliary businesses to service the branches of industry, thereby increasing general employment and hence consumption on the local scale, where the target groups and their spin-off consumers are located. The consequences of innovative and subsequent imitative production are thus the revival of the economy, the reemployment of workers with the increase in their purchasing power, and the shifting of consumer patterns so that those products unable to retain their utility in the reviving economy are phased out thereby giving the producers greater liquidity to enter other innovative or imitative production. The result is the ultimate widening and deepening of the economic infrastructure. Hence, with revived innovation and the following imitation, on a large scale, the cycle moves upward and recovery is underway.

This process continues until there is full employment—full employment being defined by the government—and most of the aggregate industrial capacity is utilized. As innovation continues, followed by imitation, purchasing patterns are established for products and not brand names because demand fluctuates as bargains are offered and as competition improves quality. Some competitive product brands are phased out because of competition and because of opting for liquidity. With employment at near capacity at this stage and with imitation slowing down because of the reduction in innovative products bringing fewer new markets, the cycle's motion continues upward, though at a decreasing rate. This is the phase of prosperity and in it are the dynamics of the impending downward movement.

Prosperity continues to increase, but entropy sets in, eventually slowing down the cycle's upward movement until this movement ceases and turns downward toward recession. Without sufficient aggregate innovation, imitation declines but for a while near-full employment provides sufficient consumer liquidity to maintain the consumption level. Competition increases in its rigor as firms not investing in new products vie with each other for customers; products of low competitive utility are phased out, which brings about unemployment, reducing the aggregate level of purchasing power. This sets into motion the phasing out of other products as purchasing power declines and as competition continues in its full rigor. The period of prosperity passes its peak and the cycle turns downward toward recession and if not checked, ultimately to depression.

Recession is marked by increasing numbers of unemployed, increasing bankruptcies among the secondary and auxiliary businesses, and the big firms' being weakened to the point of threats of takeover being realistic; and inflation high, as prices are raised to protect profit levels as much as possible to compensate for the reduced production levels resulting from the phasing out of the increasing number of low-utility goods and services. Fixed costs remain, however, and must be paid out of the increased liquidity, and with production and hence revenues declining, the liquidity level also declines. Innovation has all but ceased and imitation is mostly unprofitable because those products that are phased out are not readily replaced by other potential competitors due to the decline in consumer liquidity. This process of recession continues and is dynamic, moving downward until the cycle reaches its lower plateau of depression, after which a time lapse is required to begin the cycle's upward motion.

When the cycle's upward motion begins, the economy is not of the same composure as in its previous cyclical completion, but is altered due to its product composition. Its secondary and auxiliary businesses are different and as the cycle moves upward they are oriented toward promoting and servicing different products. Moreover, the processes of distribution have been altered as new businesses replace those which, as a result of bankruptcies and mergers, no longer remain. The big firms differ in the sense that their technologies have been altered to cope with the new production and competition that will develop. Target groups for new products are different to cope with the different socioeconomic income groups that have formed as a result of the cycle and the consequences of recession and—perhaps—depression. The economic infrastructure has been broadened by the new products and the technological changes incorporated in businesses to produce them.

Left on its own, without government intervention, therefore, the dynamics of economic growth will move the economy through the four cyclical phases, with the level and content of prosperity different each time, so that if illustrated graphically prosperity would be on a different set of coordinates, moving upward and to the right. Indeed, each cycle must be represented in comparison, indicating the unique growth bases for each cyclical motion.

The point made by Keynes and accepted by every macroeconomist ever since, that the downward swing should be minimized and the upward swing extended, is certainly the goal of both industry and government. It is to industry's best interests to keep the downward swing minimized because this allows it to maintain its liquidity and the trade-off between production and liquidity. It further allows for shortened periods of declining demand and increased periods of rising demand so that the options for innovation and imitation can be analyzed more carefully and the decisions made with less immediate economic pressure. Industry also has available its labor force, which will not migrate geographically or seek employment elsewhere if the low phase is short, because labor will soon be employed again. This is the goal for the government: for the obvious political reasons of maintaining its offices and good will with the voters; for maintaining the support of industry, for preventing destructive social unrest and for maintaining a strong socioeconomic infrastructure in light of international competition; and for keeping a strong posture in light of realpolitik confrontation.

In contemporary economies, which are managerially based, the depression phase of the cycle is neither necessary nor wanted. This phase does not lead to the clearing of the markets, as it does for the neoclassical model, but results in massive unemployment and the lying idle of productive capital; it provides no liquidity for strategic maneuvering and is self-perpetuating because of the psychological environment it generates. With its high unemployment and almost no economic activity, it is a period of stagnation, where innovation has ceased and there is no imitation. The depression is, nevertheless, a period of temporary duration, but one in which much socioeconomic suffering exists and for which there is no economic nor philosophical justification for its existence. Looking at our present situation with an awareness of our past, it is clear that since the depression phase of the cycle is an extention of the recession phase, depressions can be halted at the opportune moment, by restricting the dynamics of recession. This is a situation that did not exist prior to World War II, for the dynamics of industrialization were not fully comprehended as demonstrated by the Pigovan assumption of full employment. The mechanistic view of the world that the merger between science and technology into industry allowed, excluded one very important point: There are no real perpetual motion machines and the neoclassical cycle what was a manifestation of this view also broke down. For contemporary economics this mechanistic view has been altered by the government's taking action to maintain the mechanism, keeping the cycle in motion. The questions are, therefore, how is the opportune moment for cutting off the recession phase to be determined, and what actions are to be taken for doing so. It must be remembered that no absolute criteria exist for these decisions, as each cycle is unique. Each cycle carries with it its own goods and services, its own widening of the socioeconomic infrastructure, its own international competition generated by its dynamics.

Hence, the extent of unemployment must be gauged against the aggregate liquidity requirements necessary for the undertaking of innovative projects against organized labor's willingness and ability to tolerate unemployment. Moreover, these decisions must take into consideration the current utility of consumer purchasing power as assessed against the unknown potential future purchasing power as predicted by big businesses and organized labor in bargaining new wage structures. Government officials must assess when to cease underwriting unemployment, given the costs for doing so as the employment rate decreases with the cycle's downswing and given big businesses costs of reemployment at the cut-off point for revitalizing the economy. Thus, for these considerations, the socioeconomic costs of approaching stagnation and increasing inflation as means of reducing economic activity must be assessed, along with the levels determined sufficient for recession to have served the objectives of clearing the markets, thereby eliminating redundant and competitively inefficient products through their being phased out for the liquidity trade-off. These actions must be carefully assesed, analyzed, and agreed upon by big business and government officials.

While it is best for these power blocs to discuss their respective views on these issues, it is somewhat naive to suggest that an agreement can be easily reached. It must also be considered that while discussions are taking place, the cycle's dynamics are continuing, serving as a means of pressure, to be used accordingly by the blocs. Organized labor and big business are historical and natural protagonists; government, while relying on the support of big business for funding elections campaigns has not overlooked the fact that labor has also become big business in its own right, with its own orientation. Labor controls the strike weapon and to a large extent determines the degree of consumer liquidity for its members through wage bargaining; it accumulates its funds through membership dues, which are invested.

An important reason for reaching such an agreement—one strictly from the power-bloc self interest—is that business have to confront strong competition, domestically and internationally, and neither depressions nor sharp recessions are to their advantage. The liquidity trade-off is very short-run because of the payment of fixed costs, so that as the cycle moves downward a point is reached where the trade-off between the costs of employing and maintaining liquidity is no longer to the firms' advantage, occuring when the fixed costs of upkeep and expenses begin to equal the amount of revenues from current sales.

Labor's interests are also served best when the cut-off point is reached because this results in wages being restructured and employment maintained without resulting in further unemployment due to the cycle's recessive phase. This is also to the advantage of big business because while maintaining employment, its revenues are not eroded further, because consumer liquidity is maintained at least on this level and the incentive (i.e., the profit motive) for some degree of innovation and imitation still exists. Furthermore, it reduces the pressure for government action to reduce unemployment and to inject money into the economy, a move lacking in industrial backing in the form of goods and services, so that consumer liquidity is increased and further demand generated with supply fairly stable, resulting in increased inflation.

Reaching the cutoff point is also important to the government, which is democratically elected and therefore must act to ease the economic crisis or face an angry electorate at election time. The standard procedure of injecting money into the economy without industrial backing in corresponding output, is perhaps the easiest response in this crisis, but it is illusory and merely feeds the inflationary flame. It does, however, have the tendency to placate the electorate and is, at best, a very short-term operation—short-term being used here to describe the impact of the added inflationary currency on demand.

Within the post-Keynesian era, governments act to maintain the economy in equilibrium, seeking to defuse an inflated economy and to stimulate the economy when deflation becomes a threat. Taxes and government contracts are tools governments employ to achieve their desired goal of equilibrium and growth. The consequence of applying these tools to contemporary economics can be seen with the diseconomies of the current prolonged recession and were evident in the severe overcorrection of the stock markets in October 1987. The worldwide dynamics of these situations, especially with the political unrest in the industrialized and developing countries, also demonstrate that the old conceptions are out of date.

It is like trying to cure a disease with medicines that were once effective, but to which the disease no longer responds. Not that these post-Keynesian tools have been applied indiscriminately; rather, they are no longer effective for the objective they seek to achieve. Since the firm is the generator of economic growth (the government being the underwriter), the firm's behavior does not comply with the conditions of neoclassical equilibrium, nor Keynesian and post-Keynesian equilibrium-and-growth programs, no matter how hard it tries to conform to the heuristic law of markets. The firm can never achieve equilibrium between supply and demand over the medium-and long-run periods because of the necessity to phase out certain products, to opt for liquidity over production, and to open new markets or imitate in those markets already established and successful. There is the rescheduling of production quotas due to competition and the ordering of consumer incentives to increase sales—the direction of which cannot be predetermined. If economic stability exists—either because of the circumstances of the economy or because of its imposition by the government— if the disequilibrium situation of growth is stilled, it is only in the real world of economic dynamics when the phase of depression is reached. In contemporary economics, should a depression be allowed to occur, it would be short-lived as compared with those depressions of the past, and most certainly compared to the Great Depression, because management will seek and find ways to stimulate production and generate demand once more. The heuristic law of markets is a managerial goal, an ideal for stabilizing production, and as such it is in conflict with the reality of economic competition and consumer fickleness.

The Keynesian-cum-post-Keynesian policy of taxation—conducted in an ad hoc manner, increasing taxes to siphon off excess purchasing power or lowering them to increase aggregate liquidity—is certainly ineffective as a policy on its own. Liquidity should be regulated according to the requirements of business and not from the government's point of consideration alone. When recession increases in intensification, firms tend to trade off liquidity for employment and production in the real world, because liquidity will be short-lived as costs have to be met. Thus, to reduce their liquidity through taxation firms are forced to lower their prices temporarily so that they can maintain a competitive position for consumers' dwindling liquidity. This has a short-term effect of increasing sales, but with goods and services fixed, this results in further price rises. Tax increases in this situation result in extreme economic distortions, the inefficient application of money, and the diseconomic utilization of resources—themselves economic costs that have to be repaid socially when the cycle moves upward again.

For example, the cycle's upward motion will be delayed due to the inefficient application of money because of the lowering of prices, which is an artificial step, induced by government policy of tax increases, leading to reduced liquidity that must be compensated-for by artifically reducing prices. Demand is stimulated, but not supply at the same rate, which raises prices soon after that much higher. The economic distortions and the diseconomic utilization of resources are two sides of the same coin, as it were, because instead of consumer liquidity being conserved in this period of uncertainty, the initially-reduced prices provide a *sense* of security that does not in fact exist. Lower prices paid at time t under these circumstances will result in significantly higher prices in time $t + 1$, prices that compensate for the initial price reduction and for the the forced increases in supply at costs higher than during recovery. These prices will be met with insufficient consumer liquidity, moving the cycle downward further, perhaps into depression. The distortions arise when supply is forced, due to the initial increases in demand, for resources are allocated into supply when they should not be, because the aggregate conditions are not right for this increase. Costs are too high and labor not readily available for the manufacturing and distribution of these goods and services supplied; those who are employed will be getting wages not commensurate with their work as determined by the conditions of recovery. Moreover, increased liquidity because of tax breaks may encourage the further trading-off of production and employment for liquidity, which is to be held to avoid future borrowing and to reduce and perhaps eliminate interest payments on loans. The option for liquidity may also be based on uncertainty over economic conditions since imitation has become unprofitable and innovation infeasible due to the lack of consumer liquidity and the reluctance of consumers to get into debt to finance future purchases. This option for liquidity, understandable psychologically, is like chasing after an illusion, because, as has already been stated, meeting fixed costs eats up the liquidity and without production, it cannot be replaced.

Supporting industries by placing orders is usually a method to stimulate *ad hoc* production on the assumption that money injected into the economy and backed by production is a viable method for providing liquidity based on productivity and is therefore important for reviving a recessed economy and ensuring a degree of employment significant enough to make an impact on the economy and bring the cycle moving upward again. This reasoning is founded on the multiplier effect, where money earned is partly saved and partly directed toward consumption. That money saved is invested in industry and that part directed for consumption stimulates industrial production—so the argument goes. This is not necessarily so, because increased production in one sector or in one industry may stimulate investments that may not be directed toward financing other industrial projects, since unsuitable interest rates may preclude investors on both sides of the transaction from reaching an agreement: Subjective and objective utilities may not match, thereby rendering the transaction entropic. Moreover, the stimulation provided to production may not be sufficient for output to become increased to the level of offsetting prices rises, but may lead to further inflation if demand exceeds supply. There are no guarantees here either, unless massive industrial support is allocated, in which case productivity will increase and competition will set in. Such funding would have to be of such great proportions that it would not pass through the political channels to be accepted.

Regulating interest rates is also a technique employed by governments. This measure is taken on the assumption that if rates are low, investments will be required and sought after by the firms for project financing, which will stimulate output, which in turn will reduce unemployment and move the cycle upward. The difficulty with this is that low interest rates relative to current economic conditions may encourage firms to seek investments, but will not encourage investors to opt against the liquidity position. Thus, interest rates will not remain low, but will rise according to the demand for liquidity, to a level suitable to the market conditions. Interest rates respond to the supply and demand for money, with respect to the markets and productivity potential as expressed in the quality and quality of products.

The opposite effect may hold, so that governments raise interest rates to encourage investors to find markets for their liquidity. This does not encourage firms to seek investments because of the rates being high. The economic conditions will therefore force rates down to the level where managers and investors agree to enter into business transactions.

The difficulty with these approaches is not that they are ineffective per se, but that their applications make them ineffective as tools solving the economic problems. For example, the post-Keynesian ideal of minimizing the cycle's downward swing and maintaining the economy on an upward path of growth is unattainable because of the very dynamics of innovation and imitation. New products will always appear on the market, and if successful will be followed by close imitative competitors. Markets will always reach near-saturation with unemployment rising as products with low profits due to intense competition are phased out and firms opt for short-term utility. The cycle in a democratic society cannot be prevented.

Nor can attempts made by governing authorities to minimize recessions and maximize recovery and prosperity be prevented, but as the current crisis demonstrates, these approaches are of little utility. They are post-Keynesian in orientation and designed for equilibrium growth, and therefore have no great impact on the economy. What is required is a concerted effort by organized labor, the managerial staffs of the big firms, and government representatives to reach agreement on how low the recessive phase of the cycle is to move—and where the cutoff point should be.

Each cycle is unique because it is based on the conditions established in the previous cycle. They are, of course, common with respect to the general conditions of unemployment, idle capital, and liquidity without utility. These, however remain abstractions until placed in the context of each specific recession-phase of the cycle, in which their content, composition, and extent are determined. The point is that government measures placed on the economy to ease recessions may make sense theoretically, but in fact the government alone can exert very little control, so that the consequences of these measures are not necessarily those that are pertinent. The regulation of interest rates, without discussing the perspective of those who work with these rates to discover how they consider the results of such regulation, merely results in artifically changing the liquidity in the economy, without industrial backing sufficient for absorbing the consequences. Supporting specific industries with the intention of reviving employment and stimulating the economy, without considering the consequences of productivity on those supported firms and those firms that are supposed to benefit subsequently from the money injected into the economy as a result, may only complicate the difficulties and increase inflation, although this is not the intention. Furthermore, taxation policies have yet to prove themselves as viable forms of economic regulation because of the loopholes in tax programs and, more important, because of the ways of not paying taxes—not recognized by the authorities. Money is drained out of the economy and placed into accounts that have no macro utility, thereby depriving the economy of sources of investment.

The question to be considered here is, how is the cutoff point to be determined? The cutoff point should be determined by assessing the extent that business opt for liquidity rather than production, given current economic conditions. From the perspective of those businesses that opt for liquidity this depends on consumer willingness to shift from current purchasing patterns to those that have yet to be established through marketing; in other words, the determinant must be the viability of possible innovative products, given the present consumer preferences. This is also a potential trade-off position between present certainty about market conditions and future risk over the possibilities of market potential due to innovation and subsequent imitation. This depends on the amount of liquidity held by consumers for demand as compared with income already allocated for consumption and savings. The risk for businessess is that by opting for liquidity, they will not fall for the liquidity illusion, in which liquidity as a buffer against uncertainty is lost through paying fixed costs.

Labor's perspective differs, of course, because it is to labor's disadvantage that unemployment should not be other than marginal, in the sense of being frictional and, in part, seasonal. Unemployment increases in phases of recession and organized labor finds itself with disillusioned supporters who withdraw their financial backing and their votes for those whom they elected for representation. To minimize unemployment in recession, labor's cutoff point on the cycle will be higher than that opted for by business. This difference provides a basis for negotiation.

The government's cutoff point will be based on a combination of factors. First, the government must take into consideration the theoretical and practical post-Keynesian factor of preventing all major economic disruptions—the specter of the Great Depression still stalks us—by taking measures for keeping the economy in an equilibrium growth position. Second, the position of business must be considered since business provides employment and growth. Third, the government must consider the position of organized labor, because this political bloc exerts considerable influence on voters and discontented labor is a force to be reckoned with. Fourth, the government must consider how the "common" voter, unaffiliated with big labor or business, fares in the economic recession.

The difficulty is, given the uniqueness of every cycle, on what basis can a cutoff point for halting the cycle's downward motion be reached, given the conflict of vested interests as well as the common ground for reaching an agreement? This can be determined by assessing the percentage of unemployment tolerable for organized labor (excluding seasonal and frictional unemployment which have no political weight), the degree to which unemployment is preferred to nonproductive liquidity for business, and the extent to which low productivity and unemployment remain harmless for the government. Labor economists, government statisticians, and business economists can pool their resources, stating their respective views, to place these considerations into a working formula, find the cutoff point agreeable to all concerned, and take actions appropriate to the situation.

This is surely a better way of spending money, time, and intellectual energy, than combating recessions in ways which have so far been ineffective and of no utility. So far, using post-Keynesian procedures, the cycle has been resistant when the "cures" have been applied and has moved in its own natural way in spite of the attempts to restrain it. Hence, labor, government, and business decision makers should direct their efforts to determine where the cutoff point is for stopping the recession and which methods should be applied to achieve this end.

Of course, the consideration should be to find and apply those methods that will not only stop, but reverse the cycle's path. But for this to be done, decision makers must agree to a cutoff, because if not, the measures taken will be of little or no effect. The forces of the cycle will negate those policies introduced to reverse the cycle; indeed, they will override these policies. If there is less than full cooperation between labor, business, and government, the efforts will be futile and the cycle will ride out its course unperturbed.

In the early phases of the recession, businesses opt for liquidity as a trade-off against productivity, to maintain flexibility during the uncertain period. The cutoff point in the recession is that period when businesses begins opting for productivity over liquidity—whatever liquidity remains after fixed costs have been paid. This is the signal for government and labor to cooperate with business. It is business that stimulates economic activity. The government is the underwriter of business, and labor is the force that makes business work. But managers in their decision-making processes and in their mustering the resources and channeling them into production, and in developing markets and strategies in light of competition, are the generators of economic activity. When managers seek to resume productivity, they do so because either their liquidity has become small, so that trading it off for productivity is not such a risk, or because they view the market conditions favorable for resuming operations, or perhaps for a combination of these.

This is the cutoff point and is the signal for the government officials and the labor organizations that business will allow the cycle to fall no further, but this can be achieved only with the government's and with labor's assistance. At this point, governing bodies should ease consumer taxes so that money can be increased for spending and saving. Furthermore, money should be injected into the economy at a rate equal to the previous cycle's inflation so that the economy will not experience a shock that it cannot tolerate due to this monetary injection. In any case, this money will not be available until the next fiscal year, during which it will be allocated according to the economy's response to the reviving measures. Production and consumption, which follows, will therefore be stimulated by the productivity option and by greater consumer liquidity; the injected money will take effect only after, increasing consumption and output that much more.

Labor's cooperation is essential here. Businesses have to introduce more efficient ways of producing in order to withstand the rigors of the ensuing competition. This may result in the short-term layoffs of still other workers, those who managed to retain their jobs during the early periods of the cycle's downswing. It is a fact, although not so comforting to those affected, that where short-run unemployment results from improved production techniques, medium-run employment increases as production increases and competition places demands on the labor market. Moreover, those who are employed during the later stages of production acquire the skills that have been developed during the earlier stages and thus tend to have the advantage over those employed earlier in that these skills are relatively free from the difficulties of a "breaking-in" period.

Labor's cooperation is also necessary where wages are concerned. Labor's wage position should be in line with the economic conditions and business should compensate labor accordingly. Too excessive wage demands in light of these conditions only result in work conflicts when rejected by management, which may affect the industry's operations. Wages that are too low rebound on management because consumption is at levels according to consumer liquidity. Proper compensation, including proper salary scales, can be worked out within the terms of the economic situation without industrial action being taken and industrial output halted. This may reverse the cycle's upward path as liquidity is reduced due to the halt in production and the reduction of liquidity held by those workers engaged in the industrial action; also, there is the uneasy economic climate generated by such action, which may induce strikes in other industrial sectors.

During this period unemployment benefits must be maintained to provide a basic consumption level for those not being compensated by industry for their being unemployed. This will be discussed further in the next part, but for now, it can be said that should the government embark on welfare-oriented projects, this could be done as a means for relieving the unemployment situation only after the cycle begins moving upward. This happens because it not only injects money into the economy at levels higher than the unemployment rate; it also requires the cooperation of the private sectors to supply the government with goods and services, which these sectors could not supply had they not begun to retool and produce for the private sectors. Their machinery is turning out products and their labor structures are geared for working. Only with these conditions operating can the government turn to these industries for their goods and services.

During this resurgence of economic activity, interest rates pose problems on their own. Here, the government's influence should be marginal, acting on banks, government-backed savings and loan associations, and building societies. Interest rates fluctuate according to the aggregate utility of liquidity and investment. The government should act by providing incentives in the form of lowering the banks' and other institutions' capital-investment ratios so that liquidity is that much more easily accumulated. Any attempt to force interest-rate mobility will result in distortions in the supply and demand for money, and will retard the benefits of the other programs. Imposing interest rates of which the economy is not prepared to take advantage, will, in the case where the rates are lowered, result in borrowing for projects for which the utility of money is very low. The employment situation will not be able to respond to this money, and the markets will be unable to absorb any significant production increases as a result of the money being channeled into production. Should the interest rates be raised prematurely, then investments which were to be made will be cancelled or postponed, retracting from the economy money whose utility is high, given the receptivity toward innovation and imitation on the part of the targeted and secondary consumer groups.

The interest rate, as a regulative tool, must be implemented with awareness and with caution, in response to the economic climate. The government's regulation of the capital-investment ratio should therefore be considered with respect to aggregate business activity. Where businesses begin retooling for production, where innovation is being considered and funding sought, when labor organizations consider programs of retraining those affected by unemployment (more on this in the Part 3), then the capital-investment ratio should be regulated to make the lending institutions more liquid. The lower cost of money will be compensated by the increased borrowing and the returns paid on the money. As the cycle begins its upward motion from recession, the utility of money increases and the failures of projects and businesses are reduced accordingly. There is greater liquidity held by the consumers and, after a period of restricting consumption because of the uncertainty of the recession, spending will increase again, making business more profitable.

The capital-investment ratio should be regulated with respect to the agreement among business and labor as to the cutoff point of the recession. Depending on the circumstances, the government may implement a time-inducement factor in its use of this ratio. For example, having reached agreement with the other two sectors, it may reduce interest rates before business makes serious attempts at borrowing for financing projects. This step can be taken, for example, as a response to a "scenario" in which the three sectors, during the recession, seek to formulate the cutoff point in the near future. Such a step will encourage business and labor, making money more available, and stimulating activity just prior to the agreed time.

This ratio can also be used as an economic "weapon," as it were, to bring business and labor around to the government's position, should hesitation or opposition occur. While each sector views the situation from its own perspective, only the government is accountable and answerable to its electorate and citizenry in general. A prolonged recession is not favorable to public opinion about the government and to alter this, the capital-investment ratio can be changed as a stimulant, even though business and labor may express reservations. There is a caveat here, however: Premature altering of the ratio may affect the utility of money and stimulate activity before it is adventageous to the economy in general. Market saturation may still exist and innovation may still be inactive. Releasing money at low interest rates may stimulate borrowing, but the money's utility may not be as high as it could have been, had the proper time been considered for so doing. This explains why the use of the ratio as a weapon may have distressing affects on the economy and why it is best to employ this ratio in agreement with the other sectors. Sometimes political expediency clashes with economic good sense.

The consequence of these methods, when acted upon in concert and with the approval of the three sectors, is that they stimulate production and consumption at the proper stage in the recession phase of the cycle. Prior to their enactment, imitation was still functioning, but only on the part of those brave firms willing to chance entering a market that had already experienced saturation. Innovation, if existing at all, is nil and certainly insignificant with respect to the dynamics of market development; that is, the likelihood that it would draw with it imitation is low because business liquidity, together with consumer liquidity, is low (there would most likely be no Slutsky substitution effect because of committed consumer loyalties and the unwillingness to experiment in the aggregate during difficult times) and firms prefer in these circumstances to stay as they are. However, with production stimulated and consumers possessing additional liquidity because of increasing employment and government incentives such as project building and the capital-investment ratio, the processess of innovation and imitation can begin anew, thereby moving the cycle upward to recovery and prosperity.

One more point has to be considered. During prosperity, should an upper cutoff point on the cycle's upswing be determined, so that measures can be applied to curb prosperity or to maintain it to prevent the cycle's tending downward? The answer is that the prosperity phase should be left alone because it is increasing at a decreasing rate, thereby allowing industrial activity to slow down. The downturn eventually sets in, allowing the markets to clear themselves, offering sales as consumer liquidity becomes restricted. Labor, business, and the government will then have sufficient time to consider where and when the cutoff point should be, each with respect to its specific interests. Moreover, consumers will have time to reasses the utilities of their purchases and be psychologically receptive to the new products of innovation. Labor will be sufficiently ready to work and the strike threat minimized as the cycle moves upward. Governments will be prepared to take unified steps, together with business and labor, to maintain the cycle's movement into recovery, thereby eliminating the onesided *ad hoc* policies that have proved to be ineffectual. Applying these methods in a unified manner, working with the government, business, and labor, can limit recession and extend prosperity, the objective since Keynes stated this point.

# Part 3

# ECONOMIC WELFARE AND DYNAMIC DISEQUILIBRIUM

# 8

# Preliminary Remarks

> Although philosophers have sought to specify equity in universal principles, the basic thrust of the economic profession has been to seek specification of economic equity in the aggregation of individual preferences rather than in universal values. Unfortunately, the process of aggregating preferences ran into an intellectual dead-end and came to a halt in the 1950s. Although the dead-end is real, the attempt to find economic equity in individual preferences illuminates the concept of economic equity. There may also be an escape.
>
> Lester C. Thurow
> *Generating Inequality*

## INTRODUCTION

When reading Thurow's words, the philosophically trained economist may be somewhat confused by their meanings—not in the sense that each word has to be defined, but in the import and significance of them. For example, the terms "aggregrate preferences" and "universal values" appear to be somewhat confusing in Prof. Thurow's context, when he holds them up as contrasting sentiments. Granted, the very concept of "aggregate" is diminished when compared to "universal." "Aggregate" is the common, the conjunction or collection of particulars formed into a whole mass or sum; it is the total or universal but subject to change, in the way that, for mathematics, a group or combination of numbers or objects are axiomatic set-universal, subject to the dynamics of the system and its operators. Thus, aggregate demand for a product is the sum of demand, its total, its conjunction, its collected demand expressed as an economic force. Aggregation changes, however, adjusting to the reality for which it is expressed. As a product is phased out, the aggregate demand declines; likewise, a declining aggregate demand may bring about a product's demise.[1]

"Universal," however, is not subject to change; it is permanent and inflexible, in this sense static and all-encompassing for its defined and delineated range and domain. In this sense, then, there is some ambiguity between "aggregate" in its sense of being the set-universal grouping, and "universal," independent of changing permutations, or sets included in it. This ambiguity may be excusable, however, because two different concepts of the universal are being discussed.

But what about "preferences" and "values"?—do they differ that much? In discussions of ethics, there is a difference. Preferences are personal, though they may be held in common with other people; if so, they are held independently. Values, on the other hand, are also personal, but more than likely, developed by the society and taken for granted by those who hold them as the correct approach, the best method of conduct. But for economics, in which the context of Thurow's sentiment is expressed, value and preference tend to be equal. A person's value depends on his or her utility preference; therefore value and preference are strongly related. A good preferred over another good for consumption has a higher value for the person; therefore, he or she chooses that good if affordable.

This does not negate Thurow's assertion that the process of aggregating preferences came to a halt in the 1950s. Such a process relies on statistical compilations, which were made extremely difficult—indeed, increasingly so—by the quantity of innovative products and the extent of imitation that followed, competing for consumer liquidity. This was unprecedented in the history of economic development and the statisticians, viewing the economy from Keynesian glasses, as it were, were not able to comprehend the situation of the postwar economics of managerial capitalism.

Furthermore, Thurow states that as each person determines the amount of utility that flows from his or her income, no one gets to impose his or her preferences on anyone else.

Social welfare is found by aggregating individual utilities. Since no one is given a zero or negative weight in the social welfare function, every time an individual is better off (i.e., has more utility) and no one else is worse off, social welfare must increase (even if only a little).[2]

Thurow then states that, given a social welfare function and knowing individual utility functions, economists would be in a position to pronounce on the equity or inequity of any economic change. Anything that makes the social welfare function go up, he maintains, is good; anything that makes the social welfare function go down, is bad. Therefore Thurow maintains that the obvious economic goal is to maximize social welfare.

This argument is reminiscent of Pareto's argument, which is one of the pillars of accepted socioeconomic welfare theory. As such, it is not without its difficulties. For example, is social welfare really a function of aggregate individual utilities? And consider Pareto's position—that welfare improves if at least one person's economic position is better, while everyone else remains the same, represents an increase in *social* welfare—is this valid? Can the people still unemployed be considered in a better aggregate welfare position because one person's welfare has improved while all others welfare remains unchanged? Alternatively, can welfare be considered to be worsened if one's position is worsened, while all others' positions remain the same?

The tenets of neoclassical welfare economics are no longer valid, if they ever were. To consider welfare in terms of aggregate welfare functions or universal standards, is not to realize that since the end of World War II a new and unique set of economic conditions has been formed, one that does not respond very well to the neoclassical, Keynesian, or post-Keynesian conceptualizations and prescriptions. The attempt to find economic equity is, indeed, real; it is based on a genuine concern for the welfare of peoples as citizens of their respective countries and as participants in the economic processes that maintain their countries viabilities. But to assess this noble concept of equity in terms of aggregate welfare functions is to do little to come to grips with the real economic issues. Even the Marxists, with all their human feelings for their fellow worker and human being, sought equity, subjecting the people to the will of the state and thus making them equal within the state's conceptualizations: equal, yes, but not different—not to the point of being innovative and imitative economically, generating economic growth and prosperity.

This does not mean that those who think of welfare in neoclassical or Keynesian or post-Keynesian terms are seeking to prevent economic growth, leaving the mechanisms of growth to the state bureaucrats. There is another issue here, however, one that is just as devastating in its own way. While seeking aggregate welfare functions, becoming involved in advanced statistical computations and econometric models, there is an oversight being made. This is the lack of consideration for those very conditions and circumstances that constitute the problems of economic and social welfare.

The terms ''economic welfare'' and ''social welfare'' are used together and often interchangeably in the literature, because of their dependence and their conditions. Is unemployment, for example, strictly an economic consideration, or is it a social consideration? Indeed, it is both economic and social. The same holds for the lack of education—although the reasons for this may be strictly social and familial. Slums, the blight of our cities, are social and economic— social in their circumstance and economic for their reason. Poverty, the scourge of our peoples, is economic and social. The solutions to these situations are, however, first economic and then social; this order is necessary, for without the economic resources, there can be no real social development and these problems would remain. Is there another way?

## FURTHER COMMENTS

In this latter part of the twentieth century we have achieved amazing feats in the arts and sciences. Also, our economies have accomplished great deeds, even though the specter of the Great Depression remains with us. An argument can be made, therefore, for leaving the issues of welfare economics alone. After all, we use our resources in projects of national defense, into building the economic infrastructure, into innovating and imitating to maintain the system and to generate wealth. This generates a "pulling up" effect, in the sense that it does provide employment and stresses the need for education to obtain employment. It provides an increasing franchise of people who were disenfranchised previously, prevented from becoming active in the economy and receiving the benefits from this activity. The economist concerned with welfare economics should continue in the manner of considering programs for increasing the welfare function, which is good, and preventing those policies which bring the welfare function down, which is socially and economically bad.

Meanwhile, this attitude still prevails in our contemporary economy. The emphasis of economic concern is profits, efficiency, better terms of trade, and maintaining the business cycle on an even, yet upward, growth path. This is not to belittle the profit motive or efficiency, or the other objectives of seeking and promoting the better economic health. It is just this point, however, that must be tackled. Better economic health relies, of course, on profits, and efficiency, and better terms of trade. But so long as the conditions of poverty, slums, and unemployment plague our economies, this health will be fragile at best.

Welfare economics is considered the "black sheep" of the discipline. Its concern for the "good" and its attempt to avoid the "bad," brings it out of the pure discipline of economic reasoning and places it partly in the amorphous reasoning of the philosophers, for whom the arguments about the "good" and the "bad" go back as far as ancient Greece and even further, to the Bible, without any permanent resolutions being made. Economics, on the other hand, has made progress, from the time of Adam Smith to the post-Keynesians.

It must be said that the terms "good" and "bad" are ethically laden and are therefore unfortunate choices in our scientifically-oriented period. Therefore, instead of discussing the "good" and "bad" in terms of welfare, the terms "benefit," "efficient," and other such accepted terminology will be used. For what must be considered is that welfare economics is not indeed the black sheep of the discipline; it is the final objective of economics, to construct an economy in which waste is eliminated and the efficient utility of resources maintained. An economy with a low welfare profile is an economy of high growth. The lack of unemployment means high levels of liquidity and therefore high consumption. Maintained over the long run, this results in the abolition of economic poverty and its social consequences such as slums and illiteracy. Economic-cum-social welfare will then be able to deal strictly with those people who, for whatever reasons, are unable to fend for themselves.

# 9

# The Welfare Utility Function

## GENERAL COMMENTS

It is said that the gift of prophecy was terminated with the destruction of the Second Temple.[1] However, the tendency for prophecy still remains and has become somewhat sophisticated in the form of inductive logic. This is the reasoning that, given certain specific conditions holding in the past and present that yield specific results, the same results will be yielded, should these conditions hold in the future. For example, given the temperature of water at 212°F., the water will respond to this temperature by boiling. This has happened in the past, it happens in the present, and therefore will occur at all times in the future.

This is not the place to delve into the intricacies of inductive logic, and the above example has no bearing on general economics (although it did bear on the reasoning of David Hume, a philosopher and economist, and a contemporary of Adam Smith). There is, however, a bearing on welfare economics. For example, since the beginning of the Industrial Revolution, there have been slums as people migrated to the cities to find employment. Because more people moved into these centers of industrialization than there were more jobs available, there was poverty. Poverty bred illiteracy at the time when education was gaining in importance and the printed word more accessible to the multitudes.

Throughout the processes of industrialization great wealth was amassed while poverty still persisted. Those people on the lower rungs of the economic ladder were socially disenfranchised (i.e., kept out of the economic system), either by their own making or by the socioeconomic circumstances in which they were born and raised—circumstances generally frowned upon by society in general, thereby adding to the discrimination.

One important dynamic of this industrialization process is that it generated business cycles in which the wealthy could easily fall to the level of poverty and, albeit much more difficult, in which even those in poverty, if having imagination, daring, and economic sense, could raise themselves out of their condition and achieve great wealth. The business cycle became ingrained in the industrialization processes; it came to be expected, yet its severity in the recession-depression phase could never be anticipated, while its recovery-prosperity phases were too stimulating and enjoyable to be considered as subjects for economic analysis. Poverty still existed, and so did the slums in which the poor dwelt. In good times, some of those slumdwellers managed to get out; in bad times, some of the wealthy found their way in. But in general and real terms, the slums and all they contained still remained.

Business cycles came and went, and then came the downward crash of 1929, and the extreme poverty that followed. Unemployment was high and machinery remained idle. The wealthy, most of them, descended into the ranks of the unemployed and there seemed no sign of the perpetual movement upward. The mechanism broke down, only to be repaired by Keynesian theory and the Second World War.

Poverty, in our postwar post-Keynesian period, still exists, as do the slums and all they breed. While the Industrial Revolution has come to an end, the conditions of economic growth are the same in the respect that poverty, slums, and all that they breed still persist. The difference between then and now, between the pre-and post-Depression periods, is that there are institutionalized methods for alleviating poverty, such as unemployment insurance, welfare payments, and social security.

Where does induction come in? These conditions have existed since the Industrial Revolution, and the post-World War II situation did not remove them, in spite of the difficulties experienced during the depression. They most certainly exist now and, without prophesying but inducing, they will exist for still a while longer. The question is, for how long. We have the resources to remove them forever from our economies. This does not mean that, should this come about, there would be no people in a higher income bracket than others (i.e., that there would no longer be degrees of wealth). All men and women are born in the same manner, but with different genetic makeups. Talents are different, proclivities are different, likes and dislikes are different. Some people ascribe to careers in the arts and sciences, while others seek their fortunes in business. Some people earn more than others, through their occupations and by using skills that they inherited and developed. This is the way of the world. But the existence of poverty, slums, and the disorientation they breed is the way of society, and a social outlook that has not moved beyond the time of the Great Depression. These can be removed; whether or not they will be removed is not for the inductive logician to proclaim, but it is a task for the economist to frame a theory that will make possible their obliteration, to society's benefit.

## THE WELFARE UTILITY FUNCTION

The problem with the social welfare function is that it is impossible to calculate. This would require the calculation of each consuming and working individual's utility function with respect to preferences; these preferences are not stable, but change as tastes change, as people experiment with consumption and as people are influenced by others to alter their consuming behavior. The social welfare function is Paretian, and therefore subject to the restrictions discussed in the first Part on Pareto's theory. Moreover, the social welfare function cannot account for the dynamics of change in consumer preferences; it does not take into account the reasons for changing consumption patterns as does the substitution effect. Slutsky's substitution effect explains theoretically how consumers change their patterns, but it does not point out the impact of these changes in the social welfare function of utilities.

These contributions, together with Edgeworth's indifference-curve contract concept, are extremely important, for they placed the basic concepts of neo-classical welfare economics in their proper perspective and formed the basis for welfare programs today. They do, however, relate to a period of economics that is no longer relevant. The neoclassical era drew to an end when that system collapsed in the Great Depression. This does not mean that the ideas of the welfare economists of the neoclassical period are significant only for their historical value. It does mean, however, that a different approach to welfare must be considered, one relevant to contemporary economic conditions.

In Part 2, it was stated that with agreement as to the cutoff point in the cycle's downward phase, business, the government, and organized labor could act in concert to halt the downward movement and bring the cycle back up again. It is to these three economic forces that the solutions to the welfare difficulties can be found. In this sense, then, the social welfare function which attempts to describe the consumption patterns of working and consuming individuals must be replaced by a consideration of the functions of those generators of economic growth and activity. Businesses employ, thereby providing income; the government employs, as well as underwrites the economy, thereby providing the basis for economic activity; organized labor employs, as well as protects workers's rights, thereby reducing the exploitation of workers and providing political influence to see that a living wage is paid. Each worker, each consuming individual, falls into at least one of these spheres of influence, and it is to these powers that the welfare function is to be sought for our contemporary economic situation.

This welfare function is *not* a social welfare function; it is a *utility* welfare function. The greater the utility of these powers, the greater the liquidity available for consumption, the greater the business output and thus the greater innovation and imitation, and the more effective government policy is for carrying out the tasks of underwriting the economy. From a high utility, greater social welfare is derived; from a low utility, less social welfare results. The greater or lesser utility depends on the position of the trade cycle, but this must wait for clarification in chapter 10.

At this stage, the utility welfare function can be stated in a stationary setting, without dynamics. Letting W stand for the welfare utility function, $W_t = U(I, G, L)_t$, with the enclosed letters standing for Industry, Government, and Labor, respectively. As these are generalized terms, they can be broken down into their components. Industry, for example, contains the subsets of all industrial firms, secondary businesses and their auxiliaries. Government contains the subsets of all government activity bearing on the economy, such as defense, taxation, and welfare payments of all kinds.[2] Labor is organized labor in all branches of industry and government, viewed in terms of their wage bargaining and strike actions as they affect the economy.

The general utility of W is determined in the same manner as the information system $\underline{S}$; that is, the utility of W for any time $t$ is $0 < W_t < 1$. For each component of $W_t$ there are subsets. The I component of industry and business, for example, is composed of subsets for the various industries such as steel, the automotive industry, electronics, and so on. For each of these subsets, there are further subsets, such as the various automotive companies, the several steel and electronic companies, etc. The utility position of the individual firm within each of these subsets shows its ability to compete within its restricted market. This depends on the firm's information system and the responses from investors and consumers that this system evokes. Moreover, while one firm may not be able to compete effectively, other firms competing for the same market may be doing very well and thus showing a high profit rate. The total of these firms at time t gives their respective utility positions, so that if some of these firms' utilities are low while the majority are high, then for these firms, say, $F_1$ in the complex of firms, tends to 1.

The low utility rates for those several firms may be due to several reasons. There may, for example, be a reduction in their efforts to market the competing product, as their managers seek to rechannel their resources into developing other products, either innovative or imitative for other markets. Or, there may be conflict within the firm at the decision-making level and managers seek to liquidate their own positions and seek employment elsewhere. Another reason may be the opting for liquidity instead of maintaining production for achieving strong positions to fend off corporate raiders. Should the utility rates of all or the majority of the firms be low, while those of the few be high, this is an indication that the market itself is changing, in the sense that the cycle is bringing consumers to act with greater restraint in their purchasing. Hence, for all the businesses and firms in the economy symbolized by the letter I for industry, and at time $t$, $0 < I < 1$.

For the government, G, the situation is similar. There is a difficulty, however, because while the domain of business activity is clear-cut, acting within the markets, the impact of government economic activity is not so well defined. Government can order from business products that may or may not be necessary for the smooth functioning of governmental activity—a condition of all bureaucratic entities—and while business may be profiting from this order, it may be wasteful on the government's part. Another big spending objective is defense. While motivated in the best interests of the citizenry, the government's actions along the line of defense requirements and purchases may not be in the best economic interest. Wasteful defense projects, for example, may seem impressive, but their utilities may be very low in the military sphere, making these projects extremely wasteful, while the firms contributing to the manufacturing of these projects achieve high profits.

The area of governmental activity where there is not this difficulty is in the building of infrastructure to enhance long-run economic activity. Such projects as building dams and roadways, and investing in state and regional education are examples of this activity. Although these projects require the contracting of business for their realization, their utilities can be determined with respect to the growth they provide the economy—although this may be over the very long run. Measuring the G within the $W_t$ equation is thus problematic, but as the government is a powerful factor in the economy, its position with respect to utility must be considered. As the government's various economic functions are subsets of its overall economic activity, assessing the utility of each within the upper and lower utility boundaries at time $t$ provides the overall utility of G. Hence, $0 < G < 1$, for time $t$ provides the general utility of the government's economic policies—including health and welfare—for that time.

Labor's situation is not ambiguous, but very clear-cut. For labor, no distinction exists between the government or industry as employer; they are both employers, and labor has to reckon with them—as well as their having to reckon with labor. The distinction holds for those governments—and in this sense, regional and local government as subsets of the national government are also considered—whose employees are not allowed by law to take work action against the governing bodies, such as the police and fire departments as well as the armed forces: These are workers with well-defined jobs and who, in their roles as wage earners, are supported by organizations that enter into collective bargaining on their behalf. It is understood that the strike action is deprived them, and they must have good contracts to prevent discrimination and provide benefits that will continue to make their jobs attractive and motivate others to join them.

But with organized labor in the free markets, it is clear that the traditional labor-industry dichotomy still exists. Workers want high pay for their efforts and business managers want workers to work long hours for low pay. The utility of labor's actions must be viewed in light of this dichotomy. Bargaining for higher wages in an industrial sector weakened by international competition is not likely to yield the wages set by the unions, nor be within an acceptable range of wage scales, and therefore tends toward entropy as a policy. Similarly, bargaining for higher wages when the economy is experiencing recession is not very effective, because so many jobs are being threatened by the recession.

Programs sponsored by unions and management alike, allowing for retraining of workers threatened with redundancy and unemployment and providing for their reassignment to other divisions of the firm, are certainly steps in the direction of keeping able workers off the dole. Like every other labor and business action, however, they too must be evaluated for their utility and entropy. For some of these programs it might be demonstrated that, while the intentions are sound and the idealism motivating them very healthy, the programs are of very low utility and must therefore be abandoned. Other programs might be of high utility, thereby providing incentive to expand and diversify them—actions subject to utility evaluations in their own right.

This welfare utility function thus contains the three forces in the economy. When each of these forces has a utility tending to the upper limit, then welfare is operating at high utility; where their utility ratings are low, then so is the welfare utility low; and, where these utilities are mixed, then welfare's utility moves with those utility ratings that are dominant.

This approach to welfare differs from the standard neoclassical approach that is Paretian-Slutskian and considers the welfare position of the individual and his or her relation to the aggregate. For what then is welfare, if not individual welfare—personal well-being, given the individual's specific set of economic circumstances?

This approach differs from the neoclassical approach in that instead of reasoning from the individual to the general economic situation, here the emphasis is on the general economic situation, as demonstrated by the dynamics and interretations of the Industrial, Governmental and Labor sectors, of which the individual is a member or is directly affected, in any case. The individual's welfare, his or her well-being, is derived from the economic conditions of these sectors and the manner in which they interract with one another. Stated another way, the individual is a resident in a society and these sectors are the society's economic forces, from which the goods and services are produced, from which the socioeconomic infrastructure is derived and generated, and from which employment is sought and maintained as best as possible, given the unique economic conditions at any one time.

The individual can compute his or her utility functions with respect to income earned, the goods and services available for consumption, the labor possibilities and opportunities, and, for those able to vote, for casting the vote for that person or party whose election platform tends to coincide with the individual's utility function. For ultimately, in the industrial sector, the contemporary individual's utility function with respect to the goods and services available determines, when taken on aggregate, which firms will survive and which will not, which firms will continue their production lines and which will alter them, which firms will maintain their labor composition and which will hire more workers, and which will fire or temporarily lay off workers. With the vote, the consumer can determine the type of government he or she wants, and if disappointed, can vote for the opposition during the next elections.

By not considering the consumer influence as a sector, however, this does not mean that the consumer as a force has been neglected. For the consumer is the ultimate beneficiary and the subject of all economic activity. By so being, the consumer at the same time is intrinsically involved in the economy, either in industry, in the government, or in the labor movement. Welfare economics is thus of great importance to the consumer, and the welfare utility function reflects the consumer's position with respect to the economy as it relates to the dynamics of innovation and imitation *in toto*.

There is another sector of the economy that has not yet been dealt with here, and this is the sector of the economically (and hence socially) disenfranchised: those people who are poor or indigent and without assistance other than welfare; and those people who are homeless and who must beg for their livelihoods. For these people the concepts of neoclassical welfare economics do not apply, for they compose no forceful sector that can exert influence in the markets by substituting products (Slutsky) or by being considered within the Paretian concept of the optimum.

In the era of knowledge and contemporary economics this sector should not exist. It should be absorbed into the mainstream of economic activity (i.e., into employment) and earn its livelihood by contributing to the economy and society, instead of either avoiding the economy or taking from it without giving in return.

This sector is a vestige, a remainder, of the era past, the era of industrialization. It is a vestige of a time when the social and economic welfare systems were inadequate to cope with people suffering from these extreme problems, and left them to fend for themselves as best they could. It left them in a vicious circle of being unable to help themselves out of their situations because they lacked the means for so doing, and they could not get the means because none were available to them. Of course, in our postwar situation our welfare agencies have developed and acquired a great deal of sophistication. Assistance is there, but these people have to be able to reach out and ask for it, and our societies are not traditionally geared for those who ask.

A theory of welfare economics that does not treat this sector is certainly inadequate. The argument that these people are marginal and could have no possible bearing on the economy, that their intelligence levels and potential skills and abilities are low, which is why they remain where they are, is completely false. Sometimes—and these people bear witness to this—the weight of events, the circumstances, are such that there are no real opportunities available for change, no possibilities for one's improvement of one's position. As people, indeed as individuals, their intelligence has yet to be tested and yet their skills are tested every day in their living on the streets and maintaining life in spite of their marginal situations. The point is that an economic theory that leaves this sector out cannot really make a contribution in the welfare sphere. It is therefore maintained here that a theory can be presented that will allow these people to be absorbed into the dynamics of disequilibrium innovation and imitation. Those people who will then remain outside this dynamic framework will be those who for physical or mental reasons cannot be absorbed into the system.

For those who are able to be absorbed, our economies are open and will provide them with opportunities. This is one of the qualities of our contemporary economic system, unique to our time. As a vestige of an earlier era, this sector can be removed and its people brought into the productive dynamics of our economies.

# 10

# The Welfare Utility Function and the Business Cycle

## THE DYNAMIC WELFARE UTILITY FUNCTION

In Chapter 9, the welfare utility function was stated with respect to a moment in time. Its components of Industry, Government and Labor were also thus frozen at that moment. Analyzing these components with respect to a moment in time cannot give a clear view of the positions and situations of their subsets, for only *over* time, that is in a dynamic setting, can these subsets be studied and their utilities and entropies be understood.

The static moment in time captured by the subscript $t$ cannot therefore explain the dynamics of the welfare utility function. For example, in explaining the Industry component, it was said that some of the firms may have low utility, because of opting for liquidity or of changes in production being undertaken. As utility is with respect to the markets and as these operations bring the firms in question to a weakened market position, the static $W_t$ cannot provide for the explanations for the low utilities and attempts to explain the reasons merely moves W from being bound by the static $t$, to a dynamic $t + n$ ($n \geq 1$).

The same holds for the Government and Labor components. Capturing them in a single moment of time can allow for no explanations of their utilities. The government, for example, may undertake to provide economic infrastructure in a regional area of the country where economic growth is lagging behind the other areas. In time $t$, how can this action be evaluated? Or government investments in an industry of such a region—how are they to be analyzed with respect to utility when the reasons may be for enhancing weapons systems as well as providing income and employment in that region? Labor policies are also not understood in the moment of time captured by $t$. Strike action, for example, may seem to be counterproductive when viewed in the moment; the longer-term view may realize that protectionism is evoked to a certain extent and that domestic labor is not threatened so much by cheaper foreign products. Or it may be advantageous for labor to resist new and efficient technologies that threaten the employment situation as it now exists in certain industries. Capturing this resistance in the moment $t$ gives no indication of the reasons for this strategy.

For a welfare function to be viable, it must be therefore dynamic, moving with the changes in the economy and offering the opportunities to evaluate these changes with respect to utility and entropy. An automobile firm, for example, may embark on a new image for a car and seek to use this new car to capture the markets of its competing firms. In the static situation, this may seem to be good marketing and indeed an innovative product; over time, however, this project may be a drain on resources as it neither meets expected sales from the customers generally loyal to the firm and from those consumers that the firm sought to attract from its competitors.

The government's investing in infrastructure in a depressed region may be sound as far as planning goes, but only over time can this be assessed. The region may respond due to the injection of money in the form of wages and the purchasing of goods and services locally, so that the government's objective is obtained, or it may continue to rely on its traditional attitudes and approaches in its industry and labor position so that in spite of the initial stimulation because of the money injected, the region reverts to its previous level of economic activity and in the long run there is no difference in its economic situation.

The welfare utility function is a measuring function of the utilities of the industrial, governmental, and labor sectors over time; it also takes into account the fact that as the economy is not an entity in which these sectors operate independent of one another, but that these sectors are intricately related in the dynamics of economic development and expansion. The function does, however, measure the utilities of each of these sectors as they operate with the inclusion of the other sectors in them. For the purpose is not to isolate these sectors, but to assess their utilities in their dynamic settings over time.

The notion "over time," refers to the time period of cyclical fluctuation, for their utilities depend on the cycle's position. For example, during prosperity, just as the cycle's upward motion is increasing at a decreasing rate, innovation may not yield expected profits for a firm. Saturation is setting in, and in spite of the optimistic situation, profits for the industry in which the firm belongs are declining, albeit slowly. Innovation in a similar market will then yield declining profits, in spite of the expectation of higher profits, and the firm's utility thus declines with respect to the innovative project. This is measured by the particular industry's welfare utility function, and may have a bearing on the I sector, depending on the weight that the industry has.

Government projects during recession, for example, tend to alleviate difficult economic conditions, because—in Keynesian terms—the increased money in terms of wages and investment stimulates demand, and this generates restocking of inventories, bringing about further employment. It also stimulates innovation as the element of risk is reduced because of the increased liquidity. These projects over the time of the recession phase have high utility, and their influences on industry and labor are noticeable and positive for economic growth.

Labor unrest during recovery may be of low utility for a specific industry because of the foreign competition with that industry. The electronics industry, for example, may be experiencing demand due to aggregate liquidity's having been increased because of the recovery and because of innovative products within the industry. But as innovation generates imitation and as there is an international imitation effect in which foreign companies seek out the newest in domestic products and attempt to manufacture imitative substitutes at lower prices even when tariffs are considered, labor unrest will not be beneficial to that part of organized labor engaged in sanctions, or strike action, as the case may be.[1]

As $W_{t+n} = U(I, G. L)_{t+n}$ and as the utilities of these components depend to a large extent on the cycle's position at the time of measurement, then the welfare utility function is, to the same extent, dependent on the cycle's position. This dependence is as weak or strong as that of the component during the measuring period and indicates the utilities as a result of this dependence. Moreover, as the measurement relies on the time factor, circumstances considered relevant during one part of that time may not be so significant during another part. Hence, this utility measure does not account for the real events that have occurred during that time; it merely assesses the utility of the sector over that time range.

In general, then, the welfare utility function $W \approx 1/C_p$, where $C_p$ is the cycle at its phase during the measurement, and the approximation sign indicating that a strict equation does not exist because of variations in the subsectors due to responses which are not general but specific. For example, a single firm during recession may generate demand because of its innovation and also bring imitation into the dynamics. But for the industry in general in which this firm is included, the utility rating may be very low due to the cycle's recession phase. Thus, as $W_{t+n} = U(I, G, L)_{t+n}$, then $U(I, G, L) \approx 1/C_p$. Joining the cycle's phase p with $t+n$ allows for the time element as well as the cycle's phase to be considered. Should the time element for a given imitation be one year, and during that very time the cycle has moved from recovery to prosperity, then as $p = t+n$, then this time period can be substituted by recovery.

The consequence of substituting the cycle's phase for the time period is that this substitution allows for the isolation of each sector for observation, and indeed, the components of each sector for further scrutiny, evaluating these performances in their general compositions and for their specific utilities. For example, consider the I sector, during recovery. Partial derivation allows for I's isolation from the other components, and the corresponding partial derivative of $C_{recovery}$ allows for I's position in the cycle during recovery to be evaluated.

Hence, $O < \delta I < 1/\delta C_{rec}$. Moreover, this also allows for looking at a specific industry in I, to consider its evaluation, so that for I, i$\epsilon$ I can be substituted. This also provides for the evaluation of a single firm in an industry, so that (F$\epsilon$i)$\epsilon$I can also be evaluated.

Another advantage of this approach is that for the cycle's phase, say, recovery, can be further broken down. Recovery, for example, may be a very long-term process, but the I is being considered for only the first two months (or for whatever period of time considered necessary for evaluation), the approximation welfare utility function takes the form $W_I \approx 1/l_{C\,t(2months)}$ from which can be derived the utility position $0 < \delta I < 1_{t(2months)}$.

Moreover, this equation can take into account two of the three sectors, so that, from time $a$ to $c$, for, say, industry and labor, the situation takes the form $W_I, L \approx 1/C_{I,L\,t(a-c)}$, so that $O < (\delta I \delta L) < 1$ can be evaluated. Another advantage of this welfare utility function is that it provides for the breaking down of each of these sectors into their components and subcomponents for still further evaluation. As $\Sigma(F\epsilon\,i)\epsilon$ I, and as $\Sigma$ (gp$\epsilon$ g)$\epsilon$G—*gp* being a specific government policy— and as $\Sigma$(lp$\epsilon$l)$\epsilon$L—lp being a specific labor policy—with the "sigma" sign being a summation of these policies and the "$\epsilon$" being the inclusion sign, then such breaking down is readily accessible.

For example, consider a specific firm in an industry, for which its utility is sought over the past two months. Firm$_1$, the firm in question, can be placed in this equation in the following manner: As $W_I \approx l/C$, and $\Sigma(F\epsilon i) \epsilon$ I, then this summation can be substituted for "I" in the approximation equation. As $F_1$ is one of the subcomponents of I, then the equation can be written $W_{FI} \approx l/c_{t(2months)}$ for which the derivative is stated $O < [\Sigma (F \epsilon i) \epsilon I] < 1$, and as $F_1$ is a component of the summation, then it too can be placed within the utility evaluation separate from the other firms and industries. Isolating the I and L sectors, or any other two sectors, also provides no difficulty. Substituting the specific industry and specific labor policy for the generalized I and L notation above yields the results. This can show the influences of labor on industry and/or industry on labor, as the case may be, by way of the isomorphic relationships of each's utilities on the other, as was discussed in Part 2. The reason why only three sectors at a time can be treated at the most happens because, should all three sectors be treated at the same time, this would give the general W approximation and no isolation could be undertaken.

It must be understood that so far the discussion has pertained to the welfare utility measurements over time *past* up to a point in time, from the past to the present. This itself involves a dynamism because the measurement—in the examples above it was two months—takes into account the changes over the signified time, and the point of the present is somewhat difficult to capture, without the dynamics surrounding it. If the present were to include today and the next five days, this is a very small time, but it is far from static. Other firms, other government policies, and other labor issues are very likely to come up and be implemented during this time period, but the greatest dynamic lies, again, with the "engine" of economic activity, the single firm in the industry, where programs of innovation and imitation are devised, planned for, and acted upon.

The present, in this sense, is a sufficiently small amount of time not to allow for cyclical considerations in *most* situations; the qualified "most" in this case is to allow for considerations not really expected for in the general run of economic events such as the October 1987 market crash, which, while not cyclical in nature, was certainly an extremely disturbing event. Events, unpredictable and unexpected, cannot be ruled out and their effects will certainly be made known in the very short time of even a few days allowed by the concept of "present" in the welfare approximation. In general, then, the use of the past in relation to the present, or whatever the cutoff point should be for analyzing the welfare utility position, refers to a period of time in which, while there have been changes in the economy, there have been no radical deviations from the path in which the economy has been running. This includes events that are expected to occur, such as a president's or prime minister's speech reporting on the conditions of the country and perhaps proposing tax reforms or replacement of finance ministers or secretaries of the treasury due to previously known clashes of opinions or because of indicated plans of retirement.

The question remains: if the past and the present as defined above can be treated in this manner, what about the future? Cannot the future utility of a program be stated, and cannot the future utility of a firm and its extension, the industry, be predicted? This brings up the issue of expectation discussed in Part 4. While a firm's project can be assessed with respect to internal utility, that is, there are no contradictions in its formulation and the resources and technology exist for its execution according to its planning, its overt utility can be assessed only with respect to its market performance. Hence if the consumer response is within the range acceptable according to the program, then utility approaches 1; if the deviation is outside the allowed boundaries, then the project becomes entropic and should be treated in the appropriate manner, of either altering it or rejecting it, should the costs of alteration be too high or should the resources involved be considered better used elsewhere. So, while the firm is included in the industry, the future of the industry cannot be predicted by the extension of the firm's policies on the industry. Utility is assessed according to performance and the individual firm's performance is no indication of the industry's abilities in its markets.

But cannot the industry's utility inself be predicted, even in the short-run? If we had the power of prophecy, the answer would be an unqualified yes. But even in such an arbitrary time-span as the short run, too many difficulties lie in the path. For example, assuming that the short run is delineated by no industries undertaking either innovative or imitative projects and that sales are going as expected; in this situation there is no market disturbances and stability exists. This short-run stability can be disrupted by labor actions or by a shift in government policy that were not accounted for in industry's calculations. There is always risk involved even though it may not be apparent or in the offing. Utility in industry can be estimated, based on current conditions and projected expectations, but not more than this.

In this sense, industry is in the most volatile of positions. As the driving force of economic activity, industry sets the pace of innovation and imitation; with respect to labor and government, industry attempts to exert control over these sectors through market operations. By this, it is meant that industry employs labor and generates the conditions for which government can act, in either a corresponding or contrary manner, depending on the calculations of the governing officials.

While industry generates the conditions, it has very little control over them. In instances of innovation, labor, realizing that a profit is to be made above the current profit level, may consider this as grounds for demanding a new contract, as the terms of the present contract can be interpreted as being isolated or altered, as the understanding may be. There may be an agreement that prevents difficulties but that reduces industry's potential earning power, or there may be conflict, thereby setting back the innovative process and resulting in a loss because innovation was being conducted due to reduced profits because of market saturation.

Government policy may also hinder industry's operations. While such issues as tax policies and investing in various regions may be the subject for public debate, such policies as devaluation, or the replacement of officials unexpectedly, with the consequent effects on the stock exchange and the uncertainty in the markets that this so often causes, may result in the postponement of innovative or imitative projects, or depending on how serious these policies are and how extensive they are for industry's long-range planning, may bring about major revisions in industry's operations.

Of course, not all responses to these policies are negative. For example, labor may propose the adoption of profit sharing programs, with the consequence of stimulating work rather than considering sanctions and strikes. This may also bring some workers to undergo retraining where necessary to learn to handle the new technologies being introduced as well as those technologies that will result from spin-off processes, thereby upgrading their competitive positions with regard to the rest of the total work force—this too is an aspect of welfare.

Government policies of devaluation may be positive for industry if devaluation increases the medium-and-long-run competitive price positions of domestic industry with regard to foreign competition. Reducing the domestic currency's value makes it more expensive for foreigners to maintain the present purchasing patterns and they will tend to opt for the cheaper-quality domestic products of the devalued country's currency. The effectiveness of devaluation depends, of course, on the responses of the other countries. Leveling tariffs against the devalued goods and services removes the advantage, but this could set off a trade war, because such actions are reciprocal, with tariffs set up against those countries that reacted in this manner. These countries can also devalue, wiping out any advantages gained from this action. Devaluation is undertaken, then, with the point of view that while such actions may be taken, there is no necessity for this happening. For example, other countries may consider it politically expedient to maintain a higher valued currency for such internal political considerations as advocating pride in the national currency—especially during election time—or responding to industrial pressure to prevent a devaluation in kind because of a strong industrial base, backed by potential labor unrest pressuring for higher wages to offset the losses due to devaluation. Political considerations can allow for the rejection of devaluation against international pressure for doing so when the industrial base is sufficiently strong to allow for a trade-off of holding a strong currency against marginal declines in sales, offset as much as possible by offering discount rates for the goods and services.

Replacing officials may not necessarily be to industry's disadvantage, if the reason for so doing is that the replacement is more sympathetic to the problems of competition, environment at the cost of growth, and the effects of foreign trade on domestic industrial development. In all cases such a replacement will bring about slight tremors because of the unexpected, but these tremors will soon subside if the replacement is pro-industry and seeks to promote it, bringing it into regions in which it is lacking but where feasibility studies show it can be beneficial to the region and profitable to management.

Government policy toward labor can be positive, especially during downward swings of the trade cycle, when unemployment begins to set in. Financial relief in the form of increased unemployment benefits, the encouragement of early retirement age thereby allowing younger people with greater obligations to move higher in the union pay scale and in the jobs, and provisions for job retraining under various government schemes, are measures that are beneficial to labor. Furthermore, by government supporting industry, more jobs are provided and guaranteed. Support comes by way of orders from industry and these orders must be supplemented by industry from its various subsectors supplying the materials and basic components. This requires employment and by so ordering from industry—be these orders for military or civilian purposes—both industry and labor profit. Government support can come indirectly by way of the research supported by grants. This research yields technology that is acquired by industry and worked by labor so that not only does this research result in employment, but labor's skills are developed and kept up with the advances in technology and its industrial applications.

These situations occur as part of the activity of economics and, because they are within the realm of economic activity, they must be accounted for in responsive ways. Devaluation, for example, requires one of several alternatives and at least one of them must be given expression. Labor sanctions require affirmative responses. Government decisions on taxation, although anticipated to a certain extent, have to be taken into consideration by both business and labor, each sector being affected differently.

The question to be considered now is, can there be some degree of planning for these sectors? The welfare utility equation was able to describe utility and entropy for the past and present as defined above. What, however, can be said with respect to the future and this approximation equation? Stated another way, while the future is unknowable, is there something of the future about which we can know and, more than this, on which we can apply our technology and exert some control over our activity as a result? The answer to this is affirmative, for while economic activity deals with the problems of everyday commerce—with the tasks of developing projects and planning them, and bargaining for higher wages and offering better and modern work techniques as a result; and doing more than trying to determine what the government's next steps are to be, and to attempt to find protection against them and avoid them if they are detrimental, and how to exploit them to the best advantage if positive—economic activity occurs within the phases of the trade cycle and this can be understood and addressed.

## THE WELFARE UTILITY FUNCTION AND THE BUSINESS CYCLE

The cycle is repetitive in the sense that its phases are the same, even with the final phase of the neoclassical cycle of depression removed. The cycle moves from recession to recovery, to prosperity, and finally to recession once again. But, as was mentioned in the discussion on the cycle in the part 2, no two cycles are the same because each cycle leaves the economy with its own conditions, as well as its own goods and services, and its means of using the natural resources in production have been altered. In an earlier expression of this position, this writer stated:

When the cycle does begin its upward motion, the economy is not of the same composure as its previous cyclical completion. It has been altered due to its product composition. Its secondary and auxiliary businesses are different and oriented toward promoting different products; the process of distribution has altered as new businesses replace those that as a result of mergers and bankruptcies no longer remain. The big firms are different in the sense that their technologies have been altered to cope with the different compositions of socioeconomic income groups that have formed as a result of the cycle and the consequences of recession and depression. The economic infrastructure has been broadened by the new products and the technological changes incorporated to produce them.[2]

But here the similarities among the cycles cease. The socioeconomic income groups differ to some extent, as determined by those who benefited and those who lost as a result of the cycle's motion. The broadened economic infrastructure contains products that hitherto did not exist and it has technologies unique to the cycle's movement, while those products and technologies that were no longer relevant were phased out through the disequilibrium dynamics of innovation and imitation. Except for those products that survived the cycle's motion, the new technologies incorporated in innovation and imitation have become established, only to be threatened by the dynamics of the cycle to follow.

The dynamics of the cycle to follow are based on the previous cycle, and in this sense there is continuity. During the recession phase, innovation can only be constructed on the infrastructure already established, and using the resources that already exist. The newness comes with the ideas as incorporated into projects, and this sets the "tone," as it were, for the cycle's movement upward, through the process of imitation, should the innovation be successful.

With successful innovation, the inertia is broken and once the cycle begins its upward movement, new technologies are formulated for producing new projects and the period of recovery gets under way, leading into prosperity. It has so far been the situation, however, that even with recovery and prosperity, the difficulties of welfare economics have remained. Poverty has not been eradicated, slums still exist, and people are still sleeping on the streets for lack of housing.

The challenge to the theory of welfare economics is expressed in this dilemma of the economy's moving in cyclical phases while at the same time there are basic conditions remaining unchanged, unaffected by the dynamics of disequilibrium growth, and by the expansion of the socioeconomic infrastructure and by the impact of the new technologies on living standards. Yet, the conditions of poverty remain, in spite of the attempts to remove and abolish these blights, which are relics of an era past and seem to be impervious to these attempts.

The point is, however, that slums are inanimate and the concept of poverty is highly abstract.[3] What really counts are the people affected by poverty and those who dwell in slums and on the streets. The problem is, how can these people be brought within the dynamics of the cycle? Once this is achieved, the slum dwellings will be removed and in their places will rise adequate homes with safe environments. Poverty, with its self-perpetuating dynamics, will disappear. This does not mean, however, that social welfare cases will, or can, be abolished forever. But in our present era of high technologies, of better understanding of the government's role as underwriter of the economy, and of the dynamics of industry and the relationship between industry and labor, there is no reason for poverty and its ramifications to be justified on grounds of economics. The "dismal science" of economics has now in its power to raise the standards of living and contributing to society to the extent never before possible; in our contemporary era the techniques for contributing to our welfare are almost unlimited. Those situations that do not respond to the economics of the cycle remain within the scope of the social welfare boards assigned to address them, for their causes are not economic, but derived from other origins.

For this to be achieved, it must first be shown how the welfare utility function can lead to predictions about the economy for the short- and medium-run future, after which the application of the welfare utility function can contribute to the elimination of economic poverty and its ramifications.

For this to be accomplished, the cycle must be considered once again. It was argued that the depression phase has been eliminated in the aftermath of the Great Depression. The technique for this elimination was discussed in terms of the cut-off point of the cycle's downward phase, as agreed to by government, industry, and labor, each sector acting in its own interest and, because these sectors compose the economy, then acting with the interest of the economy. Depressions are thus ruled out, for they can occur only when shortsightedness prevails or narrow interests replace sound judgment; but as each sector exerts checks over the others, these conditions are highly unlikely in contemporary economics.

Thus, the cycle is three-phased, with recession, recovery, and prosperity completing its motion. The cycle is not to be considered mechanistic in any sense because the timing of its phases and their dynamics and extent cannot be foreseen. The cycle can, however, be considered deterministic, but only in one sense, that being the recurring nature of its three phases. The questions of when, and to what extent, have to be evaluated during each phase. There are no prophets in economics, just economists working with given situations and trying to understand how things will develop over time.

The concept of the welfare utility function can be applied to the cycle in its phases to enable predictions to be made about the short- and medium-run future with respect to the conditions and the phase of the cycle during which the predictions are made. It must be clear, however, that as predictions, they are subject to unreliability and uncertainty. They are useful within the context of planning and considering further operations on the current markets; they are invalid as certain steps to be taken, as reliable bases for decision making.

For the situation here is one of a business cycle undergoing its phases and of the general economic activity of industrial, governmental, and labor decision making and other activities that occur and affect the behavior of the economy within its phases. With respect to these occurrences, the welfare utility function is past-oriented, allowing measurements of utility as these events have occurred over time past, with this time being delineated according to current conditions as interpreted by the decision makers. However, with respect to the business cycle, the welfare utility function is future-oriented, because it is on the basis of the cycle's phase that short- and medium-run decisions should be considered. For example, entering into an innovative project when there is much unemployment and liquidity has been diminished because consumers are unemployed and using their savings—that is, during a prolonged recession—might not make good sense unless there are target groups that will consume, no matter what the economic situation, and that resources and labor to work them are guaranteed in this period of great uncertainty. In other words, not only must the conditions be favorable, but the means for working with these conditions must be available.

But, if it were not for innovation, the recession phase of the cycle would never be moved upward into recovery. This requires innovation on a serious scale, involving the financial institutions, the accumulation of natural and productive resources, and the assembling of labor, much of which was hitherto unemployed and receiving assistance. Innovation during this phase would not have been undertaken on any significant scale had the decision makers of industry not considered innovation viable. During this period of the recession phase the cutoff point was reached, so that industry could take the risks, with the understanding that both labor and government were ready for the cycle to begin its upward motion. Thus, for this recessive phase, the welfare utility function takes the form $W_r \approx 1/C_r$ (with r representing the recession phase), with the approximation signifying that dynamics are existing even though the phase is of recession. While for time *tr* $O< (I, G, L)< 1$ and that $(I, G, L)_r \rightarrow O$, the cutoff point is reached at time tr $+ 1$, so that at tr $+ 2$, innovation is being considered and even undertaken to a fairly large extent, bringing in its wake imitation.

This brings about a shift in the welfare utility function so that $W_r \approx 1/C_{r+2}$, as the recession phase has not yet moved up, but its cyclical response is being felt. As innovation and imitation increase, bringing more people into the disequilibrium dynamics of shifting markets and employment and consumption, the cycle moves into its recovery phase. But, industry begins to undertake such programs as trading liquidity for short-term investments and/or imitation, in which case a major attempt is make to enter a market, with the intention of a serious withdrawl if short-term profits are not realized. Government, during this phase, seeks to invest in depressed regions, but only in projects that are viable as determined by feasibility studies. Labor is regaining its position in both industry and government, and while it is still quiet because of the emergence from recession, it is beginning to realize its strength in the renewed dynamics of recovery. Hence, from time r $+ 2$, the cycle has moved into recovery so that $W_{rec} \approx 1/C_{rec}$, with all the dynamics of the period function accordingly. Thus O $< (I,G,L) < 1$, but there is no tendency toward entropy of recession or utility of prosperity. The situation pulls both ways in the sense that while the economic climate is favorable for innovation and imitation, and indeed such activities are taking place, at $W_{rec}$ a major commitment has not yet been made to the dynamics of innovation and imitation; the economy has moved into recovery but the cycle's upward motion is still hampered by the inertia of the recession.

Innovation and imitation have to continue and intensify for a new period in the recovery phase to be reached. Such a period will be realized when innovation and imitation gain momentum as the conservatism of the recession phase yields to profit motivation. Industry begins to increase its pace of developing new projects and entering into markets that are new and promising. These new markets bring competitors into their domains and, in the case of competition, profits can be rechanneled into innovative projects. Government investments in regions considered needy increase as industry becomes more daring and willing to invest in these areas, given their newly found strength because of the cycle's upswing and because of government incentives such as tax considerations and potential purchases. Labor, as well, becomes more daring, seeing that its position is obtaining security because of the demand for employment to produce industry's goods and services. Labor action usually begins during this period, but it is still subdued, with sanctions and strikes occurring only in those firms that are in a weakened bargaining position because of the upsurge in consumer demand for their products and the need for workers to fulfill the orders.

During this period, government officials are reconsidering the tax structure.

During the early period of the recession, taxes were high and were used as a means for reducing liquidity for consumption and for innovation and imitation. Industry, during this period, was cutting back on its production as innovation was slowing down to almost none and imitation was also being reduced because of the market saturation and great risks further imitation held. These high taxes were held over from the final periods of the recovery phase, in which inflation was gathering momentum and taxation was used as a means for reducing aggregate liquidity. The imposition of these high taxes, together with the high inflation, are two important causes of the cycle's turning downward into recession, but these will be discussed momentarily.

The point of note right now, however, is that there exists a time-lag between the cycle's period within its phase and the rates of taxation levied by the government to absorb or release liquidity. This is necessary because taxation is a corrective procedure, employed to regulate the cycle, and the cycle's periods within their phases have to be studied and understood. As these periods become entrenched within the phases, each period carries its own dynamics which the tax authorities have to comprehend in order to devise programs to either accommodate the period within the phase, or to counteract it, as the case may be. This has to be done without affecting the phase's motion, so that it cannot be halted. There must be a time-lag, therefore, so that the period's special conditions can be understood and programs formulated to deal with them. The difficulty is, that once these programs are initiated, the period most likely shifts to another period along the phase; in any case, the dynamics of the period have to work themselves out and thus tax programs for a certain period are rigid and do not allow for the flexibility necessary for the periods to realize their full dynamics. For example, with innovation occuring in a specific industrial branch and its spin-off moving into another, yet closely-related branch—such as lasers in communications and in computer technology (which is a form of communications as information is requested, sought, and obtained)—taxing these sectors removes both liquidity and, to some degree, incentives that are necessary for further research and the applications of research into industry. However, taxation cannot be flexible, moving from one industrial sector to another as shifts in these sectors are generated. Because they are formulated to pertain to specific situations over time, and because these situations do not remain static but are subject to the dynamics of the time, the tax policies are inadequate and are hindered by the time lag.

The point now to be considered is that tax incentives for industry to invest in new regions, while encouraging, do not allow for sufficient protection against the risks involved during this period of the recovery phase. While industry's moving into these regions may stimulate economic activity because of the very construction of the industry's firms and the consumption of the relocated employees, there must be suitable employment in the form of skilled labor to work for the firms; there must be available supplies of the necessary resources to allow for production, and there must be adequate infrastructure for acquiring the resources and for the distribution of the finished products. In this sense, while these risks are real, there is an optimism as the cycle moves upward, and the government uses this optimism to encourage firms to move into these areas.

This optimism is due to the increasing innovative and imitative projects that are successful. Greater employment provides greater liquidity and this, together with the profit motive, stimulates innovation and imitation. Consumption increases as liquidity increases, but also savings increase, so there is a demarcation between disposable and consumption liquidity, absent during the recession as aggregate liquidity was diminished, with savings reduced considerably to maintain living standards. The disposable and consumption liquidity demarcation enters at the second period of the recovery phase and is sharpened further as recovery continues. This demarcation also contributes to the optimism as it provides backing for both individuals and firms to expand consumption and enter into innovation and imitation, respectively.

During this period, $W_{rec} \approx 1/C_{rec+2}$ with $O < (I,C,L) < 1$ and $(I,C,L) \rightarrow 1$. The recovery phase is gathering momentum as more firms enter into the dynamics of production, either on the side of innovation or imitation, opening new markets and expanding those that have been opened. Employment is increasing and government activity is trying to follow industry and maintain the momentum of growth and expansion.

The recovery phase moves into the prosperity phase when the dynamics of innovation and imitation are fully active. No industry, and no firm within an industry, is *not* engaged in one of these forms of economic activity during the early period of prosperity. This is important, because as the move is made from recovery into prosperity, this is the period in which most of the citizenry in the society are gainfully employed and active in one form or another within the dynamics of the activity. But it is also significant to note that during this period government begins to withdraw from active intervention in the form of infrastructural building and tax incentives, because it assumes that industry is no longer in need of its support. Indeed, this is so, as sales are up and profits good, with employment and consumption, as the consequences of innovation and imitation, being at levels that reinforce the production and the opening of still-further new markets.

However, the opening of additional new markets relies on the liquidity available to the target groups, and most likely this liquidity is committed to either savings or to established consumption patterns. For successful innovation, therefore, consumers have, at this stage in recovery, to be taken away from established markets. This results in strenuous competition, taking the forms of price reductions, enacted by the firms that lost customers, in order to compete with those firms that took the customers; trade-offs of production for liquidity, adopted by firms in order to enter into new or established markets, thus leaving the previous markets for marginal producers; and aggressive advertising, chosen by firms as the final and perhaps most effective means for competing.

During this period of the prosperity phase $W_p \approx 1/C_p$, with $(I,G,L) \rightarrow 1$. At this time taxes are low, reflecting on the previous phase of recovery when they

were reduced to aid in stimulating business activity and for providing greater
liquidity for consumption. Low taxes also assist in prosperity, because for a time
they allow for increasing consumption and production to support it. Labor is
either quiet and working, or discontented and expressing it in sanctions or strikes;
these may affect certain industrial sectors but they have no major bearing on the
economy itself. The economy has become buoyant during this period and is
resilient in the face of labor unrest, having the profits to back it when labor takes
sanctions or strike-action.

However, during the next period of this phase, signs of decline start to set
in. Innovation begins to decline as consumer liquidity is accounted for in the
purchasing patterns established by imitation, so that the risk of innovation becomes incommensurate with the opportunities of profit-making. Imitation itself
begins to decline as market saturation cannot allow for further competitors to
any extent. Labor's restiveness begins to subside as its leaders recognize that
industrial activity is either standing still or declining, and it is not opportune to
resume conflicts during this period. The government begins to understand that
business activity is slowing, while consumers still enjoy high levels of liquidity.
Inflation sets in as the production of goods and services declines but demand
remains high. During this period the government considers levying higher taxes
to reduce consumption as a means of curtailing inflation. With prices increasing
and production declining, these extra taxes act as an extra push on the cycle's
momentum. Innovation ceases almost entirely and imitation declines considerably as those established markets are reaching near-saturation. Prices continue
to rise and, in spite of the competition, the lack of adequate new production is
the cause for high prices.

During this period, industry has become aware that innovation is not viable
and therefore to be avoided; imitation can be undertaken, but only in those
industrial sectors that provide more than a marginal profit on the investment in
imitation. Moreover, these markets are becoming increasingly scarce, reducing
imitation that much further. The government is levying higher taxes on both
industry and the consumers, reducing still the motivation for risk-taking and
lowering the consumption levels that much more, over what the high prices have
achieved. The situation with labor is uneasy. While unemployment has begun
to appear, it is only very small because of the need to maintain near-constant
production levels. But signs are beginning to indicate that larger levels of unemployment are in the offing. Labor is quiet industrially, but is somewhat restive
because of the realization that the cycle will begin moving downward. Workers
seek to maintain their positions of employment but others seek employment
elsewhere, in other regions. This is somewhat difficult because by this time
period government begins to withdraw support for the depressed regions (another
form of taxation), bringing about a decline in employment in these areas through
the cancel of orders and withholding of funding. The restiveness that labor
experiences finds no relief; those workers who are able to hold their jobs are
well-off, while those who cannot and are unable to find employment elsewhere,

turn to the dole. The cycle has peaked and begins moving down toward recession. $W_{p+2} \approx 1/C_{p+2}$ with $O < (I,G,L) < 1$ and the next time period $p + 3$ equals the first period of the recession, with $(I,G,L,) \mapsto O$.

## COMMENTS ON POVERTY

Before pursuing this argument further, some comments on poverty are in order. The most glaring comment that has to be made is that as poverty exists in our era it is a blight on our societies and puts our sciences to shame. It should not exist. The question remains as to why it exists. Our industrial societies have developed refined systems to treat poverty, conceived of originally during the Great Depression and improved-on as industry and government, together with labor, have sought to better the socioeconomic positions of their constituents. "Constituents," in this situation, means those people to whom the sectors are responsible. For industry, it is the managerial staffs who build the industry and plan innovative and imitative projects, and who increase industry's productive power and wealth. For the labor organizations, the constituents are those union members who pay dues and who vote labor leaders into power. The constituents are those who vote for workers benefits and follow their leaders' orders to achieve the desired results, be it through sanctions or through striking.

These constitutents can be considered as distinct entities, each motivated by the uniting special interests. Historically, this distinction was sharp, with management being separated from labor, meeting only on the shop floor. Now, however, there is a flexibility, so that workers who have developed understanding of the broader systems of the firm and its production projects, and who can make viable contributions outside of the restricted domains of their work, can move up the ladder into the decision-making process of managerial activity. Moreover, managers are also workers who are answerable to the owners of their firms, these being stock holders and other investors. Their jobs are of a different nature than the other types of jobs, but the risks are taken by them and while they enjoy the profits, they often fail when lossess are excessive, whether due to the impersonal dynamics of the market and the cycle, or because of incompetence and faulty judgement.

What can be said about the government's constituents? They are the citizenry, and those who reside within the political territory and geographical boundaries of the country. They include, obviously, managers and workers alike. These people are franchised within the system; they work within it and contribute to it, so that the system takes care of them. The system, in this sense, is the government, which underwrites the economy through the money supply, through taxation, through investments in socioeconomic infrastructure. The government finances and regulates national insurance (social security) as well as pays unemployment insurance. These are expected from the government and are part of the system's benefits, when in need. The government also provides welfare payments for those who have been unemployed for too long, including those who have never been employed. For those people in the last category, they are not part of the system, but certainly part of the system's benefit receivers.

These people are usually uneducated in the common sense of this concept; that is, they lack the reading, writing, and computing skills that are the prerequisites for viable employment. They are, however, very "street-wise" and able to fend for themselves—and this includes receiving money from the "system."

That these people live in poverty means that their situation is relative and traditionally absolute. It is relative in the sense that poverty is relative to the low and minimum living standards—medium and high living standards do not even figure here—so that even the low living standards are not in the same category as poverty. Poverty is absolute in its traditional concept of being irreversible, a concept that will come under scrutiny and be placed in a setting appropriate with the dynamics of contemporary economics. Poverty is not limited to our contemporary economics, however, and is certainly more pernicious in the developing and emerging economies. This situation in these economies will be discussed in part 4, and methods to remove poverty will then be explained.

The condition of poverty in the postindustrialized societies, those of our contemporary era, is somewhat ambiguous, in the sense that it is traditional, a part of society since the Industrial Revolution and certainly much older, and solvable, as will be shown in this argument. The difference between poverty prior to and during the Industrial Revolution is, that prior to industrialization, poverty was mainly a result of caste systems, of the lower classes being relegated to their status in perpetuity, with those very few who managed—by their skills in their work, or in battle—to lift themselves from their situations being the great exceptions.

These lower-caste people were easily recognizable by their manner of speech and dress, and by their lack of education, which made itself obvious to members of the educated classes in the form of perceived inabilities at reasoning and higher discourse. Those who found employment worked only at the most menial tasks and as they raised their families, they too were brought into the world in this status. It seemed to be a curse of perpetuity, but most of these people most likely never realized the differences because they were taught to respect and worship their superiors, and often did so without question.

The difference between this kind of poverty and the poverty of slavery is that the slaves were once proud peoples, forced into their situations by the slave traders who captured them and tried to subdue them. Their living conditions were no better. Those societies that kept slaves and were not originally founded on a class basis sought to treat their slaves as did the older established aristocratic societies. This was an imposition of an alien attitude on soil unreceptive to such an attitude, and on a people who opposed the very notion of the system they themselves tried to adopt. The result was the decline of slavery and the eventual absorption of these peoples into a dynamic thriving society.[4]

Both for the aristocratic societies and for the slave-keeping societies, however, there was no ideology which prevailed to remove these classes from existence.

There was a process of economics in the form of industrialization that required a reorientation if success in the application of science to manufacturing was to be achieved.

And this, too, had its paradox. On the one hand, the machine was a replacement for manpower; on the other hand, the centers of manufacturing brought into their spheres many more people than had originally lived in these areas. This paradox can be explained by the new wealth that these regions generated and the breakdown of class discrimination as labor was required for industry. Labor mobility was thus instituted and people moved from agricultural areas to the cities to take part in the great process of industrialization, either through working in the industries themselves, or by exploiting the secondary and auxiliary businesses formed to support the industries. Also, industry centered where industry was proven successful, so that as one industrial sector opened up and brought in labor, others soon followed and the processes of industrialization gained momentum, only to be interrupted by the downward swings of the business cycles.

Still, poverty remained, but gradually, the racial, ethnic, and class-oriented traits prejudicially associated with poverty lost their significance and, as all people were acceptable in the industrial processess, all people were also susceptible to the consequences of poverty—this being one of the equalizing forces of industrialization. The composition of the impoverished changed, but poverty remained.

At no time was this more prevalent than during the Great Depression, when vast fortunes were lost and many wealthy people joined the ranks of the poor. Machines, once producing goods and services of high quality and at great speed, stood idle while those who were trained to work them and those who managed the organizations for their production stood on line at the soup kitchens. Economics broke down, and with it fell the theories of Edgeworth, Pareto, and Slutsky. The bargaining position that Edgeworth formulated lost its significance as people were concerned with keeping themselves alive, and as the opportunities for bargaining were deprived them. Pareto's opthelimity was rendered inadequate as most of the people were poorly off and the notion of increasing the welfare of one person while that of all others remained unchanged had lost its significance. As for the substitution effect, there were no longer the vast quantities of goods and services among which the consumers could choose, because of the breakdown in production.

Governments became active in the economies, basing their activities not on the esoteric theories of "some academic scribbler of a few years back," [5] to quote Keynes, but on the basis of hardcore sociopolitical pragmatics, on policies for preventing the breakdown of society and to quell the cries for revolution— cries that were not stopped in Germany with the rise of the Nazis.

The premise underlying neoclassical welfare theory was that of full employment, a premise which excluded the unemployable and impoverished populations of society. As Keynes pointed out, this premise was certainly inaccurate and its inaccuracy became glaring and obvious during the depression. In the post–World War II years welfare considerations had gained considerable importance for two important reasons. There was the demobilization of troops and their reorientation into society, and this represented a threat of mass unemployment, and perhaps another depression similar to that which followed the demobilization after World War I. The second reason was that the scars of the Great Depression were so deep that the fear of this kind of situation's recurring moved governments to act to prevent it. Social programs were instituted and social security was improved as a means of providing a buffer between employment and retirement. The governments took actions to enable regions of their countries to develop economically, even though many subcultural attitudes came into conflict with the concepts of modernization.

But these programs did not rid the trade cycle of its recession phase, and while recession is not as severe as depression, it still brings out the soup lines and imposes on the governing institutions—local, regional, and national—to provide for those afflicted with poverty because of the cycle's downward phase and to ease their burden of support for themselves and their families.

In our contemporary era poverty takes two forms (again, the post-industrial economies are being discussed and the emerging and developing countries will be treated in part 4). There is the poverty that results because of the recession phase of the cycle, in which people are unemployed and must rely on the amenities of the governing institutions for unemployment insurance, welfare payments, and the soup kitchens when necessary. The other form is that which remains outside the pale of the business cycle. It is the chronic poverty of those dispossessed by society, or those who disposed themselves from the obligations and responsibilities that society placed on them. These are the dropouts, the misfits, the street people, the beggars, of every society.

For the first form of poverty, the situation can be alleviated by the cycle's upturn toward recovery. During this phase, employment is reinstated with demand increasing and stimulating innovation and imitation. While this form remains a blot on modern economic activity, it is subject to the control of industry, government, and labor as they reach agreement as to the recession's cutoff point and rejuvenate economic activity.

The second form of poverty presents its own difficulties. The people in this classification are either incapable of taking part in contemporary society, or refuse to be so active. Their economic requirements are food, clothing, and shelter, and they have no great desires concerning the qualities of these necessities. For these people, then, it seems that the laws of economics do not apply, as they reject these laws; still, they receive assistance from the welfare agences when they apply to them. The problem is to bring those who want to be brought into the dynamics of modern economic activity, while continuing to maintain through welfare agencies those who are incapable of being so incorporated. The challenge is to reduce both these groups in numbers and make them active and participating members of society, perhaps enabling them to make changes in the social orientation that they deem necessary. The streets should be places for walking and not for being accosted by the poor.

# 11

# The Welfare Utility
# Function and Dynamic
# Disequilibrium

At the "microscope" or "molecular" level, a fair-sized competitive capitalist economy presents a picture of enormous complexity and disorder. Tens of thousands of firms and tens of millions of workers and individual consumers are engaged in producing and exchanging a huge assortment of commodities. It is estimated that about 60,000 different chemicals are regularly produced for the market; the number of different commodities of all kinds must run into millions. The actions of any two firms or consumers are in general almost independent of each other, although each depends to a very considerable extent on the sum total of the actions of all the rest. Each investment of capital, each transaction in the market, is affected by a great variety of social, technical and economic causes, influenced by innumerable individual motives and volitions and subject to countless imponderable accidental circumstances.

Emmanuel Farjoun and Moshe Machover,
*Laws of Chaos*

## GENERAL COMMENTS

"A scientific theory," write Emmanuel Farjoun and Moshe Machover, "cannot confine itself to dealing with what is directly observable, to the exclusion of abstract theoretical concepts. The attempt to expunge theoretical concepts, such as labour-content, from economic theory, leaving only directly observable quantities, such as prices, is a manifestation of instrumentalism, an extreme form of empiricism, which is destructive of all science. Without the concept of labour-content, economic theory would be condemned to scratching the surface of phenomena, and would be unable to consider, let alone explain, certain basic tendencies of the capitalist mode of production.'' [1] Whether instrumentalism is an extreme form of empiricism, and whether it is destructive of all science, are questions better left for works by philosophers on epistemology and scientific method. But the attempt to expunge theoretical concepts from economic theory, is a matter for economists to confront. [2]

This is a contradiction, for to expunge theoretical concepts from a theory reduces the theory to nothing. If, however, Farjoun and Machover mean that to expunge theoretical concepts from *observation,* then they have a valid point. The quote at the beginning of this chapter describes the micro economy from a macro perspective, and description is certainly a part of scientific theory. But it is only a *part*; for *explanation* is the other part, that which completes the theory. For this, theoretical concepts are required, for they are means for working with the vast descriptions and become shorthand terms for a vast array of events, and for their descriptions and explanations.

The theory of welfare economics stated here is based on a broader theory of the modern economy in dynamic disequilibrium. By this, it is meant that during the recovery and prosperity phases the dynamics of innovation and imitation are fully operative, with markets being established and other markets being phased out as they reach near-saturation.

For this theory, there is no equilibrium; the economy is in a state of continuous dynamic disequilibrium, with new markets initiated, existing markets expanded through imitation, and still-other existing markets having reached the condition that further imitation is not profitable being phased out. Hence, on the ''microscopic'' level of the fair-sized capitalist economy, where there are tens of thousands of firms employing millions of workers and there are also individual consumers engaging in producing and exchanging a huge assortment of commodities, the theoretical and practical dynamics of such an economy are those of markets expanding and contracting, of new products being introduced—while others already introduced are attracting close imitative competitors, and, while still others are being phased out because of too much competition and too little profits, and by the decision to enter other new markets. Firms are not stable in their manufacturing plans; their managers consider the dynamics of the markets and how to exploit them in the long run, even though their short-run projects are on the markets. Thus, on the ''microscopic'' level the fair-sized capitalist economy shares the same situation with its larger counterpart: Both the fair-sized capitalist economy and the large post-industrial capitalist economy are undergoing disequilibrium changes, fluctuating between innovation, and imitation, and opting for liquidity as the situation may be for every firm, while at the same time moving with the business cycle according to its phases.

What of the ''macroscopic'' level? On this level the theory of the economy in disequilibrium holds—here the theoretical constructs of the firm, the government in its capacity as economic participant, and labor, are unified into a single approach to contemporary economic activity. The relationship between the "microscopic" micro level and the macro level involves the micro components of specific firms, specific government policies, and specific labor policies—the (F∈ i)∈ I, the (gp∈ g)∈ G and the (lp∈ l)∈ L, with I, G, and L, the components of the macro economy—so that with the I, G, and L, and with the foreign trade restriction removed, there is a good working model of the macro economy with its micro components functioning in dynamic disequilibrium and moving along with the cycle.

## THE WELFARE UTILITY FUNCTION AND ITS MACRO-MICRO COMPOSITION

The welfare utility function states that welfare is an approximation measurement with respect to the cycle's phase at the time the measurement is taken. Statically, it was stated that $W_t = U(I, G, L)_t$, and that as (F∈ i)∈ I, (gp∈ g)∈ G, and (lp∈ l)∈ L at time $t$, to determine the utilities of these components, either the sectors themselves can be evaluated, or, more tedious but more accurate, their specific components can be evaluated and then be assembled into their sectors.

While examining the sector, only a general picture can be obtained. Industry as a whole may be healthy when considered with respect to its sector, but specific firms within each industrial sector may be inefficient and it may be worthwhile to consider these, to see how their situations can be improved. This is important if it is management considering their positions with respect to the rest of the industrial sector, so that their positions can be understood when considering further steps in competition, or whether to opt for liquidity or innovation.

What it means for firms to be not doing well while the rest of their sector is flourishing, is that they are in markets in which saturation is approaching. The situation is that these markets are information systems for both the firms and their consumers. As they approach saturation their utilities decline, for they have been exploited almost to the limit, in all the variations that the firms' managers can construct. Further alterations will lead to only marginal sales increases at best, and at worst, no changes in sales. This is significant, because those firms with declining revenues in these markets have either entered the markets too late to take advantage of their viabilities, or else their prices are too high, reflecting either inefficient production or the requirement of receiving exaggerated profits with respect to the market conditions, or perhaps their promotion is inadequate, from either advertising, packaging, or both. Thus, while the markets are approaching saturation and the utility positions of most of the markets are high, those with low utility positions can either reconstruct their production programs or opt for liquidity, channeling their resources into projects where, upon evaluation, the markets appear more favorable. If the former decision is taken, there are the difficulties of reprogramming, given the loss of competitive time and the dynamics of the market which may render such reprogramming entropic, as the market's further decline brings other firms into the same decision situation. The decisions are taken on the basis of the open utility considerations, including the cycle's position and phase.

The cycle's position and phase are of great significance because of the general conditions prevailing within the cycle. For example, government economic policy depends on the cycle, so that when the cycle is in the period of peak recovery and moving into prosperity, welfare programs such as unemployment insurance and welfare payments tend to be entropic, as the reasons for their being applied have diminished with the reviving economy. When the cycle is moving from prosperity into recession, the government's policies on unemployment insurance and welfare payments become entropic with the cycle's downward swing if they are not activated to cope with the impending difficulties.

Likewise with labor. Strike actions and sanctions are of utility as the cycle moves into peak recovery and into prosperity, for the markets provide the firms with revenues that can be channeled into higher wages and better working conditions, if they are not already designated for innovative or imitative projects. For labor, timing is important. As workers produce, they know when projects are new, and whether they are innovative or imitative. They also know when the general economy is healthy, whether the cycle is moving upward, as this can be judged by the ratio between the employed and unemployed. These are considerations which must be evaluated before strike actions or sanctions are to be undertaken. If these are avoided or misinterpreted, the strikes or sanctions are most likely to be counterproductive—entropic—because the economy will not be able to meet their demands and wasted hours of work, which could go into strengthening the economy, thereby making their demands more reasonable in light of better economic conditions.

Both industry and labor act affirmatively with the cycle's movement. With the termination of recession and the beginnings of prosperity, the firms begin engaging in innovation and imitation, requiring greater working forces to get the industries going and manufacturing again. The government, however, should move countercyclically, so that as industry begins its recovery through innovation and imitation, the government should ease-off from its policies of welfare support, according to the conditions as they develop regarding employment. This counterbalancing, as it were, assists in keeping the economy in disequilibrium because of government's withdrawing of funds that are no longer of utility and keeping the money in the economy based on productivity instead of welfare. This allows for inflation to remain low, because money in circulation is related primarily to productivity, so that wages and revenues from sales can be channeled into consumption and the liquidity option without unnecessary distortions from excess and unproductive money affecting prices. Liquidity as a result of revenues can be rechanneled into production and/or savings for future production as the case may be, with inflation resulting only as the cycle peaks-out at prosperity, and innovation and imitation slow down and eventually cease. Inflation and the disturbances of unproductive money in the economy—disturbances such as preferring the dole to being employed and adding to production, or consuming without considering the possibilities of saving because the recipient's position is almost untenable as a result of the difficult straits of being on the dole—are unnecessary during times of recovery and prosperity; inflation occurs only when the peak of prosperity approaches, and innovation and imitation decline and eventually cease.

The mirco components of the welfare utility function are the industrial sector, government economic policy, and organized labor operating in their individual programs, projects, and markets. The micro components of the government are those policies such as regional development, the building of infrastructure, and the support of specific industries that can be evaluated in the same manner as all other utility systems, either open or closed, as the case may be. Labor action in the various industrial sectorials is also to be so considered. The advantage of micro utility is that it provides a basis for analysis prior to the initiation of action and policy. Consistency in mapping of the operational language onto the area language allows for sound reasoning and the isomorphism restricts the degree of ambiguity in the languages, until entropy sets in. Once these information systems are established, they provide the basis for alteration, expansion, and maneuvering, according to managements' perceptions, governmental decision makers' considerations and labor organizers' understanding of their situations in the economy.

From the microcomponents, the macrosectors are constructed. From the sum of the firms in a single sectorial, to the sum of sectorials into general industry, the I component is constructed. From the specific types of government economic policy summed into a single sectorial to the more general policies and finally to the monetary and fiscal policies overriding the lower level decision making, government policy can be summed into the G component. For labor, from the individual management-labor contracts and conflicts when the contract time expires, to the sectorial labor relations and to the general labor attitude and policy, the L component can be constructed.

These constructions can be made from the general to the specific as well. Taking the abstract concept of industry, for example, by stating what the industrial sectorials are and then breaking them down into their individual firms, from I, F can be derived. The same holds for government policy. Beginning with the general monetary and fiscal policies, specific policies can be derived, and the basic regional policies can be still broken down. As for labor, the situation is a little more complex, because as well as being an overall labor policy, the unions also act according to the conditions within each firm. The guidelines for such action must be broadly stated on top, so that specific actions with respect to the broad guidelines can be taken, if necessary, without clashing with the major unions, so that in grievances over transportation, the local teamsters must have the support as well as the agreement by the higher union authorities to initiate strike action or sanctions.

Even though this welfare utility function takes into account industrial, governmental, and labor policies—and their decision making, too—it remains incomplete if it does not include the individual in the economy. While the firm is the generator of economic activity, the target groupings of each specific firm's projects are composed of contemporary individuals, and it is to the individual that the firm ultimately seeks to program its project—to appeal to the individual and to attract his or her consumer loyalty. The government's economic policies must gain the contemporary individual's support, for if dissatisfaction is too great or if government programs become entropic and fall far short of their objectives, the consumers as voters will register their negative opinions where it counts most for the government—at the polls. Labor's situation is somewhat different because by closing down firms which are not union workplaces and preventing nonunion workers from gaining employment some workers may suffer; union members have the only recourse for expressing their dissatisfaction by means of union meetings and voters options against their leaders at election time. However, even this situation is changing because of the dynamics of contemporary economics, but this will be discussed in section 4 of this chapter.

For the completion of the welfare utility function individual utility and its relation to the welfare utility function has now to be discussed, after which welfare in general will be treated.

## INDIVIDUAL AND GENERAL WELFARE

The welfare utility function treats industry, government economic policy, and labor policy in light of the phases of the business cycle. Of these three, industry is most volatile, as it generates growth—and growth is subject to consumer purchases of industrial output. In this sense, labor serves industry and government regulates the growth process in light of the cycle's phases. However, both government and labor have their constituents—these as with industry being the consumers, the contemporary individuals to whom industry, the government, and the labor movement are ultimately answerable and accountable.

Individual tastes and opinions vary among people, and within the individual himself or herself over time. Tastes are therefore not fixed, and this is exploited by industry through innovation and imitation. Opinions are not fixed, and this is utilized by the government in formulating its economic policies. Moreover, workers' opinions are made known in labor meetings, and these are taken into consideration by labor management and given expression in the formulation of differing and newer policies.

There is, then, a relationship between individual utility functions based on information systems and the greater welfare utility function based on the cycle's fluctuations. The relationship is different from Edgeworth's contract considerations as these pertain to agreements among individuals. It is different from Pareto's utility optimum, for the welfare of the economy does not depend on one person's position being better or worse-off than the rest of the economy, but the economy's welfare and hence its individuals' depends on the cycle's phase. This relationship differs from Slutsky's position in the sense that, while there is substitution of products—and this depends to a large extent on close competitiveness and price—again, the cycle's phase is more important: Consumption must continue but innovation and imitation, bringing new and competitive products into the markets, depend on the cycle's position because they will not occur to any significant extent during the peak of prosperity and the phase of recession.

The relationship between individual utility functions and the greater welfare utility function, therefore is the following: Individual utility functions are formulated on the basis of information stated rigorously and placed in an operational-area language isomorphism; this strict relationship exists because of the expectations to be derived in the reality of the situation. Such utility functions are attempts to impose on a seemingly chaotic reality an order, derived from individual tastes, wants, and desires. With respect to firms, governmental agencies responsible for economic policies, and labor organizations responsible for their workers, this poses little or no difficulty. The leaders in each of these sectors and sectorials, including the micro level of the firm, the specific agency, and the specific labor branch or local union, are managers and their decisions are made with respect to their positions in their organizations and their individual conceptions tempered by the opinions of those with whom they work.

Often, these information systems clash and are thus subject to entropy, the extent of which depends on how well they perform in the conflict of systems. The managers of firms often have to consider the responses of their workers when new projects are placed into operation. Workers have to consider their strategies with respect to management's predicament in the firm's competitive position. Both business and labor managers have to consider the effects of government policies on their operations, and these considerations influence their relationships with one another as well as with the government.

When considered important, therefore, this information is included in the system. The system is open-ended if longer than the immediate very short-term period is being considered; this open-endedness allows for alterations and responses to alterations generated within the system by the influences of the marketplace. Changes can be made within the system, either by management's intentional alteration of the operational and/or the area languages to cope with the reality for which the system was formulated, or because of the reality's imposing changes within the system for which alterations have to be made in one or both languages. This process is dynamic and continues until the alterations outweigh the original system and entropy is too intense, or until the system is abandoned for other projects. This holds for the information systems of the firm, the governmental agencies, and labor management, and the systems of each of these must take into account not only their competitors in their respective markets, but also the information systems of the others.

As was stated in the previous section, the decisions of business managers, governmental managers, and the labor organization managers are dependent on the cycle. Innovation and imitation, for example, will most likely not be undertaken when the cycle approaches the peak of prosperity. Governmental decisions tend to be countercyclical, in order to eliminate as much as possible the difficulties of unemployment and the problems of welfare when the cycle declines, and to prevent too much liquidity, hence inflation, when the cycle rises. Labor realizes during the peak of prosperity and the movement toward recession, as well as the obvious situation of the recession itself, that it has to refrain as much as possible from taking sanctions and striking, and that the best time for these actions is when the cycle moves well into recovery.

The question to be dealt with now, is how does the individual as consumer relate to the welfare utility function? The contemporary individual as consumer, outside the framework of employment and managerial-level decision making, does not have information systems formulated with respect to rigor, as do the managers of business, industry, and labor. Consider, for example, the contemporary individual as a manager in a large firm. This individual constructs the information system, using operational and area language to attempt to define the problem situation and form a working relationship, one that will provide the conditions for using the system effectively—a relationship that is constructed for expansion and alteration as the conditions prescribe.

Consider this same contemporary individual as consumer. This person has tastes, preferences, income limitations in his or her allocation for consumption, and is open to try new products in spite of these tastes and preferences—this last condition being necessary in our expanding markets. In one very important sense, this individual shares with the general economy the property that his or her consumption is influenced to a great extent by the cycle's phase. When the cycle is in the depths of recession, goods and services are still limited in quantity and their prices are high—hence the combination of stagnation and inflation, or "stagflation" as the term has been named. The business managers then share with the government managers and those of labor the same property as with the employee of the firm, the government, and the rank and file union member— this being that consumption is restricted to the *relatively small* amount of goods and services available at prices that are fairly high. The consumer, no matter what his or her job may be, is then restricted by this condition. The restriction is one of degree and this requires that each consumer budget his or her purchases according to the liquidity possessed with respect to alternative purchases.

When the cycle begins to rise, the opportunities for consumption increase, and competition forces prices down. This process continues throughout the various stages of recovery and into the prosperity phase, until innovation ceases and imitation follows suit shortly after, plunging the cycle into recession once again, only with a broader-based socioeconomic infrastructure, so that the next movement to recovery will bring a greater variety of goods and services due to innovation and imitation into the markets. The completion of each cycle enriches the economy that much more.

From this, it can be stated that the consumers' utilities are cyclically-oriented, so that setting UC for consumers' utilities, it can be stated that $UC_p \approx 1/C_p$, where the subscript $p$ stands for the period in the cycle's phase. $p$ could also be substituted by $t$ for time, but it is important to note the cycle's period in its phase when discussing consumers' utilities, for this indicates the general pattern of purchases from the available goods and services with respect to income.

It will be remembered from part 2 that income Y is separated into $Y_c$ and $Y_d$, with $Y_c$ being income in circulation and $Y_d$ being disposable income. Income in circulation is income for consumption, as it is through consumption that money is placed into the economy in exchange for goods and services. Disposable income can also be placed into circulation through consumption, but can also be saved (and if rationally, invested to earn returns) as the consumers see fit. The point is that while income Y holds for the entire economy (Money $= Y_c + Y_d$), $y_c$ and $y_d$ hold for the contemporary individual as consumer, so that his or her money supply is equal to personal income for consumption as well as the disposable income that exists after the usual consumption is completed and that can be directed toward further consumption or for savings, as the case may be.

Just as consumption relies on the cycle's periods in its phases, so do individual savings, which influence the direction to be taken by disposable income as well as consumption. This is important, for on the basis of the cycle's period and phase, investments are made. Of course, there is the element of risk not associated with the cycle's movement, and this is manifested in expectation on the returns of the investment. This is based on the utility of investment and is associated with the rate of interest expected, so that E/U (*idnr/ldn*), with $i$ being the interest, $dn$ being the deferred number of time-units, r being the rate of return, and l being the currency in which the investment is made. As the velocity of money is equal to the utility of money, and as $M = Y$, the velocity of money invested is equal to its utility as investment. But as this utility cannot be evaluated with a high degree of certainty due to the disequilibrium dynamics of shifting markets and the demand for loans as a consequence, then utility has to be of an expected value, with the interest rate an expected percentage of the investment and the money value of the return determined by the conditions of the market. The exception to this is guaranteed returns at a fixed rate over time such as offered by banks and savings and loan institutions. But these rates also fluctuate after the fixed-time saving period expires.

From $UC_p \approx 1/C_p$, the individual consumer's utility function can be further explained. As $UC \equiv \Sigma UC_1^n$, then $uc_i \epsilon UC$, and therefore $uc_{ip} \approx 1/C_p$. Having isolated the individual consumer utility position, it can be analyzed further: $uc = m(yc + y_d)$ that is, individual consumer utility is a money function of consumption income and disposable income. The main component in this function is $y_c$, for from this, most if not all of the consumption is made. Hence, it is used for the the purchases of individual goods and services having the set-elements $< 1, 2, \ldots, n >$ for time $t$. At $t+1$, there is no necessity that the elements of consumption will be identical to those of time $t$, but as people tend to be creatures of habit, the deviations will not be too profound. This, of course, depends on depends on the impacts of innovation and imitation. The deviations from the habitual purchasing patterns, therefore, depend on the impact of the innovation made on the consumer. Imitation, on the other hand, affects the purchases, not in the type made but in the competitive variation of the type. The reason for change may be price, a better packaging, good effective advertising, or just a better product of the same type, such as two different vacuum cleaners, one offering more options than the other and having a longer guarantee.

The assumption that each consumer knows what is best for him or her, is upheld in this argument. For this reason, consumer tastes differ as much as do the consumers themselves and this renders any attempt to quantify over the individual consumer impossible. Tastes are as fickle as the weather: General patterns can be established, but individual details escape the pattern. On this basis, innovation and imitation are undertaken, to influence the consumer to change the direction—in the case of imitation, perhaps slightly—the direction of purchases.

This does not mean that general statements cannot be made about the consumer, statements which are valid for all of the consuming populace. For example, the consumer's purchasing patterns are influenced directly by the cycle's period and phase. On the basis of this type of reasoning, the substitution effect takes hold, as, for example when inflation is high due to the peak of prosperity or the beginning of recession, the consumer will then seek substitutes of lower-priced goods for the higher-priced ones. Substitution is not limited to inflation, however, for it forms the basis for imitation, as firms compete for consumer liquidity— this, as a variation of substitution, is another generality.

Another generalization is that as the cycle moves up in recovery, less of the consumer's income will be directed toward consumption, because prices decline through competition and more consumption can be undertaken at fixed rates of income alloted for consumption, thereby releasing disposable income for investments. This does not have to occur throughout the cycle's upward movement, but the tendency exists for savings to be undertaken during this time. For this reason, fixed rates of return are popular savings incentives, as they allow for hedges against uncertainty, even though the rates of return are far lower than the risk-investment rates.

There is still another certainty about the consumer as a member of consuming groups. The term "group" is used loosely here in the sense that it refers not to organizations or organized behavior set by others to be followed. It does mean that certain standards of living, certain appliances, and certain modes of consumption, are expected by people on differing income levels; at these levels, commercials are directed, packaging is oriented, and innovation and imitation vie for the consumers' liquidity.

Nor are these groups rigid, for while they are targets for production, they may—or the consumers may—prefer to venture into the purchasing patterns of other such group levels. Hence, expensive wines can be enjoyed by those who have the money, and by those who decide to "splurge" and cut back on consumption later. This mobility is not always upward, but can be downward as well, as in the case of wealthy people preferring a common brand of cigarette.

What determines these consuming groups, and how does a consumer decide to which group he or she belongs? These groups are socially oriented to the status of salary and position within the economy. A banker has a higher status economically than a street cleaner and the banker's consumption patterns based on the salary received allows for vastness compared to the street cleaner. The contemporary individual decides to which group he or she belongs by his or her aspirations, but the grouping is also determined by the common property of the salary range. This determinant is socially oriented and quantifiable, while inner feelings, expressed openly through aspirations, are strictly personal and hence nonquantifiable.

What is quantifiable, moreover, is the total consumption of the contemporary individual and this is expressed by the uc function over the time considered. As consumption varies with the cycle's period and phase, then for each consumer, $uc_t = m = (y_c + y_d)_t = m <1, 2, \ldots n >_t \approx 1/C_{Pt}$. Hence, the consumer's utility function is identical to the welfare utility function, which approximates the economy's position with respect to the cycle's period and phase. This is so, intuitively, for in times of recession and unemployment, the consumer cuts back on consumption and during recovery and prosperity, when the economy is active with innovation and imitation, the consumer expands consumption. That this is so, logically, has been derived from the argument.

With both the contemporary individual's utility function and the general welfare utility function being approximations of the cycle's period and phase, it can be seen that the economy's welfare requires both the individual as consumer and the organizations—be they business, governmental, or labor—in which they work. Their work generates income and part of this income is directed toward salaries, which generates liquidity for consumption of the products of innovation and imitation. But while this is so, business, government, and labor each has a specific role to play in the maintenance of the economy.

It has already been stated that business is the generator of economic activity, for the firm initiates programs of innovation and imitation, producing for consumption. Moreover, through the firms' activities, the cycle is generated and the firm responds to the cycle's dynamics through innovation and imitation when the cyclic conditions allow.

While the firm generates cyclical dynamics, the government's role, through policies of investment in infrastructure and in specific projects, is to counter the cycle in its extremes and hold it steady when moving from recovery to prosperity. This means the the government has to prevent the cycle from moving too fast during recovery, so that firms cannot maintain the pressures of production to the extent that inflation rises with increased demand generated by increased liquidity obtained through employment. For example, should the psychology of the recession be one of caution even though recovery is progressing, then the liquidity option for firms will be stronger than otherwise. While profits are gained through successful innovation and imitation, the liquidity option acts as a form of security, but this is unrealistic because fixed costs are reducing unproductive liquidity. Other firms act on production, and with demand increasing supply does not follow the pace. The result is inflation and the government has to take steps at this time to reduce inflation.

Taxation is not the measure to be undertaken, for this restricts spending only marginally, but mostly reduces the rates of personal income allocated for savings—monies necessary to maintain the liquidity flow for businesses. Consumption levels are largely maintained, applying increasing pressure on limited supplies and hence increasing inflation still that much further. As the problem is psychological, so is the solution. The government should invest in social infrastructure and maintain the current tax levels, thereby stimulating a more positive economic picture, one that will encourage the liquidity option to be dropped for production, so that supply can be increased and the full dynamics of disequilibrium, through changing production orientation by innovation and imitation, can be realized.

Labor's policies are perhaps the most important for our contemporary era. The tradition of labor is to use strikes and sanctions to gain workers' rights, and with various government legislation, labor's policies have become fair play when they correspond to the requirements of this legislation.

There is another aspect of labor which must be considered, however, and this involves the changing approaches of labor to the changing industries. There are the traditional industries that evolved as a result of the Industrial Revolution, such as the steel industry, the automotive industry, and the aviation industry—although the latter developed greatly only after the World War II, when the advantages of air travel were increased through jet propulsion. However, in our contemporary era of economics, new industries have developed, those not requiring "blue collars" and "hard hats," but demanding skills at extremely high levels of perfection. These are the computer industries and those industries that are necessary in their development and manufacture, and in maintaining their competiveness in light of foreign contributions.

Because of their hard-fought struggles and the concessions gained from business, labor has tended to become conservative, requiring stringent procedures, such as long periods of apprenticeship and long waiting-time before such apprenticeship can be obtained, as well as the restricted mobility of workers within plants, to maintain labor's own positions of authority and bargaining power with respect to the firms.

This conservatism is understandable historically, but has little bearing on our contemporary situation. Contrary to popular opinion, technology does not have to be specialized in orientation; as it becomes advanced and increasingly sophisticated, technology requires the conceptualizations of mathematical and physical disciplines, among others, as the case may be. The point is that the traditional concept of the blue-collar worker, hard-hatted and assembly-line oriented, is being replaced by workers who are acquiring higher degrees in education and further sophistication in their labor. The necessity of innovation and imitation imposes on labor to maintain its competitive edge in order to remain employed. Labor unions cannot, therefore, rest on their traditions of the struggle in the earlier decades of the twentieth century, but must make efforts to ensure that their members are kept abreast with the latest in technological developments and their applications in industry.

Labor is thus in a period of transition. Many of its older workers received on-the-job training in the aftermath of World War II and though techniques have developed since then, these workers have been slow to catch on to the new ways of working. The is not a situation of being unable to "teach old dogs new tricks," as the expression goes; it is that these people have not grown up within and been educated by the school systems of contemporary society. Their training background is post-Depression-oriented and, except for the extremely eager and motivated, the older patterns of work tend to dominate. There may be some rationale to "kick these people upstairs" into managerial positions because of the knowledge and wisdom they have amassed through their years on the job, but how many of these people can be moved to higher positions? How many positions for these people are available?

The period of transition in which labor finds itself can be exploited to its best interests if, instead of wasting valuable money and time in sanctions and strike action, the money and resources be directed toward providing courses for workers involved in the technologies of industrialization. As the cycle turns downward, those funds previously allocated for buffers while strikes are being undertaken or while sanctions are being applied and employers hold back payment, could be invested during the profitable times and applied to reeducation during periods of unemployment. Moreover, this should not be be considered a policy of discrimination against workers unskilled in technology, for in our modern economy, technology and its related improvements in the state of the arts imposed by industrialization demand a technological awareness from workers. During the recession phase of the cycle, workers receive unemployment compensation and, in situations where unemployment is prolonged, welfare payments are made. These types of funding, together with the retraining and updating in the techniques of work in the specific fields, will allow the worker to maintain a level of self-esteem, instead of being idle, and prepare him or her for the next upturn of the cycle.

The demands of industrialization vary from one cycle to another, with the economy being that much more enriched as the cycle is completed. This places demands on the labor force that in the case of individual workers could not be met—to the detriment of industrial development. As members of unions concerned for their workers, retraining and reeducating can only result in the labor force in general and the individual worker's being prepared for the next upswing and the demands that industrialization will place on the labor force and the individual worker. This is not merely the case of robots operating an assembly line; it also applies to those workers, technologically oriented, who construct the robots, program their operations, and relate these processes to the products being manufactured. Blue collars and hard hats are being replaced by college-educated workers who are developing new methods and materials for industry. They are members of unions and when the circumstances of the cycle bring them into the ranks of the unemployed, they should receive the further training to allow them to advance in their careers when their services will be demanded again by industry.

There is another service that the labor organizations can provide their membership, and this is the educating of those workers who, for whatever circumstances, were unable to complete their formal educations. This will allow them to move up the wage scale and improve their personal positions, perhaps to the point of entering the technological levels of employment. Not only will they benefit, but industry will also benefit by having a higher level of skilled workers employable, so that projects requiring advanced technologies can be introduced into the production process with little difficulty and need for adjustments. The question is asked, then, what happens to those workers on the lower wage scale, for someone has to do the menial work? One of the advantages of technology should be to remove the drudgery of labor, to replace it with the challenges of work, challenges that can be met and their dynamics absorbed into the information networks of other systems. The fact that some forms of work remain laborious is a remnant of the earlier economic eras and with rational planning and retraining by labor organizations, they should be abolished.

This brings up the issue of vested interests in the labor organizations, the desire on the part of some labor leaders to maintain their hold on the rank and file. That the political aspects of organized labor often dominate the decision-making processess cannot be denied, and indeed, politics can be beneficial because it provides a form of internal competition, so that a single force tends not to become dominant, and if so, not for too long. But this politicking should not be at the expense of the rank and file membership, which should be encouraged to seek advancement in job positions. The status quo, being maintained, can allow for the leadership to maneuver among themselves in their power plays, being comforted with the knowing that there will be no changes in labor policy that could upset their power bases. In earlier times, this attitude would result in no damage to the unions, because there was no real demand from labor to be skilled in then-contemporary technologies. This is not the situation now, and that labor still relies on sanctions and strikes to influence business managers to provide higher wages and better working benefits, demonstrates that the unions are still operating according to the conditions of the earlier era. Granted that these methods are still somewhat effective in gaining the priviliges demanded by the unions, but for the most part, they refer to a bygone era and have little to do with our contemporary economic situation.

Just as firms innovate and imitate, they require new technologies and different approaches to work in order for their projects to be economically viable. Labor should not merely adjust accordingly, seeking retraining whenever possible, but the unions should become dynamic in the introduction and expansion of the retraining programs, indeed even developing their own contributions in technology that can be provided to the firms. The point is that this type of cooperation will make the firms more profitable and improve labor's position as a consequence. There will be then little need for sanctions and strikes as a means to achieve labor's objectives, because cooperation will be rewarded with higher pay and better working conditions. Should management not be so forthcoming, however, leaving labor's contributions unrewarded or not sufficiently remunerated according to labor's calculations, then the older methods of sanctions and strikes can be implemented, with the backing of the general public in most cases. Moreover, this policy will provide higher levels of technology that can be translated into greater productive efficiency, freeing resources for other projects and allowing for the liquidity option when considered necessary.

There is another advantage to technological education in its manifestations in work. Greater available technologies can prolong the cycle's recovery and prosperity phases, because these technologies are transformed into innovative and imitative projects. The duration of these forms of production and the expansion of the economy that they allow, maintains the cycle's motion upward. Markets can reach near saturation but so long as the technological means exist for new markets to be open or for the firms to shift into other yet competitive markets, the cycle's upward motion is maintained. Technology tends to release resources for other purposes, so that the greater the technologies, the more available are resources for other projects. Labor can retrain its members to keep them skilled in the latest technologies, especially during periods of cyclical decline and unemployment, so that when the cycle begins its upward movement again, labor's contribution will not only be in the execution of the work plans, but perhaps also in contributing to the efficiency of executing these plans through the introduction of technologies that are then approved my the firm's management and incorporated in the working project. The time has come for management and labor to perhaps yield on their traditional roles as antagonists and begin working together for the benefit of the both, and for the consumers alike.

## THE WELFARE UTILITY FUNCTION AND DYNAMIC DISEQUILIBRIUM

Because the welfare utility function depends on the cycle and the economy fluctuates in a condition of dynamic disequilibrium, with markets expanding and closing and with innovation and imitation opening up new markets and bringing about near-saturation in existing markets—resulting in shifts in market orientation—another point remains to be discussed with respect to the welfare utility function and dynamic disequilibrium. This is the point about economic welfare and the abolition of poverty.

But first, it must be clear about what is not being considered. The issue of the eqalitarian society, based on merit and accomplishments as the recognition of respect and honor, is fine, for in such a socioeconomic state there would be no differences in pay for labor no matter what the type of labor would be; only merit would be the determining factor for social status, so that those people with little or no accomplishments would have a corresponding status in the society. This is fine, but it is also utopian, with no basis in history nor in our contemporary economic era. A society based on merit would be one in which there was no poverty and those who stood outside the pale of society would be those who are incapable of being within it for reasons of illness, either mental, physical, or both. In the egalitarian society, means would be allotted to provide for these people, just as they are provided for, to some extent, now.

A society based on merit, however nicely it could be constructed, could never exist. Industry, government, and labor employ merit in the quality of their people and their individual, their talents, skills, and knowledge, but only as economic contributors. Their salaries are paid according to the evaluation of their meritorious qualities, as manifested in their work and output. This results from the very nature of economics as the allocation of scarce resources among competing ends, and merit, no matter how impressive, cannot serve as a means for achieving this allocation, but money can and does. This is one reason why money is the basis of economic activity. But resources, especially in our contemporary era, refer not only to materials and machinery, but also to the talents for exploiting these objects to yield productive capacity and revenues. Without reverting too much to the basic principles of economics, it should be noted that talent is also a resource and it too is allocated by money in the form of wages.

We have evolved our societies in this manner and as with all forms of evolution, it has succeeded and thrived because it is the most efficient method. And as with evolution, it is not stagnant. We have made great strides not only since Adam Smith, but also since John Maynard Keynes and not doubt will continue to do so—if we are not interrupted in our activities by the final war.

One aspect of this evolution is that poverty, in its traditional, i.e., depression-oriented concept of people out on the streets, food lines, slums, poor medical services and lack of education for the underprivileged, and so on, can be removed from our presence for ever. Our modern economies have the strength, the resources, and the means for accomplishing this.

One of the reasons for such slow progress along these lines is that the abolition of poverty has been considered to be a burden on society. Resources for accomplishing this can be better used for purposes that will expand economic activity, and these people in their poor straits are considered to be liabilities in the economic sense. This sense, however, is nonsense. It would be much better to have these people gainfully employed, taking their places in the dynamic economy, than to have them improverished and on the dole. Moreover, monies provided for such welfare recipients are not used efficiently and hence have almost no utility. Money should be paid for productivity and not for subsistence. Of course, the government has an obligation to look after its citizenry, and this includes people who are down-and-out. The easy and least productive way is just to provide welfare payments, i.e., maintaining these people on their sub-sistence living standards.

There is, however, another way, one that initially presents difficulties, but will eventually yield the results desired: making these people productive workers, each according to his or her specialities and proclivities. This way is the intro-duction of compulsory training programs and education for these people—forcing them, as it were, to enter society as productive members. Not only can em-ployment be guaranteed after the training and educating processes are completed, but money for maintaining well-being can be provided in the interim. Moreover, the natural tendencies of these people can be evaluated and developed, so that the training will not be wasted.

The expenses of running these kinds of programs can be calculated. The best available teachers can be provided and the subjects demanded by industry and the society in general can be taught. What cannot be even estimated are the benefits that society would receive by having these people become productive citizens, contributing in their various ways according to their talents. It can be said *a priori* that the costs of these programs will be paid-for many times over in the time-span between the training program graduation and job placement of participants. For the dole as a means of easing the welfare burden is really a waste of money and resources; changing the dole to a real welfare project, that of ridding the causes of the need for welfare and enabling these recipients to become truly productive, is certainly a much better approach, for the government agencies responsible for welfare programs and for the recipients themselves.

Consider the welfare utility function. As $W_t = U(I, G, L)_t$ partial differen-tiation on G isolates it from the equation and allows it to be examined closer. $G = \leqslant g_1, g_2, \ldots, g_n$; and in time t, its welfare programs can be evaluated. If these programs maintain the dole—perhaps as a means of preventing unrest on the part of the recipients and perhaps because of the lack of initiative to attempt to resolve the welfare problems—then the status quo is maintained and as for G in the welfare utility function, its position will not move to the upper limit at the same rate as Industry and Labor.

However, if $g_{rehabilitation}$, $g_{education}$, and $g_{future\ employment}$ are elements providing for the recipients' welfare, then as they increase in efficiency, the elements of $g_{unemployment\ insurance}$, $g_{welfare\ payments}$, $g_{subsidizing\ industries}$, and $g_{investing\ in\ low\ utility\ regions}$ can be reduced and phased-out as the efficient programs become entrenched in the government welfare policy and decision-making processes. Rehabilitation can take the form of working to abolish chronic poverty through inner-city programs and financial incentives for businesses. This would help counteract unemploy-ment insurance by providing employment to these people in their areas of res-idence. Welfare payments can be reduced through these programs, by taking the chronically unemployed and providing employment in these business. This often requires some basic education so that basic and advanced skills for businesses are learned and developed, perhaps coordinating this education with the actual business and employment experiences. People with qualifications can then find employment in industries outside their regions so that labor mobility can be established in those areas where proverty had previously held them fixed and immobile, with little or no hope for improvement. As G moves with the cycle, its programs will be intensified as the cycle turns downward and eases during the final period of recovery and into prosperity. But these programs will remain, nevertheless, until the contemporary economy finally, if ever, sheds its shackles of the previous historical era and moves into its own, generating its own economic dynamics.

As $W_t = U(I, G, L)_t$, and as government policy bears on Industry and Labor, the improvement in the welfare situation due to rehabilitation, education, and future employment leads to changes in industries' and labor organizations' planning and strategies. First, these people enter the mainstream of economic activity as consumers and producers. They have acquired consumer utility functions as a result and this has to be considered by industry. As employees, they also contribute to the economy but compete for positions as well, and this has to be considered by labor. Moreover, with respect to labor, their union membership provides greater strength to the unions and their dues expand the coffers. Because these people have come up from the pit of poverty, they can be assets as individuals in the labor movement and as employees in industry. They know the feelings of economic impotency, of the "system" that had previously perpetrated and perpetuated poverty, and these feelings can often be channeled and directed by these very people into increased work motivation and labor activity.

While the government is the underwriter of the economy, industry should also pay a part in the removal of the dole and subsidies on poverty. This is not for any altruism that industry should acquire, nor because of the necessity for industry because of social dictates to act benevolently toward welfare recipients. It is for the good of industry, however, and for this it should be done. For example, by investing in those deprived areas, industry provides the stimulant for secondary and auxiliary businesses to develop there. This requires infrastructure that the government will assist in developing and employment will result, so that demand generates profits. Of course, no philanthropy is expected from industry and only those areas with appropriate basic infrastructure and cost advantages should be considered. Goodwill, however, should never be a main motivating consideration for such a policy, as it is not based on sound economic reasoning and the considerations of plant location, and is therefore liable to result in financial losses and the demise of a very good intention. With more people employed, there is greater demand and therefore greater sales, resulting in greater revenues and profits. Moreover, with more people employed, more skilled workers are in industry and job competition will maintain the development of skills. Labor organizations can do their part to maintain efficiency in work and improved skills when unemployment results from the downward turn of the cycle.

Finally, because the welfare utility function is inferred from the individual welfare function, and because the contemporary individual's utility function is derived from the welfare utility function, with both being derivable from the business cycle in its periods and phases, both these utility functions are far from stable, but are in a state of dynamic disequilibrium, just as is the economy. Tastes are influenced by the types and quantities of products on the markets, but as these products fluctuate due to innovation and imitation, tastes respond accordingly, as manifested in demand. Thus, the contemporary individual's utility function is dynamic and in disequilibrium.

With government policy being formulated to cope with a changing economy, its institutions are maintained until they are no longer adequate to deal with the economic realities. This does not, of course, mean that the finance ministries or central banks will be closed down, for they are the overall institutions for handling the economy. It does mean, however, that some of the agencies within these institutions may be either closed down or restructured to allow for greater efficiency in handling the economy. Also, other branches may be added, such as the value-added tax authorities to the tax department, so that greater control can be exerted through specification and functional specialization. Government policies are thus altered with the economic situation, if this situation deviates too far from that for which the agencies are currently set up to handle. It is therefore the case that an economy operating in an atmosphere in dynamic disequilibrium exerts its influences on the government agencies responsible for its overseeing and alters them accordingly.

What about labor? Here, again, is an institution strongly rooted in its past and having a great future in the economic situation; it has to take the distant stand and look at the economy and itself, to see where the economy may be going and how it can contribute to its progress. It is no longer the case of taking to the streets, of having to confront "scabs" and strike breakers, for the battles have already been fought and the war won. Organized labor must now come to terms with itself, with its somewhat archaic system of quotas, apprenticeship, and seniority ranked above talent. Not that the older workers should be turned out, but that they should be retrained where necessary to allow industry (and government, for that matter) to develop new products and compete effectively on the domestic front and in international competitive markets. Labor should certainly not neglect its past, for its past is a period of great struggle for a worthy cause. But the past holds no promise, while the present has to be dealt with, but this in the manner best considered for the future, making the future more controllable and profitable. Labor holds a promise for the future that it never had previously. It is no longer the case of business versus labor, but of business and labor versus poverty, the lack of education, the striving against corruption in the ranks of organized labor and the removal of internal obstacles, the presence of which renders the labor organizations stagnant and inefficient, in the name of their rank and file.

As $L$ is a component of the welfare utility function, it relates to the cycle and to the influences of business and the government. The cycle's downward movement means that unemployment rises and its upward movement means that employment is reabsorbed into the economy. But the point is, what kind of labor is required, what quality of worker is available, and what are the skills of those who are entering the labor markets? In the early stages of recovery, industry does not rely on its past technologies entirely, but develops new technologies that it expects the labor force to be able to work with. If not, then the cycle's upward motion is slowed that much more as industry must retrain labor to a certain extent to work the technologies. This also results in higher prices as time is translated into money and passed on to the consumer at every stage of the production process. This can be eliminated if, using the funds at their disposal, perhaps insured to bring greater dividends and also subsidized by some of the governing agencies, workers are reeducated in the state-of-the-art techniques. A certain consequence of this is that the cycle will move up not only more swiftly, but also expand the industrial base, and hence the employment situation, that much more broadly and productively.

We live in a world united to a large extent economically, and to no small extent, the economic events of one country or region have direct effects on the rest of the world. The United States Federal Reserve Bank raises or lowers interest rates and the economies of the rest of the world are affected. The Organization of Petroleum Exporting Countries agrees on cartel prices for crude oil and the effects are reverberated throughout the world. Moreover, these policies affect the cycle and hence welfare, as the high oil prices in the 1970s demonstrated all too clearly.

There is an international disequilibrium effect associated with these policies that influences the welfare of each country. This must be discussed, and finally the problems of welfare in that special category of the developing countries must be considered. These are the subjects of the final part of this work.

# Part 4

## THE WELFARE UTILITY FUNCTION AND ITS GLOBAL CONSEQUENCES

# 12

# Welfare in the Developed Economy

An uncoordinated government has produced uncoordinated programs with gaps, overlaps, cross-purposes, inequities, administrative inefficiencies, work and family support disincentives, and a waste of taxpayers' money.

Rep. Martha Griffiths of Michigan

## GENERAL COMMENTS

The concept of the developed economy is somewhat misleading, for it tends to imply that development has been achieved and that it has ceased, that the state of technology is such that no further advancements are necessary, that in the neoclassical and Keynesian sense of development the stationary state has been reached and that the high levels of consumption and production require no further economic expansion.

Of course, this is not so. That the developed economies have achieved a very high standard of living is not in dispute here. But that their technologies have decreased or even halted in their development is not the case, nor has a stationary state been achieved. There are dynamics in the developed economy in which dynamic disequilibrium functions, phasing out markets for which demand has declined and developing new markets for products that are demonstrably commercially attractive; indeed, one of the criteria for considering an economy to be developed is its ability to expand according to the phase of the business cycle.

Another criterion for considering an economy to be developed is its set of standards in the realm of welfare. A country with programs covering all aspects of its welfare needs is considered to be advanced and developed, in the sense that its legislative bodies have enacted regulations to alleviate the pressures of poverty, unemployment, and the absence of education on the lower classes of society.[1] Welfare systems are thus maintained in the developed economy for two reasons. One reason is to reduce social pressures for reform that are not acceptable in the country's political system. Rebellion, for example, always fermenting below the social calm when times get economically difficult, has to be avoided in order to prevent the body politic from disruption. Outbreaks of street rioting, occurring in the United States (in the Watts area of Los Angeles and in Detroit in the 1960s), and in France (Paris during the late 1960s and early 1970s), and sporadically in Japan and in South Korea,[2] are expressions of such rebellion. These forms of protest, with their destruction and loss of worktime, can be reduced or eliminated by welfare programs suited to current economic conditions. Welfare has thus become a method of relieving social pressures on a system that cannot be changed; it is a substitute—sometimes an effective one—for immediate legislation geared to alter conditions that have led to the building up of explosive social pressures. Legislation is immediate in its impact and, where the political system can absorb such legislation, or when the alternative is momentum into social conflict that may be irreversible (such as race relations in the 1960s in the U.S.) then legislation is mandatory. When the system is unable to handle the pressures, for example, those which occur during recessions with increasing unemployment, the welfare programs are necessary for relieving the pressures and unrest brought about by unemployment.

The other reason welfare systems are maintained in developed countries the presence of an economic-cum-social dilemma present in these countries. This dilemma is manifested in the following manner: The developed countries possess productive wealth and levels of output and consumption unprecedented in history. Yet, when prior to the Great Depression welfare programs were sparse compared to those now in operation, with all the wealth and relative luxury present in these countries there seems to be a social and political drive to not only maintain these programs, but to alter them and expand them when necessary. While the economic aspiration of the developed countries *should* be to maintain levels of economic activity so that all the potentionally productive citizens can be self-sufficient and not rely on the government for sustenance, welfare is increasing; both government and business policies on welfare—in the form of pension schemes, Social Security, Medicare, and socialized medicine encourage early retirement and the loss of productive hours of skilled workpower in production.

Of course, the reasons for this are perfectly logical when viewed from both a historical and a modern perspective. Historically, in spite of the lapse of time and the subsequent pertinent economic changes, the developed economies are still functioning in the shadow of the Great Depression. This is not only man-ifested in the types of welfare programs, such as The Social Security System in the United States (with its surplus estimated at $100 billion in 1993[3]), enacted in 1935 to eliminate the problems of poverty in retirement, and also in the types of job assistance offered to people seeking employment and assistance in re-training for employment in modern industry,[4] but also in the tense, almost near-panic reactions when the stock market fell in October 1987 and comparisons were readily made with the crash of 1929. The ghost of the Great Depression still haunts the developed economies but without reason, as their resilience demonstrated. Whereas in 1929 the economies collapsed and welfare programs were required to reemploy and stimulate demand, no such collapse occured in 1987—even though many businesses were seriously affected, especially those which brokered on the markets trading in stocks or investing heavily in the exchanges. There are no guarantees that another such unexpected and sudden sharp decline can be prevented and, should the market fall again, the comparisons between that time and the Great Depression will be once more readily made. The difference is, however, that the contemporary developed economy will again recover and continue in its processes of development. These welfare programs serve as a psychological buffer against such economic shocks, by providing financial assistance for those in need who are covered by the respective programs.

From the modern perspective, along with increasing wealth there is increasing population. This is not manifested so much in families having large numbers of children, although this situation still persists somewhat in the most rural sections of the developed economies. For as wealth increases and people attain the education and sophistication that accompany wealth, couples tend to limit the birth of their children, to provide those who are brought into this world the luxuries that wealth can provide, and thus not divide their income among too many children. Population increases in the developed countries take on the form of many couples having few children and, in turn, these children when reaching maturity, marrying, and also having few children. Many families expanding at this rate increase the population more than do the few rural families with many children. Moreover, migration, while marginal, also has its impact on population growth, even though the first and, to some extent, the second generations tend to rely on more welfare assistance than those people who have roots deeper in the countries.

This increase results in a young labor force, some seeking training, some going into their own businesses, others still already acquiring skills, which places pressures on industries run by relatively young administrators to pension-off those employees who have reached their early sixties and are still able to make significant contributions in their occupations, partly because of the high level of public health care affordable in the developed economies and partly because of the improved working conditions in industry as a result of the awareness that costs in improving plant and working conditions are more than repaid in the workers' output.

This situation places the developed economies in somewhat of a dilemma. Talented and trained people are being retired earlier than before so that young people can be put to work, being trained at lower wage scales to compensate for their training costs. This is a reduction of efficiency in industry, because the older workers have the necessary skills to meet current production requirements. Thus, productive workers are removed from the work force, paid a reasonable pension according to their work, and receive Social Security (National Insurance) as a percentage of their earnings. Retirement is thus made easier, but at the loss of still-productive workers capable of making still-significant contributions in their respective areas.

However, industry can employ only so many workers. Young people of working age seek employment and should be so employed. But with limited space for workers in industry, it seems that there is a trade-off between older and still-productive workers and the young and largely untrained work-potential of the newly emerged seekers of employment.

This situation is compounded by the fact that industry is not in a state of permanance, but in a state of flux, expanding and entering into new or established markets, and contracting, phasing out those markets that are no longer profitable. Workers established in their patterns, restricted in their learning abilities because of age and considered by management to be of pensionable age are thus retired and the labor force is altered by the acceptance of into industry young people who are trained at the cost of receiving lower wages than those already skilled. The problem is that those young people who are not employed by industry and not able to enter the business world on their own, remain unemployed and are subject to the dole. Thus, even the developed economies, with their high levels of output and consumption, with their ever-increasing sophistication in production and marketing, and with their emphasis on exporting as well as supplying the domestic markets, are plagued with the difficulties of seeking a fair distribution of monies and services to assist the underprivileged and uneducated, thereby to bring them into the realm of the contemporary economy and its dynamics of production and consumption.

It must be remembered, however, that welfare is a function of the general economy, subject to the bureaucratic processes dealing with national and regional problems and the distribution of services and funding accordingly. When the economy is moving toward prosperity, peoples' reliance on welfare is diminished according to their rate of absorption into the economic processes; when the economy declines into recession, the reliance on the welfare system intensifies, according to the extent that business activity slows. Cyclical fluctuations are unavoidable and welfare needs expand and contract according to the downward and upward cyclical movements. Nevertheless, there is a level of welfare that each developed country must maintain in order to provide assistance for the lowest income stratum as well as for those who are unable to find their places in the economic system, either temporarily, as in the case of some types of unemployment, or for longer durations, because of social distinctions and inadequate education resulting from them or for other, individual, reasons. Whatever the situation, much truth holds for Rep. Griffiths's remarks, especially as they were stated in 1974, when the developed world economies were experiencing the effects of the OPEC (Organization of Petroleum Exporting Countries) oil embargo and the subsequent slowing-down of economic activity.

In this situation the need for welfare became important as the governments of the developed world were caught off-guard. The tendency was to complicate the welfare system as economic recession continued and unemployment increased. This situation was critical even though it was not brought about by the downward movement of the cycle but by the artificial, yet severe impact on the economies exerted by the oil crisis. The effects of the price rises were immediate and it is no wonder that in light of this situation governments were producing programs with gaps, and uncoordinated programs with overlaps,—each fraught with cross-purposes as well as administrative inefficiencies. Families thus found it to their advantage to receive help from welfare agencies rather than seek work in a dwindling employment market. Whether such programs, in spite of their faults, were a waste of the taxpayers' money is certainly debatable, for social crises were avoided and eventually the developed economies established their own energy priorities and systems, leaving the OPEC countries in disarray.

In the following section comments will be made on the United States welfare system and in the third section the system will be approached from the perspective of the welfare utility function. As a model of the capitalistic market system, the United States presents some interesting features of the real issue facing the developed economies, one being the dilemma of retaining the welfare system or phasing it out, thereby absorbing those who would be on welfare into the economy.

## THE UNITED STATES: WELFARE AND ITS DILEMMA

Throughout the history of the United States, two dominant themes have run through its political system. There is the Jeffersonian theme of the government that governs best governs least, and there is the Hamiltonian concept of a strong central government with the states subservient to federal rule. These very themes also run throughout the welfare system, because the system is federally-oriented even though the states participate and distribute federal funds according to their perception of their requirements, with the federal government exercising final control through the allocation of funds. But the states retain their independence to some extent by funding their own welfare systems with revenues accumulated through taxation.

Such services as schools and public universities, for example, are both state and federally funded. These could be considered as part of the welfare system because they assure education for those eligible for education. Highways and waterways are also federally and state-funded: as are the uses of the highways and the waterways-their availability and servicibility. However, education, while in the public domain, is not strictly so, because private schools that set their own tuition and establish their own curriculum are also allowed, and these may or may not receive state and/or federal aid, according to their charters and financial needs. Highways are sometimes privately owned and waterways may infringe on personal private property, the service of which sometimes requires a toll from the users.

The problems of welfare in the United States become more complicated because of the history of the capitalist ethos that has prevailed in the country. Since the writing of Adam Smith calling for free enterprise (in the Jeffersonian esprit, it should be noted) the intervention of the federal government has since been viewed askance, and in nonfederal intrastate affairs the constitutionality of such intervention has been seriously questioned.

That the federal government play an active role in the states' economic affairs is dictated by its obligation to establish the necessary infrastructure to maintain a healthy economy—one that will aid in stimulating further growth. Federal funding for education, for example, provides for the training of young people and discharged soldiers under the G.I. Bill of Rights. Cooperating with the states in the construction of highways also allow for greater population dispersion and the establishment of businesses in regions previously unpopulated. These, however, are marginal issues where welfare is concerned.

The United States has undergone momentous changes in its conception of welfare, its programs in the Great Depression. Had the Pigovian concept of the depression been correct, that is, had full employment been a fact that had suffered a temporary setback as a result of the cycle's downswing, much of the concern for welfare would not have been so dominant during that time. But full employment did not exist and the mechanical approach to the cycle certainly proved inadequate. Steps had to be taken to get people working again and to assist those of old age who could no longer be active in the realm of self-support through labor. In 1935 the Social Security Act was passed, providing insurance against the ravages of economic insecurity during the retirement period. This Act, together with the various works projects, went a long way to alleviate unemployment and uncertainty. Had World War II not occurred, the United States would have taken further-reaching measures to revive the economy and end unemployment. The war, however, "solved" that problem by absorbing young men and women into the military.

The G.I. Bill of Rights was passed after World War II to provide education and training to the many demobilized service personnel who, because of the Depression were unable to receive an education or proper training for industry that was developing in the aftermath of World War II. There was a slight recession following the cessation of hostilities, as the demobilized personnel sought work in industry that was changing over from wartime to peacetime production. However, the cycle began moving upward as people became employed in civilian industry and prosperity seemed to be within reach. Poverty existed even as wealth, however, with increased social and economic discrimination continued minorities still feeling the disenfranchisement within the system of expanding wealth.

Another step in the establishing of the welfare system was the Small Business Act of 1953, run by the newly-formed Small Business Administration. This act served to provide assistance to those who sought to enter businesses but lacked the capital and guidance, those eligible including the demobilized soldiers of the Korean Conflict who preferred business opportunities to the education provided by the G.I. Bill. As well as providing financial assistance, this Act provided guidance in acquiring the benefits of research and development sponsored directly by federal agencies, or through government contracts or grants. It also provided literature on new technologies and assisted in small business selection of the relevant technologies to boost their competitive edge in commerce. In 1958, the act was reaffirmed and reformulated into the Small Business Investment Act, to be further authorized to delegate certain responsibilities of assistance to state and federal agencies under Chapter 3 of the Trade Act of 1974 (88 Statute 1978; 19 U. S. C. 2101).

Whereas the Small Business Act was established to serve those interested in going into business, in 1979 the Secretary of Commerce established the Minority Business Development Agency to assist minority-owned businesses in achieving effective and nondiscrimination participation in the U.S. economic system of enterprise, and to overcome social and economic disadvantages that have hindered their participation in the past. Besides assisting minorities from all different cultural backgrounds, this agency enabled businesses to be established in areas that had hitherto been sidestepped because of their low profit potential and, in some instances, because of the high incidence of crime in the neighborhoods, so that people who were streetwise and knew their neighborhoods could prosper and make economic contributions to others in these areas.

As the United States developed its concept of welfare, not only was the economic aspect considered vital but health care, too, became a crucial concern. With increasing medical costs and a population comprised of larger numbers of elderly, the Medicare Act was passed as an ammendment to the Social Security Act, to provide basic medical care for the elderly over that amount of regular health insurance. Medicaid, also a part of this act, was formulated to provide medical payments to those not of retirement age but unable to afford the costs of medical treatment. This act, however, was met with opposition by the American Medical Association, which proposed a means test for those who were to receive its benefits. The AMA considered government infringement on its domain as an attempt to establish a form of socialism on American soil, but a more rational argument was put forth, that being that payment delays due to the filing of papers and the bureaucratic system necessary for processing and re-imbursment, would represent a loss to the physicians, as they would be deprived of using the money due to the delay in receive it for treatment. The issue is now open, with each physician accepting Medicare and Medicaid, or accepting payment and not using the federal system of compensation.

In the 1970s, the welfare system was deplorably disorganized. World events which caused havoc in the American economy consequently affected the welfare system. The recession brought about by the energy crisis due to the rapid rise in oil prices brought many business down. Demand for goods and services ran high in the years prior to the Yom Kippur War of 1973, unaffected by the Vietnam conflict and the racial tensions following the assassination of Dr. Martin Luther King, Jr. In the aftermath of the Yom Kippur War, the OPEC countries used their prime resource, oil, as a weapon to exact from the world's economies high prices and pressures against Israel. Industries were confronted with rapidly rising costs, which they sought to pass on to consumers. Demand declined and unemployment rose as a result. This placed very rapid and strenuous burdens on the welfare system. The federal government sought ways to educate the unemployed—such as the concept of the workforce, dating back to the Poor Laws of sixteenth century England, which provided work as a welfare benefit. Federally authorized, the workforce concept became mandatory as a means of relieving the burden of unemployment; people worked in menial jobs in the federal and state governments and received their upkeep.[5] This and other work programs, such as the Comprehensive Training Act, which provided vocational training in coordination with other projects (and which was terminated in 1983, to be replaced by similar federally sponsored job training partnerships offering employment and training assistance for dislocated workers) were certainly overlapping. They often operated at cross-purposes, resulting in administrative inefficiencies because of the bureaucracy involved. There was also an unavoidable human factor involved in the consideration of the applicants skills and selection of the best retraining and vocational program for the tenuous market circumstances.

As for housing, the Housing and Urban Development Act of 1965 provided rent subsidies for the lower middle and middle income classes. There were soon difficulties with this situation, however, as rent subsidies were in the form of fixed rent rates, to be altered by the cities and states subject to federal government approval. While this provided relief for these income groups, the property available for such renting was insufficient to match the demand for living in these rent-controlled dwellings. Moreover, landowners found their profits reduced significantly, compared to what they could earn from rent on the regular markets, and many sold out, either at break-even or at a small profit with the property being taken over by management companies. Nor did this Act reach the core of the poverty line to which welfare should aim, that being the slums. Lower and middle income families were not housed in these dwellings and those that were could not reap the benefits of appropriate subsidies. Another difficulty with this Act is that in spite of its name and intention, the people who were without housing did not come under its aegis. As recessions intensify and unemployment increases, those out of work and out of pocket often have to resort to finding sleeping quarters in abandoned property that is hazardous because of its derelict condition and dangerous because of the crime risks, or on the streets where both criminals and the elements show little discrimination.

In the 1970s, the situation in the United States was one of recession, with high levels of unemployment and uneconomic uses of industrial capital. Moreover, the fairly liberal approach to international trade allowed foreign manufactured goods to enter the market, thereby reducing the sale of domestically produced goods. Corresponding tariffs in these exporting countries did not allow for reciprocal activity and the U.S. citizens paid for their government's generosity to foreign countries with unemployment and reduced output.

Hence, when the Reagan administration began its first term in office in 1981, there were high expectations among the business and consumer communities that the tight money-easy fiscal mix, that favors consumption at the cost of capital formation, thereby retarding growth and maintaining high unemployment, would be examined. Furthermore, with high unemployment, a desired growth rate had to be established that would reduce unemployment, but with the balance-of-payments deficit in the U.S., it was thought that tax incentives for investment would stimulate capital formation, lead to increased production, and provide stronger competition to those countries exporting to the U.S. Also, further examination was required to deal with the output-inflation situation, where increased output was at the expense of increased costs that were passed on to the consumer in terms of higher, yet marginally so, prices. With the overburdened welfare system and its overlapping programs, the administration's approach was to reduce welfare programs. It advocated restimulating effective investment conditions so that production could increase in a cost-reduction economy, as a means for absorbing welfare recipients.

One step taken in this direction was the Budget Reconciliation Act of 1981, which directed monies into drug and alcohol rehabilitation and primary health-care, thereby eliminating the duplication of overlapping programs by pooling and streamlining funds. However, as a consequence, this led to the reduction of the number of programs that benefit the poor, in spite of their overlap and duplication, leaving those programs untouched that benefit the middle and upper income levels.[6] Thus, there developed inadequate financing for unemployment compensation, leaving pockets of unemployment and subsistence living in urban areas throughout the country. Moreover, in the attempt to streamline the welfare system, interest rates were charged on federal loans made to state compensation systems; the reasoning for this was that with interest charged, state compensation would be deployed more efficiently, with the costs of administering in the states reduced accordingly. With these interest rates on the state welfare administration, however, the requirement for assessing the unemployed became more stringent. Each state adopted its own system, but in general the principle or the willingness to be reemployed, no matter what the job offer might be, was accepted among the states. Moreover, the compensation for unemployment was often inadequate in light of the purchasing power of the monies provided and the economic situation in general. Again, the middle and upper income levels remained untouched because they were unaffected by the market conditions to the extent of being compelled to approach the welfare system for assistance.

In the 1970s high inflation and diminished economic growth drained the Social

Security Trust funds. Even though the ratio of beneficiaries to workers had dropped from 1:40 in 1940 to 1:33 in 1980 and prediction was that the system might collapse because of the amount of payments made. In 1982 President Reagan appointed a bipartisan National Commission on Social Security Reform, which in 1983 recommended delays in the cost-of-living increases, taxes on upper-income recipients, and a gradually higher retirement age in the twenty-first century; these were adopted, reflecting short-term tinkering with the system rather than considering its long-term financial and ideological problems.

The 1983 amendments to the Social Security Act quieted the situation for only a short while, for soon after Reagan's reelection came the issues of old age security and financing healthcare. The humane healthcare of Medicare and Medicaid had become so costly that, in real terms, for people over sixty-five the total healthcare cost is expected to be $200 billion in 2000, compared with $50 billion in 1978. The proportion purported to grow from public expenditures is expected to be about $114 billion in 2,000 as compared with $29 billion in 1978.

The Social Security Act allows for the collection of taxes distinct from, but running palallel with, other business and personal taxes. The system pays pensions to retired and disabled Americans and until 1982 its outlays exceeded its revenues, which increased the government's overall deficit. This motivated President Reagan early in his administration to take the Social Security off the budget, arguing that because it is a trust fund, and is managed as such it should be kept separate from the rest of the government's transactions. As this was accepted early in the Administration the budget deficit certainly appeared smaller. That Social Security should be off the budget was accepted in principle by the Gramm-Rudman-Hollings Act of 1985, which requires that the budget deficit be reduced over the years and be brought into balance by 1993.

The Gramm-Rudman-Hollings Act kept Social Security off the budget, but then redefined the deficit to keep the status quo, so that the overall deficit applies to the on-budget deficit such as international trade and defense and the off-budget social security taken together. With the current budget deficit estimated at between $146-$150 billion, the government is searching for extra sources of money to reduce the deficit.

One answer is Social Security. In 1982 the Social Security Trust stood at a deficit; during the past six years, however, because of higher payroll taxes social security is at a surplus, estimated to be $40 billion in 1988 and reaching more than $100 billion by 1994. By 1993, given present policies, the budget deficit is projected to be $220 billion, and as a possible approach to reducing this budget Social Security monies can be transfered into the government coffers.

While this is feasible, it is far from practical for two reasons. First, even though with social security taxes and benefits at their present levels, adjusted for inflation, and its estimated surplus lasting for 25 years or so, the surplus would have to be of such proportions as to move the budget deficit toward surplus in the years remaining for the Gramm-Rudman-Hollings Act to be effective. The Social Security surplus is far from being sufficient to achieve this. However, even if this policy were adopted and the overall deficit falls—for this and other possible reasons—the political pressures on the government to cut taxes and increase spending become harder to resist, thereby moving the budget into extreme deficit again. The second reason is that while the Gramm-Rudman-Hollings Act was correct in only pretending to set Social Security apart, the system is still a trust fund and while it may be in surplus now, it should remain so, especially in the next century with the possibilities of demographic trends resulting again in outlays exceeding revenues.

Still, the Social Security Act established the system as a trust fund in name only and the government can therefore alter its contributions and benefits as it sees fit with participants not entitled under the terms of the fund to the actuarial values of their contributions. Based on taxation of income, to consider that the system can accumulate surpluses in isolation from the rest of the public sector's finances is unrealistic; hence to set it off from the rest of the budget is both economically wrong and politically impractical. The government's overall deficit is what matters and, should the government reduce its contributions to the trust fund in order to satisfy the domestic and world financial markets, this would be a most questionable policy. The Social Security system is inappropriate as a fund source for assisting the government in its budget problems, even though it is effective now for assisting retired and infirm citizens.

Regardless of its surplus, however, more people are drawing on the Social Security system now than at any other time since the trust was established. This happens for two reasons. One reason is the generous retirement benefits available at earlier ages than was previously the situation. These benefits allow people who are still capable of contributing to retire earlier, thereby vacating their places for younger people and those needing to be employed. The other reason is the high costs of medical care, because of the increasing costs of education and sophisticated equipment, as well as research and the implementing of break-throughs in treatment medical and rehabilitation. Because Medicare and Medicaid were established as part of the Social Security Trust, and because insurance companies are not covering the full costs of treatment, this branch of Social Security is becoming increasingly active in financing care, to the point that the Reagan administration posited the Catastrophic Health Insurance, guaranteeing out-of-pocket hospitalization costs of $2,000 per month, for a payment of $2.49 of the pay packet. The Catastrophic Health Insurance Bill was passed on June 8, 1988, and signed into law on July 1, 1988, as the Medicare Catastrophic Act of 1988, PL 100–360.

Whether or not older workers are set in their ways, and unable to learn new methods of production, cannot be debated here. However, as a consequence of early retirement, places are found in industry for young people seeking employment. It has been estimated that formal employer-sponsored training to be about $60 billion a year and rising.[7] This has the advantage of providing on-the-job training for youth. Industry pays lower wages as a price for this training, but this sum does not include the wage value workers receive for jobs that include training, nor does it include informal everyday activities of workers and business people to improve the working environment and hence output. Perhaps this latter point is immeasurable.

In spite of the generous retirement benefits and the openings for young people for training and eventual positions in industry, 3 out of every 8 unemployed are between the ages of 16–24, with 4 million high school dropouts and 1 out of every 4 dropouts seeking employment.

Moreover, real poverty in the United States is a serious problem. It seems incongruous that in the world's most prosperous and powerful country, more than 32 million people—13.5 percent of the country's approximately 246 million persons—fell below the government-established poverty line in 1987, an amount greater than Argentina's total population. The government defines poverty according to the level of income necessary for purchasing the basic necessities of life; it is thus calculated that for a person living alone, this income would be $5,778 per annum, and as Laura Castaneda points out, by comparison, the mean income for full-time workers in the U.S. "is almost four times that—$26,896 a year." [8] Considered with this figure should be the amount of homeless in the United States, but there are no estimates of this number, other than that it ranges from 300,000 to 3 million. The government is spending $10.5 billion on subsidized housing, but this deals with only one aspect of the problem. The federal government is also spending $20.3 billion on food subsidies and $8 million on educational grants and loans for the poor; this deals with another aspect of the problem.

It is not the case that the poor are lazy, preferring a comfortable reliance on the public dole for support, for the poor have an awareness of the purchasing power of a decent wage and feel the lack of respect that a responsible position in society can provide. The situation is far more complex, representing the dynamics of an advanced economy in our contemporary era. In an important sense it represents the contemporary economy's moving into the new era with many of its citizens not understanding the changes and most certainly not knowing how to cope with them.

It could be argued that in every society there has, throughout history, been an impoverished class of people, who lived on the public purse and on the good will of the more affluent citizenry. This may be so, but it certainly has no necessary validity in our time in the United States. It may be that Manhattan, for example, is beginning to look like a second Calcutta, but it may also be, for the first time since the Reagan administration began reducing the welfare budget, that people are becoming aware of the situation, that the "Calcuttization" of Manhattan has existed for some time, and that the current cuts in welfare expenditure are not easing the situation. It is most certainly the case that poverty in the U.S. has reached crisis proportions and can very easily serve as a breeding ground for social disorder. And poverty is discussed in terms of numbers of people on welfare, the number unemployed and seeking work over a six-month period, the number of Social Security recipients, and the vague estimates of the number of homeless, sleeping on the streets in spite of housing subsidies. Perhaps thinking in terms of numbers helps us understand the dimensions of the problem, but there are also numbers that must then be considered, these being the amount of federal and state funding that goes into welfare, and another related and also serious number, that of the budget deficit.

Limited in its continuous expansion by Gramm-Rudman-Hollings to a zero on-budget by 1993, nevertheless, if the budget keeps expanding without serious cuts, by 1993 it is estimated that the deficit will be $220 billion with a Social Security surplus of $100 billion. The deficit is brought about by defense spending, by foreign aid, by financing the federal and state governments, and by welfare payments. It can be argued that cuts in defense spending can be made only when more progress in world peace and economic stability have been reached, when the emerging and developing countries have moved into the classification of the developed countries, when massive defense projects are no longer required for world stability and for providing domestic employment, when foreign aid can be reduced significantly or eliminated entirely, when countries such as Sudan and Ethiopia have strong internal infrastructures to prevent starvation, and when the United States is sufficiently developed that welfare programs can reduced drastically. These are certainly very long-range objectives and are worth working for; they are not, however, relevant for the stricture of the Gramm-Rudman-Hollings Act.

If this were just an internal restraint, placed by the Congress to get the domestic economic situation in order, the Act could be extended, or repealed, or rephrased to cope with the reality of the deficit situation. For given the current state of thinking, welfare cannot be cut without serious, indeed disastrous, repercussions in the domestic situation. For example, public housing and subsidies for housing cannot be cut because of the lack of adequate dwellings for the people who need it. The estimated 300,000 to 3 million sleeping in inadequate housing, abandoned buildings, and on the streets include teenagers, with drug problems and without anyone to care for them. If these and the others on the streets could care for themselves, they would certainly not be in this situation. Cuts in educational grants are also not socially feasible, for education is the future of the country; a strong education system provides a form of guarantee that the innovative esprit which made the country dominant in the world will continue—talent is not a matter of social strata, and it must be developed among all those who have the opportunity to learn. For the future of the country, this opportunity must be open to all. Foreign aid cannot be cut because of the disruptive consequences for world stability. Should the United States reduce its foreign aid contributions, this would not eliminate the recipients' needs for this aid; such aid would most certainly be replaced by the U.S.'s adversaries and detractors, increasing world tension and moving the world that one step closer toward another confrontation.

Defense spending has been brought into focus recently as a source of unnecessary government investment, given the Act's restraint. Not in question is the spending on foreign bases in Asia, in NATO's well-being, in the Mediterranean area, or in Cuba; indeed, these are expensive and, as the recent bargaining in Greece and Spain have once again demonstrated, perhaps replaceable by other countries. What is questionable, however, is SDI, the Strategic Defense Initiative—known somewhat sarcastically as "Star Wars"—which has expanded the defense portion of the budget enormously and has a questionable viability as a performing method of deterrence, given the inability to test it in realistic conditions and given the alternative methods of deterrence, especially the summit talks that have yielded agreements on weapons reductions.

This type of spending may result in concepts for advanced scientific and technical research, but again, the on-budget restriction of the Act must certainly be worrying those Pentagon advisers who have opted for the Strategic Defense Initiative. The budget is expanding and the date of the Gramm-Rudman-Hollings Act's becoming legal draws near. Should the "Star Wars" project be phased out, justified by Soviet responses to disarmament and the reduction of tensions in a positive manner, or by the program's costliness, it has nevertheless been very expensive and, in the name of research, has involved many countries in its formulation, thereby providing funding for these countries' research; this too has become a part of foreign aid under the guise of the military aspect of the appropriation, with the recipient countries having already initiated research into assigned projects to the extent appropriate to their funding allocations. With domestic investment and research at such a stage, it is difficult to reverse this activity, and stopping it would come about at a significant cost. Reductions in foreign assistance allocation funding would cause disruptions in those economies involved, thereby placing in question the United States's peaceful intentions with respect to this type of research and scientific cooperation. This is a price that has to be calculated, should the SDI be terminated.

It may seem that the changes in the welfare situation since the Reagan administration began in 1981 are due to the ideological considerations and political expediencies of the Republican Party. After all, that party has developed over the years to be the representative of big business, and, given budget restraints, big business needs federal support in terms of contracts and trade regulations. Those people who are need or those on the lower pay scales can benefit from big business because of the employment opportunities, the retraining, the retirement schemes, and the taxes paid to the government, both state and federal, for supporting welfare projects, among other programs, which provide employment indirectly.

Granted that the Republican party has so evolved, the support of big business is only one aspect of the changing welfare situation. The Democrats also seek the support of big business and had they won the presidential election in 1980, they would have most likely acted in a manner similar to their political opponents. It was during the Carter administration in 1977–80 that the welfare situation was called into question, as the oil crisis that brought about the recession and the very heavy reliance on a welfare system unprepared for this sudden and severe downswing, deepened and intensified. Indeed, the lack of public confidence in the Democrats' ability to solve the economic crisis weighed heavily in the decision for the country to vote for a different administration.

The difficulty is that, while the recession has ended, it has left its mark on the U.S. economy. For example, the trade imbalance, which influences the United States' standing among the rest of the developed countries is due to a large extent meeting to the government's policy of its obligations to these and the developing and emerging countries while being in a recession. This has led to even further complications with the budget deficit, as reductions in the budget will also effect that aspect of foreign grants and loans, which often have to be recycled or written off entirely. The Gramm-Rudman-Hollings Act is a consequence of the attempts to rectify the recession and the debt the federal government entered into in order to resolve the economic crisis.

The welfare system's situation is also a result of the recession and of attempts to resolve its impact on those most in need of assistance. The Carter administration sought to carry on in the same manner as the Nixon and Ford administrations, with the result being more agencies, more money being spent, and greater inefficiency in the overall administration of the system. The uncoordinated government system that produced such inefficiencies merely continued to do so, with the result not being a lessening of the public pressure on the system, but its intensification. Soup lines and public shelter, so prominent during the Great Depression, existed again in the 1970s in the world's most powerful economy.

What the Reagan Administration sought to accomplish by cutting the programs which benefited the poor was to place greater responsibility on industry for retraining these needy people and absorbing them into the production process. In this manner the reliance and burden on the welfare system were to be reduced and production increased accordingly because of the newly-employed.

Industry, however, is not altruistic when it comes to employing people it does not require. The recession prevented economic expansion, and when the Reagan administration began its first term in 1981 and the recession eased in intensity, industry was unwilling to employ more than necessary, in spite of the government's encouragement to do so and regardless of the reductions in the welfare programs. Nevertheless, such absorption of the newly-employed has increased as recovery has set in; indeed, in the Economic Report of the President in February 1988, it was stated that:

The investment in formal worker-sponsored training has been estimated to be about 60 billion per year and has been rising.[9]

But this retraining, in the framework of the Administration's guidelines, has its price, that of reduced wages and on the welfare system for additional compensation during the training period and for family support in general. Moreover, this retraining is a factor of the cycle's upward motion and not a result of the administration's program of reducing the welfare system's role in society and replacing it to a large extent with industrial employment for a continuously expanding market-oriented economy.

The Great Depression brought the realization that even the most developed of the world's economies must have provisions for welfare, that together with the greatest levels of consumerism in history and the industrial output to meet this consumer demand, there will always be strata of society that are impoverished and economically disenfranchised. That these socioeconomic strata must be brought into the realm of the general economy and participate as active consumers and workers is unquestionable. That the welfare systems of the developed economies are inefficient and wasteful reflects the many attempts to resolve the welfare issues, to reduce the levels of unemployment, and to provide housing and education to their citizens. However, that the Reagan administration has sought to minimize the waste and inefficiency in the U.S. welfare system, the methods used in so doing have not been effective and the momentous changes underway in the welfare system have not led to a reduction in the need for such a system. On the contrary, as the growing number of homeless testifies, it has increased dependence on the system, which as has been repeatedly demonstrated is unable to function effectively.

## THE WELFARE UTILITY FUNCTION AND THE DEVELOPED ECONOMY

One way to approach the dilemma of high levels of consumerism and an extensive welfare system prevalent in the developed economies is to let the situation exist as it is. As the business cycle rises, the number of people on welfare will diminish, as industry, according to this approach, seeks employees to realize its production programs. When the cycle turns downward, the system will then be intact to absorb and provide for those who will then be unemployed and in need of care and services. The system will then be able to provide for those in need because the bureaucracy is already in place with the skills necessary for serving the needy.

Another approach to this dilemma is to cut back drastically the funding for the system, to reduce its aspects and services and to adapt policies that will insure a steady rate of growth so that unemployment will be minimal in all circumstances. The welfare system, which will then exist, will be streamlined without the overlapping functions and programs at cross-purposes with gaps, overlaps, and inequities, to the extent that it exists at all. This approach may ultimately result in an atrophied welfare system, with most of the people in need of assistance left to the dynamics of a thriving economy, yet an economy not immune to the fluctuations in the business cycle.

No developed economy, given the existing burden on the welfare system, can survive with either of these approaches. As the Reagan administration realized early in its first term, the welfare system could not exist as it was. Streamlining was necessary to make the system more efficient, but unfortunately for those in real need of the system, the administration reduced funding for them and introduced programs advocating greater emphasis on industry for absorbing the poor into the production process. While the intention was good, the results were far from adequate in dealing with the problems of those requiring welfare. The number of homeless in the country, although only estimated to be between 300,000 to 3 million, or the number of people unemployed between the ages of 16 to 24 being three out of every eight, or the government's figure of 32 million people—13.5 of the country's population—falling below the recognized poverty line, attest to the ''success'' of this streamlining.

The second approach of cutting back on welfare and letting the economy operate in a steady state of growth may be a positive one but; it is unrealistic. Staunch conservative thinkers, in the guise of free-market economists may find this approach appealing. Based on laissez-faire in its most extreme sense, it is used in this context on the grounds that contemporary developed economies are sufficiently resilient to recover from all recessions in a manner that will allow the absorption into the economic processes of those who became unemployed during recession. This approach means that the more extensive the welfare program the more ineffective it is in dealing efficiently with the problems of the needy and poor. This argument maintains that, should the government establish a basic welfare system and channel funds into improving infrastructure for industrial expansion and output, there would be no need for the government to provide welfare, as industry would readily absorb those in need of work because of its expansion and increased output.

The point of these arguments is that in some respects they are both correct and incorrect. That the welfare system is in serious need of streamlining, especially in the United States, given the restriction of the balanced budget by 1992, is obvious; indeed, it is crucial, given the United States's position in the world's economic system and its balance of payments deficit in international commerce. Moreover, the welfare systems of the other developed economies take up a fairly hefty share of their national budgets, as the unemployment situations in Great Britain and France attest, for example. While these countries may not have governments that are as uncoordinated in the administration of welfare as they were during the oil crisis of the 1970s, there are certainly many inadequacies in these systems, as attested to by their very extents and intensities.

As for the second approach, there are, indeed, justifications for cutting back on welfare programs. For example, those programs that provide funding for nonproductive employment, as with the workforce programs, do no more benefit to their recipients than to provide day to day pocket money. Their work is really noncontributive and their opportunities for advancement in these occupations are nonexistent because they offer nothing to society. The existence of these programs is based on the quasi-Keynesian reasoning that once these people are given work they will be able to consume to the extent that they contribute to the demand side of the production process, that their purchases will stimulate output that much further, and that in so doing they too will become absorbed in the production process and hence find stable and remunerative employment. Of course, the fallacy in this reasoning is that the Keynesian argument held for a major depression, and aggregate demand based on wages provided by welfare funding could very well stimulate the economic processes and move the cycle upward. This quasi-Keynesian argument falls because the demand stimulated by welfare payments is not sufficient enough to influence industry—neither in production nor in future planning as industrial output is geared to projected demand, and this excludes the marginal demand of welfare recipients.

Programs that maintain able-bodied people on the dole are also in need of further consideration. By "able bodied people" it is meant those who are physically fit and mentally competent to work, no matter what the social handicaps they may have, and who receive welfare payments instead of finding employment. The immigrants, the people born into impoverished homes, those of broken families, those whose single parents, cannot afford to provide effectively, as well as those deprived of adequate education because of the urgency of seeking employment in order to assist in keeping the household and then find the lack of education a serious handicap—these are the able bodied people who should not be on the dole. But as they are in need of assistance, how should this be provided? How can these people receive welfare while helped to acquire skills that will enable them to improve their conditions and rise above their poverty?

The main problem with the welfare systems of the developed economies is that they deal with the issues of welfare by allocating funds to programs that have been formulated with the conceptual imagination of the Great Depression period. They lack the initiative and imagination necessary for the conceptions of contemporary economics. As industry has developed since World War II, its complexities have intensified and demands on its employees have certainly changed. High levels of technology are required, computers are part of the state-of-the-arts, sophistication is required in developing markets and in evaluating future projects, given the present political and economic climates, judgement is needed in evaluating existing markets in order to know when to enter them with closely competing products, and skills are needed in operating current state-of-the-art machinery to produce goods—these are just some of the requirements of modern industry. Small businesses too must command greater sophistication and higher education to maintain competitive postures in their own areas. Those people on welfare who are able to work, but lack qualifications in the sense stated above, are not prepared for the rigors of modern economic life. It is to these people—for example, the three out of every eight unemployed in the U.S. between the ages of 16 to 24—that the welfare systems in the developed economies tend to give too much help, resulting in this instance in overlapping programs, inefficiency, and the other negative effects leading to frequently-stated criticisms, including claims such as wasting the taxpayers' money.

The problems that bring about poverty and the need for welfare in the contemporary developed economy may never be abolished. Broken homes with a single parent supporting a family are not basically economic issues; nor are reasons for not receiving the proper education for living in our contemporary era; neither are problems of chronic illness and old age which the welfare systems are obligated to support, yet each of these problems has a direct bearing on the respective economies as they require funds to be channeled into welfare for assisting those effected by the problems. This money is part of the government budget and can have drastic consequences on an expanding budget, as the U.S. budget's position and the Gramm-Rudman-Hollings Act testifies.

Just as the causes of poverty and the need for welfare may never be removed from the developed economies, the welfare systems will not be eliminated as long as the need for them exists. As the need intensifies (as in the situation with the cycle's downswing), there is the tendency for welfare programs to multiply their services, indeed even to the extent of overlapping and duplication in some instances. Moreover, there is another situation that must be considered, that of a government agency continuing to operate even though its purpose functions may no longer be needed. Hence, the overlapping welfare programs that tend to keep their recipients on welfare—such as the workforce programs and the giving of relief checks.

It is no longer the case entirely that any job is better than no job, for in the latter part of the twentieth century, in the contemporary economy, a job is good only if it provides an income and an opportunity for improvement and advancement in the standard of living. The same for financial assistance, for it is psychologically easy to slip into the "dole mentality"—to know that relief checks will be provided—and the reasons for seeking adequate employment are thus diminished in personal value and purpose.

But the seeking of adequate employment is perhaps the main problem with those on welfare. How do they find such employment and how do they prepare for it?

Before approaching this question, it must be noted that the welfare system as it exists in the developed countries will need to be maintained at levels necessary to provide medical care, schooling in the deprived neighborhoods, and financial assistance for those who for whatever the reasons, are unable to care for themselves. These services should be provided on national and local levels in definitive programs with the intention of streamlining the programs and eliminating duplication and inefficiencies in their administrations. Moreover, the various forms of social security in each developed economy must be maintained and the amounts available in their funds should not be transferred to cover other government expenses, but should remain intact; there may be a cyclical downswing, which may bring pressure on these funds and they have to meet their obligations.[10]

The question of seeking and preparing for adequate employment for those on welfare can now be addressed. The welfare utility function, as composed of business, the government, and labor, can be used as a criterion for devising adequate welfare programs. The type of unemployment being considered here is not of short-term frictional unemployment where, with compensation, employment will be found with commensurate remuneration; the type of employment that places the real burden on the welfare system is that requiring the system to provide for the unemployed to receive welfare payments over a significant period of time. In cases where there is sickness or disability, these payments, in whatever form they take, cannot be reduced nor eliminated. But for able-bodied people, there is a solution. This requires making welfare payments on condition of attendance in training courses, or which these people can seek adequate employment upon completion of the courses. These courses can be provided by trained people working in academic and trade fields, in coordination with industry, and can be geared as closely as possible to individual interests and talents. After completion, the welfare boards can serve to find employment for these people—employment that does not necessarily have to be local.

The welfare utility function comes into this situation as the welfare boards, together with the unions and industry, work out programs that are of utility with respect to the various aspects of industry. As $i \in I$, with the various aspects of the productive sectors of each $i$ are considered and their problems evaluated, courses can be so constructed as to deal with these sectors. And people who would have been on welfare without being trained to become productive members of the economy would receive the training necessary for gainful employment.

Of course, the business cycle has to be considered. As the cycle turns downward there is greater unemployment and hence greater pressure on the welfare system. This pressure can be augmented somewhat by the unemployed being retrained for advancements in production and marketing techniques, which will be used when the cycle begins its movement upward.

Important is the fact that the welfare boards have to actively seek employment for those who have finished their courses. This may be difficult, given that industry may have all the employees it desires at the time. Hence, there is the need for the Small Business Administration and those supervising the Minority Business Investment Act, together with the administrators of the welfare boards, to encourage those attending the courses to join together and form businesses or coalitions. In those countries without such small business administrations, these coalitions should be established to provide this necessary service. All the resources available should be put at the disposal of these businesses, including the encouragement of established industry to work with them if possible.

The expenses of this approach to welfare can be written off in the not-so-very long run as its fruits are reaped. The object is to use welfare to take people off welfare, and the process of merely supplying them with financial assistance will not do it, as the situation now demonstrates. People are not lazy and do not prefer to be on welfare. They would rather work, earn a good wage, and contribute to themselves and to their societies. The personal motivation exists in healthy individuals and in contemporary society to express their own uniquenesses in the contemporary economy by way of employment. Our economies and societies are established on this basis and suited to this situation. The welfare utility function can serve as a measurement—an indicator as to which programs are viable, given the cycle's position.

It must be remembered that the business cycle is a fact of contemporary economics, and that its downswing invariably results in unemployment and an extra burden on the system that is supposed to handle the welfare payments and unemployment subsidies. This is not bleak as it may first appear, because by assisting people during the difficult periods of recession, these people may enter into businesses with backing from the welfare system and thus stimulate economic growth before the cycle works itself out, thereby contributing to its leveling off or moving upward, even if this is in the local area. In any case, with people who are unemployed and receiving viable educations at the welfare system's expense while receiving welfare payments, industry and business should be that much more strengthened when the cycle moves upward, for talented and trained people will then take their places in industry, providing the impetus to move the cycle up farther than before. Moreover, their salaries will be more than marginal and their tastes in consumption will spur competition to an even stronger extent.

The lesson has been learned with the Great Depression and with the other cyclical downward movements, that the modern economy has become too complex and interlocking, to the extent that when the cycle turns downward the entire economy is affected. The welfare system of the period of the Great Depression was an attempt, then, to deal with this situation, and since then the system has been improved-upon and embellished. The welfare system cannot be abolished and as the U.S. experience has shown, attempts to streamline the system, i.e., to rid it of its overlapping programs and inefficiencies, have not been successful. Thus, the dilemma, given this approach or the other approach of letting the system remain as is, except for minor changes, remains. High levels of consumerism will exist alongside extensive welfare dependence. However, with the application of the welfare utility function in developing programs designed to train and educate the unemployed as well as the healthy-but-needy, there is the chance that the dilemma will wither away. This will allow the contemporary economy to continue high levels of consumerism as a welfare system provide assistance to those who really require it; the sick, and those who cannot cope for themselves.

# 13

# On International Trade

In a world where trade patterns are not perfectly stable, there will always be the problem of changing the world pattern of resource use among various industries to preserve external balance, full employment, and efficient resource use.

R.I. McKinnon
"Optimal Currency Areas"

## INTRODUCTION

"Any region within a common currency area faced with a loss of demand for its products," wrote R.I. McKinnon, "will be forced to cut its expenditures through a loss of bank reserves and regional income."[1] Because world trade patterns are not perfectly stable, regions with common currency areas will, at one time or another, be faced with a loss of demand for their products. The extent of this situation depends on the quality of goods and services, the ability to meet delivery dates, comparative pricing for similar goods and services in other competing areas, and post-delivery servicing where necessary. If by region it is meant country, then these requirements are of extreme importance, for foreign trade is based on their realization.

As well as a country's products and requirements being reasons for international commerce, there is another reason, pertaining specifically to our contemporary economic area and era. It is the severe market devaluations—contrasted to government devaluations—bringing about radical shifts in market alignments for hard currencies. These devaluations reflect only in part the real conditions of the economy involved, but are mostly brought about by expectations of the economy's inadequate performance, leading to the withdrawal of investment and foreign currency from the country. The pound sterling, for example, is very strong compared to other currencies, but it was market-devaluated in the early 1980s to the extent that it was worthwhile for many Americans to purchase airline tickets and fly to London and buy goods and services there, rather than in their own domestic markets.

The United States dollar has also been market-devaluated because of the expectation of poor balance of trade figures, thereby worsening these figures still more. It is of little consequence that the United States has become the world's banker and the largest supplier of goods and services to the most impoverished countries, thereby developing its negative trade position. The negative trade figures resulted in the dumping of the dollar in exchange for other hard currencies.

Market devaluation may be useful for governments, to prevent them from taking the political act of devaluation. It can also be detrimental, especially as election time nears, when strong currencies are a source of national pride, and positive trade balances serve as a reflection of the economy's strength. Market devaluations are, however, beyond the governments' controls, because they reflect the expectations of people in other countries concerning the currencies in question. There is only a partial justification for this devaluation where the quality of national goods and services are concerned; it does, however, demonstrate the extreme degree to which dynamic disequilibrium has affected the world's economies. Products are only partially involved, but the countries' currencies, as reflections of their relative strengths, are full participants in the shifts in their values.

As well as market devaluations there are revaluations, not necessarily market-induced (based on expectation), but generally caused by the placing of foreign currency and investments in those economies that are expected to be strong. Again, the subjective aspect of expectation, so important in the other branches of economics, exerts its influence. Japan's currency is strong relative to that of the United States, but its currency is also being threatened by those of South Korea and Taiwan, whose markets look more promising than before and that are expected to make great strides in those very same markets in which Japan has already distinguished itself. This expectation has weakened the Japanese yen to a certain extent and only in the future will it be known if this weakening process will continue to any great degree.

The question then arises: just how important is foreign trade for an economy? The answer is that it is extremely important for a country's economic survival, and this is why the market devaluations and revaluations are so unstabling, for currencies are treated like any other commodity—but without the backing of the industrial bases for their production. The quantity of a country's currency issued is determined by that country's financial leaders and not by a managerial body of industrial decision-makers in economic competition.

The significance for foreign trade is that it provides an outlet for a country's goods and services, so that employment is maintained and profits continue to increase. This is one reason why the importing of close substitutes of a country's own industrial base is restricted through the levying of quotas and tariffs, although it would be impolitic to ban the trade totally. This is also why the trade "weapon" —for retaliation against policies that are not acceptable—is also effective, so that once embargoes are established to demonstrate severe political indignation, and then broken—as they inevitably are—it is at great financial cost to the embargoed country, because its markets are reduced and its resources restricted. Foreign trade can be both a means for achieving prosperity and a weapon against the policies of another country; in the latter case, it must be used discriminately.

## INTERNATIONAL TRADE AND THE WELFARE UTILITY FUNCTION

Our current international situation of trade is extremely complex. There are economic regions such as the European Economic Community (EEC) that trade with nonmembers according to the terms drawn up by the trading partners, while establishing quotas for common products among members—sometimes resulting in internal friction. There are the developing countries, trading with the developed countries; the emerging countries, trading with whomever they can; and the Communist bloc countries acting like capitalists and trading with the capitalist countries, while the capitalist countries trade with their arch-rivals, the communists.

While models of trading situations may clarify to some extent the dynamics of the exchanges, no adequate model, not even the Heckscher–Ohlin model of trade[2] can account for these diversified countries in their trading situations. Trade can, however, be approached from a different perspective, that of the business cycles of the trading partners, and their welfare utility functions with respect to their cycles.

It should be noted that the demand for foreign goods may be due to the "snob appeal" effect, such as the demand for Russian vodka or American bourbon, or because the resources demanded can be obtained at cheaper costs through trade, or because the products and resources are lacking in the economy and are necessary for economic development and expansion. Hence, copper, cocoa, coffee, uranium, diamonds, and gold, are just a very few examples of such products demanded in international trade, with each product having its own country as the cheapest or only producer. Of course, where no products are exchanged in return, then money becomes the means of exchange, and the country receiving the products is in a safer position than the country receiving the money because the fluctuations in the costs of money are greater than those of the products—that is, market devaluation is a currency phenomenon while product value is a function of utility that is not likely to fluctuate as do currencies in our unstable world.

   As for the business cycles, in a sense they are similar and related among the developed economies, as the crash of October 19, 1987 demonstrated. The New York Stock Exchange (NYSE) fell, and all the major exchanges rapidly followed suit. Because this was a currency decline, it had as its impact the inability to honor foreign obligations resulting from the fall in liquidity. This threw into the international network a strong element of caution and hesitation, a waiting period to see how the domestic situation would continue. The markets have since revived and so has trade, but at a somewhat slower pace because of the memories of the time-lag between the 1929 crash and the further decline of the economy then. The specter of that period does indeed still haunt us.

   In a domestic economy, the level of aggregate demand depends on the cycle's period and phase. Included in this demand is also the demand for imported goods and services, for the reasons stated above. An economy in recession will not have the consumer liquidity to express demand, even from another economy moving through recovery whose products are priced competitively. The difficulty comes, however, when the necessary goods and services for recovery cannot be totally manufactured domestically. Then liquidity must result from the lowering of interest rates and grass-roots demand thereby beginning to stimulate low priority production, until enough liquidity exists for the importation of the necessary goods and services to be undertaken. This, however, depends on the phase of the exporting economy's cycle and whether these goods and services are available and at what price. Government subsidies for these products—by either the importing country, the exporting country, or both—very often result in the price adjustments from both sides of the transaction so that the exchanges can be made. Subsidies in this case are at the cost of the domestic currency in order to gain foreign currency paid for by the exchanges. It is to the advantage of the exporting country to subsidize its prices for foreign markets in order to gain foreign currency, so that its own international transactions are not dependent on its own currency to the extent that it would otherwise be. This is important during periods of market devaluations and revaluations, for currency instability effects the domestic markets using imports, and because a strong and wide currency base provides foreign confidence in the economy's ability to fend for itself in stormy economic waters.

   The world's economies can be distinguished by three different traits. There are the postindustrial economies such as the Western economies of the United States, France, Germany, Japan and Great Britain; there are the developing economies such as Israel, Spain, Greece, and Portugal; there are the underdeveloped or emerging economies such as Nigeria, India, Pakistan, and Equador. There is no logic to these classifications other than the development stages in which these countries perform economically, so that geographical location, climate, and political systems are not considered significant.[3]

   For these types of economy there is an international welfare utility effect, manifested in aggregate demand for the other economies' products. These products take one of two general forms. These are products of similarity, such as agriculture, textile and even manufacturing, which each country produces. There are the products of difference, which distinguish the countries with respect to each other. Both these types of product are subject to foreign demand.

Importing products of similarity is undertaken because of differences in production costs, making their importing worthwhile. This eventually leads to the reduction of domestic resources being allocated toward these products, as they can be obtained at lower production costs, with the released resources being channeled to those products—innovative and imitative—which offer real domestic and foreign demand profits. This does not necessarily mean that the domestic production of these products is phased out entirely to the absolute advantage of the lower cost producing economy; the phasing-out process is a result of the market dynamics within the economy and the alternatives available for imitation as markets diminish and others increase. Nor does it mean that the cost advantage of the exporting country will be retained over time, as this too depends on that country's internal market dynamics, the phase of its business cycle, and the alternatives available for imitation. The international welfare utility effect operates in this situation from the importing to the exporting country, the import of goods at relatively lower costs to satisfying internal demand. Hence, if the demand is for textiles to be imported by country *A* from country *B,* there must be a time-lag between their cyclical periods only in the early recovery phase, because the importing country has to be able to import from a country whose economy is geared for export, and this is not the case in the recession phase because of unemployment. Thus, during recovery, country *A* imports from *B* textiles and pays with cash and/or with goods and services that A's economy is beginning to produce.

The international welfare utility effect is manifested because of the transaction having been made. The transaction would not have been undertaken had it not been to the advantage of both *A* and *B*. The advantage of *A*'s transaction is that it receives the textiles at a price it can afford, and *B*'s advantage is that it receives foreign currency and/or goods and services useful to its own economy.

Of course, for the most part this is not entirely accurate. Countries do not import and export, only in the exceptional cases where the governments are involved in political transactions, such as the United States exporting cereals to the Soviet Union. Even most of the Soviet exports, albiet government sanctioned, are conducted by exporting branches and for those countries maintaining diplomatic relations with the Soviet Union there is no need for government approval for each export shipment. Businesses export and import, so that if a firm in country *A* imports a certain kind or style of textile, it is to increase its share in the domestic textile markets. *B*'s exporting firm profits from the transaction and *B*'s treasury benefits from gaining the foreign currency involved in the transaction. Hence, the transaction benefits the firms in *A* and *B* and influences directly the domestic welfare utility functions of these countries. The importing firm in

*A* brings the textiles in and their distribution affects the domestic market. This may result in competing firms diminishing their activity in the market or to close on the cycle's period and phase.

International commerce reaches its peak prior to the cycle's peak, during prosperity. Trade is undertaken so that countries are both exporters and importers, exporting where revenues are higher and importing where costs are lower or where the goods and services are necessary for continuing economic expansion. As the cycle continues its upward movement, slowing down however because of the impending decline in innovation and following imitation, the international welfare utility effect is diminished correspondingly. Exports continue, but imports are reduced as liquidity is opted for over continuing production. Consumption is reduced according to the price increases resulting from restricted imitation and the decline of innovation. The decline in competition removes consumer liquidity to a certain extent and consumption tends to be limited to only marginal goods and services over the necessities for maintaining the living standard. The cycle's peak is reached, recession sets in, and both importing and exporting decline accordingly. The international welfare utility effect is diminished, being replaced by the welfare utility function for domestic markets.

Economies with similar infrastructures tend to be on the same or similar positions in the cycle. As the cycle develops and expands in each similar economy, the economy develops according to the types of industry, the attitudes of the government and the attitudes and work ethic of labor. But in spite of these individual economic characteristics, the similarities among these economies allow for similar products being manufactured, with the foreign attraction being stimulated by both quality and advertising. The British and American automobile industries are engaged in both foreign and domestic competition—each competing within the other's country as well as their market operations in the sector entirely; alternatively, they may also import or initiate new designs—new products in a sense—changing the competitive complexion to the detriment of the importing firm, whose assets are tied up in the importing project.

During the recession phase, little international trade is conducted. Obligations undertaken during the prosperity phase are met and business slows down soon after. An economy that has already begun moving upward will not draw on trade relations with an economy still in recession, because the latter's industries are not geared yet for production and for meeting international obligations, even though such orders would most likely assist some industries by generating employment and thus further domestic demand. But unless this is undertaken on a massive scale, the cycle will remain recessed; there will be no international welfare utility effect occuring here.

During recovery, there is a time-lag between periods of the importing and exporting recovery countries, and hereafter until the peak of prosperity the time-lags lose their significance. The international welfare utility effect then becomes an expression of the domestic welfare utility function because considerations for engaging in foreign trade depend on competitive postures and innovative and imitative programs. Goods and services are imported because they are considered necessary by the firms; they are exported because the exporting firms consider this profitable. For the importing firms, the markets are affected by the introduction of the goods and services; for the exporting firms, the introduction of the money gained from the transaction into the economy affects the aggregate utility levels, the firms' liquidity positions, and the choice for the liquidity option or further innovation or imitation. In each instance, however, the decisions taken depend on the relative strengths of the markets for the receiving products, whether these products or close substitutes exist, what the potential demand levels for the products are, and, in cases where the products are unique, what the estimated time-lag is for internal competition to be generated. Moreover, more than one firm is engaged in export and import, and they each must vie their own situations with respect to other potential domestic competitors. Exporters, not only have their own internal economies to consider, but must view with each other for markets in other countries; and this brings on competition, the intensity of which depends on the size and importance of the exporters involved.

Products in countries with similar infrastructures tend to be themselves similar and therefore must be marketed internationally on the basis of appeal, quality, and the products' market ranges, so that Cadillac and Rolls Royce are not competing for the middle-range automobile consumers in foreign countries. Appeal, quality, and the products' market ranges provide the differences necessary for product distinction, and this allows for their marketing and competitive sales.

Economies with similar infrastructures have similar but not identical cyclical movements. The advanced countries tend to move in the same cyclical patterns, entering recession, recovery, and prosperity at similar times, so that the differences are not within the cycle's phases but within the phases' periods. This cyclical dynamic allows for fairly stable foreign commerce, because the international welfare utility effect reflects each economy's welfare utility function and the conditions of aggregate supply and demand, and of innovation and imitation, within each country. These countries' exports are largely those that are manufactured, subject not to the elements of nature, but to the dynamics of industry, of government policies, and the attitudes of labor.

Economies with different infrastructures tend to have differing cycle positions, although the developing and emerging countries *tend* toward the cycles of the advanced countries because of their dependence on the advanced countries' markets. In many cases, however, their exports are not dependent on industry, government, and labor, but on the natural elements as in the cases with coffee, cocoa, and sugar exports. Countries such as Spain and Israel, heavily exporting citrus and other crops, are subject to the elements, even though the Israeli economy is diversified with a fairly strong industrial base, yet with all the problems of work and government policies associated with emerging economies. These economies will not achieve their near complete cyclical synchronization with the advanced economies unless they too have their stages of development and "take-off" to advanced industrial development. This is because their industrial, governmental and labor policies, as well as their work ethic are not on the same levels as the advanced economies. Their export mix of industrial and agricultural goods may be reenforced through sales, but until the step is taken to move, primarily into industrial exports—and this means strenuous competition with the industrialized countries—they will remain within their own cyclical movements and tend toward the cycle of the advanced countries. The benefits of trade, of profits through international commerce, will remain limited and their dependence on the importation of industrial goods from the advanced countries will be retained.

Thus, for the advanced economies there is an equivalency among their international welfare utility effects. With respect to the developing and emerging economies this effect is weighted heavily toward the advanced economies in which innovation and imitation occur at rates far greater than in the developing and emerging economies. While the latter economies have a greater export mix, the advanced economies' exports are industrial and thereby are necessary for the developing and emerging countries. This more than often results in the use of hard currencies to pay for these exchanges, and it is certainly an important reason for these countries' aligning themselves with a superpower. The economic backing by these superpowers insures a degree of security in international commerce.

The emerging countries are, however, in a situation more difficult than the one facing their developing counterparts, for they have no serious export mix of agricultural and industrial products. Their agricultural sectors are too often subject to the elements, and they lack industrial capacity sufficient for controlling these natural forces. Their industries are not firmly established at best and their markets are almost totally domestically-oriented. They are in a great need of the industrial products and technologies of the advanced and developing countries, but lack the ability to pay for them. These countries are thus susceptible to the pressures of the superpowers and, although they seek their own independence and ways of life, they have little opportunity for achieving these goals on their own. Hence, countries such as Ethiopia, Bangladesh, and Zaire, so dependent on the elements for their foodstuffs and on domestic peace for their social development, are either war-torn, or ravaged by the natural forces over which they have not acquired control. These emerging countries have very little to barter for exchange in international commerce other than tourism, which is not a very big attraction in these areas.[4] They are subject to the good will of the world's communities and on the backing of their superpower supporters for their financial and economic development. This "generosity" is actually an impediment as it is curbing their fierce drive toward genuine political independence. Should these countries engage in any kind of trade—say, tourism—it is extremely heavily weighted on the side of the developing and advanced economies, and there are no grounds for an international welfare utility effect to be established.

Finally, international trade will remain most active among the advanced economies, where the international welfare utility effects are similar, and where the cyclical movements are to a large extent synchronized. The developing countries

can move into this trading sector as they expand their industrial bases, but not through copying the industrial output of the advanced economies. Where such copying is allowed, however, it is allowed because it is imitative and profitable with respect to the issuing of licenses and rights, but this has the additional advantage of releasing the advanced economies from allocating resources into products that the developing and emerging economies can produce at lower comparative costs and thereby allow their industries to innovate further into higher technological production and the imitative production that results as a consequence. The developing economies must also rely on their agricultural and industrial bases for unique innovation and imitation, employing the techniques of advertising, quality control, and the products' market ranges in order to be appealing to the advanced societies. In this way, the advanced economies' industries will find the basis for trade in a substantial manner. The dynamics of innovation and imitation cannot be allowed to lapse on their own in these developing and even emerging societies; they must be placed within the dynamics of the business cycle, which will allow them to become synchronized with the cycles of the advanced economies, through the very processes of international trade.

These conditions have not yet been formed within the emerging countries' economies, for they have no business cycles, little welfare consciousness, and no industrial base. These economies form a significant part of our world and are special cases, which will be discussed in the final chapter, to follow.

# 14

# Welfare in the Developing and Emerging Economies

When social scientists talk of social problems, they usually mean discrepancies between social reality and what they assume to be norms. Because they are largely preoccupied with discerning, announcing and emphasizing discrepancies between their assumed social norms and reality, social scientists tend to generalize social problems rather than solve them. This way of looking at social situations and reading problems into them is evident in the persistent and extensive concern of egalitarian and economic differences.

Peter T. Bauer
"The Grail of Equality"

## GENERAL COMMENTS

Because economics is a social science, economists are social scientists. As scientists, they share with the scientists of physics, chemistry, and biology the methods of their respective disciplines and the application of theory to reality. Economists assume the norms of social and economic reality, just as other scientists assume the norms in their own respective areas of concern. Theories are developed not only to explain these norms, but to research them—to draw out consequences that would otherwise not be apparent.[1]

In this sense, social scientists tend to generalize social problems, because they try to state them in theoretical terms and concepts, which may allow for the generalization of problems, over large and often abstract areas, with the intention of solving them in the abstract and bringing these solutions to the reality of the problem situation.

This is surely the case with economics, but unlike the physical sciences, the lack of laboratories and controlled experiments places the economist in a much more difficult situation. Moreover, economics is often value-laden, with moral implications for its theories; Marxism is an example in which egalitarianism underwrites the theory, just as capitalism is underwritten by the expression of individual liberty and the seeking of opportunities to better one's own economic position. While values in economics cannot often be removed from the economists' perspectives, this limitation should not hinder the development and expression of impartial economic theory, for once these values are made known, the theory can be separated from them and analyzed on the basis of its objective claims and merits. Perhaps Bauer's sentiment is correct, that by looking into social situations and reading problems into them is the concern of egalitarian and economic differences. But these situations reveal problems, which are vast and expansive in their intensities and immediacies, so that perhaps the extensive concern for egalitarianism and economic differences is an expression of the economists' humanism as they seek to achieve impartiality concordant with the scientific ethos.

Economists seek stable theories for a very unstable world; they seek certainty and the time necessary for their theories to be explored and analyzed in a global situation where uncertainty prevails and time is uncontrollable. Even in the advanced economies, where a degree of stability exists due to their advanced stages of economic development, such situations as the October 17, 1987 stock market crash came quite unexpectedly and the economists searched their theories to find parallels with the 1929 crash. Unemployment rose for a time as markets were reduced and uncertainty prevailed. It seems that the storm has now been weathered, but the upheavals of October 17 may still be felt.

Should there be any reason, then, that the developing and emerging economies possess the same stability of the advanced economies? Without the strong economic infrastructure of the advanced economies, and given their geographical locations, the developing and emerging economies are exposed to the harsh crosswinds of sociopolitical dynamics; they are caught in the "cooling war" engaging the superpowers and they seek their own identities while the powers try to impose identities upon them. They seek to construct their own economies, relying on the assistance of the superpowers, yet without compromising their own uniquenesses, and these circumstances place them in very difficult situations.

The welfare difficulties of these economies are similar, to a certain extent, to those of the advanced economies. People are homeless, hungry, and unemployed. In the developing economies the government takes on the main burden of seeking to remove these problems; in the emerging economies there is a serious lack of resources for doing so.

The economist looking into these conditions is not at a loss for problems, and very often he or she is motivated to seek egalitarian solutions, while still understanding the differences of each economy. This is part of the scientific investigation economists undertake. This does not mean that these situations are beyond hope, subject to the whims and fancies of the superpowers; nor does it imply that the economist lacks the theoretical equipment for dealing with these conditions. Indeed, it is perfectly legitimate for the economist to look into these situations, apply the theoretical knowledge at his or her disposal, and draw conclusions. Differences among the economies are obvious and apparent. Their histories, their political systems, their industry and agriculture, and, indeed, their very locations, make them different. But as with every science, generalizations are sought in economics so that theories can be applied. This is surely the case here, and the developing and emerging economies will be approached with respect to the welfare utility function and the ramifications involved for each type of economy.

## WELFARE IN THE DEVELOPING ECONOMIES

In general, a developing economy is one in which a fairly stable political system has been established. It is an economy that, being ruled by stable government after having undergone the stage of emergence and the internal conflicts that emergence generates, is now stabilized by both the political will and by the people's will for the end of conflict and the beginning of development. The political system may be dictatorial or democratic, but the economic problems are generally the same, namely, how to bring the country's resources into patterns of sectorial and overall development. The requirement of investing in the economy's infrastructure is obvious, but how should such investments be made so that the maximum benefits can be achieved under the given circumstances? Another difficulty is that the amount of welfare the governments of these countries spend is far too excessive, given their economic conditions, and the burden has to be shifted onto the people themselves, so that they will reduce their welfare claims.

Another point has to be mentioned, and this is in reference to these countries' welfare utility functions. Of the three components of this function, government is the most developed and hence bears the major brunt of welfare. It must be noted that developing economies have business cycles, so that the welfare utility function holds; these cycles, however, tend to be synchronized with those of the advanced countries, because of the reliance of these countries on the advanced countries. For example, the advanced countries are their prime export markets and the source of their imports as well. The advanced economies supply the developing economies with the technologies, raw materials when necessary, and the economic support in general, in light of the global political situation, so that when consumption in the advanced economies declines because of the cycle's decline, production in the developing economies slows down because of the contractions of their main exporting markets. Hence, the cycle and its impact on the developing economies is subject to a large extent to the cycles of the advanced economies.

While the government carries the main burden for its citizens' welfare, the other components of the function are also responsible in part. Industry, for example, remains in the stages of development, orienting itself to both domestic and foreign markets. The emphasis has to be on both markets because the economy could not survive the extensive importation of goods and services due to the lack of hard currencies to pay for them, so that industrial production has to be for local consumption and for exporting to gain foreign currency as well. But the question is, what to export, for the advanced economies are in really no great need for the same types of goods and services they produce.

This brings up the issues of quality, diversification, and the applications of technologies in manners that make the developing economy unique. Quality, for example, must be of such high standards that the goods and services can be exported to the advanced economies in competition with those of the domestic production in the advanced economies. Moreover, quality provides incentives for investment in the industries of the developing economies, so that production costs are lower and the quality tends to be of high standard, making further investments profitable. Multinational companies are often located in these countries for the reasons of cost savings and quality in production.

Diversification in production can come about when the diverse cultures composing the developing countries are harnessed into a integral culture or nation in which the diverse attitudes and customs are relegated into subcultural status. This way a nation is formed whose national goal is the expansion of industry, which can only come about by the diversification of its product base. Again, the markets have to be both domestic and for-export, for without this, there will be only little local goods and services and negligible amounts of foreign currencies and foreign investment in the industry. Product diversification based on quality is of such importance that often innovation is required to achieve its realization. With innovation comes imitation and these are also export-oriented; with innovation and imitation come the business cycles and these provide a degree of economic independence from the cycles of the advanced societies. Once cyclical patterns are established in these economies a giant step has been taken for achieving independence and thereby moving the economy into an advanced position.

This cannot be done, however, without the understanding and application of advanced technologies. For this point, government's role is important, especially in education. Involved in education is more than just the advancement of individuals in the socioeconomic situation of development. Training for it is establishing industry and its labor force in a competitive environment by providing the ability to understand and employ these technologies in industrial output. There is still another objective, however, and this is the positioning of industry in such a manner that technologies are developed by the people, and are applied and exported to the advanced economies. This requires the dynamics of innovation and imitation, already working in the economic system, to bring out these new technologies through innovation and for further exploitation in imitation.

The labor component is very critical in the developing countries. This results from two factors, often in conflict with each other. These are the historical "roots" of the peoples forming the sociopolitical country, and the channeling of these peoples' energies into a thriving industrial sector. The conflict is manifested in both historical and modern strife, the carrying on of traditions, and the exigencies of the modern and highly competitive environment. Tradition requires a certain attitude—an ethos, based on the past and manifested in the present. The ways of industrialization, however, are only based in the present and are future-oriented in production plans and meeting current requirements, and therefore they have little to do with the past. Past traditional behavior and present and future-oriented industrial production and planning conflict with each other when the requirements of tradition—such as prayer, feasts, and the abstinence from work—confront the demands of strenuous industrial production and the execution of plans so that prayer, feasts, and the abstinence from work, are considered counterproductive for industrial output and industry's obligations in general. Because each developing country has its own subcultures and histories, these problems must be confronted and solved in a manner amicable to the interests of both factors—and this again is the task of the government.

The better educated the labor force—the better acquainted it is with the methods of production and indeed with the life styles of the advanced countries—the greater the motivation the labor force will have to achieve the types of production to earn and acquire similar life styles. Thus, the uses of technologies are of great importance to labor, and workers' abilities to use these technologies depend on the formal education received as well as the advanced on-the-job training offered by industry.

Because these countries have business cycles, the obligation of the labor organizations is the same as those of the advanced economies. They must offer assistance along with government assistance when unemployment is high, and they must provide courses for training in the uses of the most advanced technologies and in the understanding of production problems and techniques. This way, the labor force does not remain idle during periods of unemployment, but learns, gaining knowledge useful in improving its own socioeconomic position.

The use of strikes and sanctions in the developing countries must be avoided at all costs, and this requires both a skilled government and sophisticated industrial and labor managerial understanding to avoid these actions. Often there is resentment along with undercurrents of anger and jealousy, resulting from the different cultural influences and personal skills that are manifested in discrimination and imposed class distinctions. As the economy develops, these forms of discrimination are subdued and replaced by discrimination focused against other classes, such as the workers. Payment for work should be commensurate with industrial ability to remunerate and this should be explained to the labor leadership, in order to attempt to avoid conflict. The condition of the developing economies is certainly critical and any setback to output can be very damaging. Thus, labor and industry should work together and seek to avoid all conflicts of this sort, for any setback in production, any exertion of force by labor to achieve what industry cannot offer, will establish antagonism, reminiscent of the late nineteenth-century and early twentieth-century labor-industrial conflicts. These countries will then be open for the breeding of political dissention and become prey for the superpowers to control and exploit them for their own needs and uses. Labor has a strong potential promise in these countries—the promise of building an effective work force to cope with the unique innovation problems and the subsequent imitation that will follow, and to bring these economies up to the levels of the advanced economies, perhaps even to the point of setting production trends that the advanced economies will adapt and follow.

Welfare in these countries has to be coinciding with a viable industrial base of education, and on skilled manpower; these, in turn, depend on a sensitive and sensible government, one educated and concerned with its citizenry. The mistakes of the Industrial Revolution, of the Great Depression, and of the welfare systems of the advanced economies can be avoided. Slums need not be allowed, nor poverty given expression on the streets as a result of inadequate welfare thinking. These countries have to maintain their cycles, and as the cycle expands the industrial base and allows for the absorption of more manpower during recovery, poverty is still countered by welfare payments but requires retraining, so that this new labor element can eventually be absorbed in further cycles. Slums need not develop, because both sensible government and city planning can avoid this. Opportunities can be provided in these economies that the advanced economies in their own development could not have achieved. The technologies are available and the conceptualizations can be formulated for the specific conditions in each economy to handle their differences in development. Their governments must, however, be truly dedicated to their citizenries to insure that the benefits of welfare are available and provided and that economic development and growth are maintained. The countries can make poverty obsolete before it sets in, and they can prevent slum development, eliminate the conditions that allow for street people, and do away with circumstances that result in an overburdened welfare system—the blights of the advanced economies—by careful planning and industrial expansion and development, backed by an education system that is modernized and by a progressive labor force that provides education and training for its members, to safeguard against the curse of unemployment by increasing workers' skills. These economies hold this promise and it is up to them to realize it.

## THE EMERGING ECONOMIES AND WELFARE: THE CRITICAL SITUATION

The emerging economies lack the conditions prevailing in the developing economies. They have very little industrial base to build upon, no real education system comparable with those of the developing economies, and no governmental systems that can effectively handle their situations and reap the benefits of growth. These economies are newly formed and still tied to their former colonizers in intricite ways, often to the point that their independence is not real after all, but merely a show for world opinion.

These economies stand at the crossroads, in which they are subject to the elements of nature over which they have little or no control, and the beginnings of industrialization, which, if properly cultivated, will bring them into the cyclical patterns of growth and expansion.

There are two main difficulties in these countries that must be overcome before economic growth can take place. As these societies are ethnically diversified, often to the point of bitter rivalry, these ethnic differences have to be placed aside for genuine unification to occur. This does not mean that they have to be removed or ignored, for this is impossible. Their incorporation into society indeed provides the society with greater strength as differences of customs, opinions, and approaches, can lead to viable societies, so long as these differences can be tolerated without the taints of bigotry and closedmindedness to other opinions.

For this to be achieved, however, a leadership is required that has the respect of the various divergent populations. It may be composed of members from these differing populations, but it must be a leadership of great wisdom and understanding, having the ability to talk both to their peoples and with the world's leaders. Here is the real challenge and the way it is faced by the leadership determines to a large extent the way the economy will develop.

Moreover, because these economies lack the stability of the developing and advanced economies, they are often in economic and political turmoil. Rivals confront each other as often with the bullet and bomb as with the ballot. Instability must be dealt with and this, again, requires a leadership capable of satisfying the majority of the diversified populations and provide the basis for economic well-being, which for these economies is a long and difficult process.

Not only are these economies subject to the elements, with their peoples often at subsistence levels of existence; there are no cyclical fluctuations bringing innovation and imitation into play. The leadership thus has to develop a master plan for growth, expoliting the country's natural lay of the land, its rivers and streams for moving materiel, its natural paths for roadways, the talents of its peoples for building industries. The problems of welfare as understood by the advanced and developing economies do not yet exist, for the problems of subsistence are the real issues here.

Thus, the government must govern, that is, control and channel the differing factions, bringing their differences out from the fields where political differences are sought to be settled with arms, and into the governing bodies such as parliaments, where differences can be discussed and opposing factions united for the good of the country. Otherwise, the conflicts will remain in the fields and people will continue to be maimed and killed, and nature's elements will continue to control the economy, such as it is.

As there is no cycle, the welfare utility function does not exist. The issues of welfare are not those of the developed and developing economies, nor of poverty such as in the slums and with street people in the sense of industrialization and unemployment. The welfare problems are far more difficult than these, for there is no real wealth, no "haves" and "have nots," as these economies are almost entirely in a state of impoverishment. The master plan allows for considerations of industrialization, but this is insufficient. Financing is important, and this often results in multinational corporations' setting up industries, assistance with political obligations, and often the genuine altruism of aid without obligations. Again, the leadership must be sufficiently committed to maneuver within these conditions and political obligations so that financial assistance and education— sometimes supported by the multinational corporations—can be gained without compromising independence.

Talented people can be sent to the advanced countries for further education and, upon their return, be given jobs commensurate with their talents and education; the objective is for these people to be employed in building the economy and the society. These economies cannot undergo their own "industrial revolutions" so they must acquire what they can from the advanced and developing economies in order that they will be able to move from the state of emergence to that of development. Once industry is established, and after sufficient infrastructure is laid down, market dynamics will set in, leading first with imitation and subsequently with the international welfare utility effect taking hold, but this time only on the side of the emerging economy. The imitative goods and services will be similar to those considered necessities in the developing economies. They will be manufactured according to international processes and at costs appropriate to local conditions. With imitation becoming established, it will not be very long before local products, unique to the economy, are developed and manufactured. This is innovation, and with market dynamics fully established, the cycle will become firmly entrenched in business activity. The economy will then move from emergence into a developing economy, with all the benefits and problems thereof.

The question that must be confronted by political and industrial leaders is, how long will the process take before innovation becomes established? There is certainly no set answer to this question and many issues are involved for each country. Such factors as the geographical layout of the land, the natural (earth) resources, the people's inclinations and the leadership's ability to muster these talents to develop the natural resources, the savor faire for acquiring foreign assistance without compromising independence, and the difficulties of maneuvering along paths fraught with the dangers of big power interests and desires to control the country, have to be analyzed when considering this question. One issue is clear: To be politically independent without economic independence, is not to be independent at all. This does not mean that economic assistance must necessary limit independence; it does mean that in international bargaining the emerging countries are the weaker partner and easily exploitable by the powers.

True leadership will gain the benefits of such a partnership without compromising its people's independence. These goals are most certainly difficult to achieve because the bargaining power of the emerging countries is severely limited. They often suffer famine and are plagued with illiteracy and a dearth of industry. But so long as their hands are outstreched and begging for aid, they will be abused by the big powers—treated as third-class world property to be exploited accordingly. Once these societies have strong idealistic leadership that is unselfish and concerned only with the betterment of the people, then a different approach will be shown—one of genuine assistance for which the obligations are minimal, the main obligation being to move the economy into a development pattern.

This is perhaps the greatest economic imperative of our time. It makes no sense that, with the world's aggregate wealth, people should still at the mercy of nature's elements, and starving when there is prolonged drought. In our contemporary era we have the technologies to wipe out the scourge of starvation, but we need only the collective will to do so. Politics are also a source of interference; consider the senseless wars for power and control. Indeed there should still be war—but war against those forces perpetuating the sources of extreme poverty in these countries, forcing the people into migrations in search for food and water. The petty leaders engaged in combat for control of these regions should be aware that after attaining victory—whatever spoils the victors may win—they will have to confront those issues of economic emergence, but the problems will be that much more intense because of the destruction and loss of life that have taken their severe tolls in these regions. Population growth has to be allowed and the repairing of the land has to take place. These are long term processes and must occur in a world of technology and scientific achievement, impatient with long-term processes. Moreover, the people involved will also be impatient, so whatever the stability finally achieved will be fragile, and the sparks of dissent, and of impatient protest are liable to set the entire process of political conflict off again.

There are many challenges confronting these emerging economies, but none is as great as the necessity for true leadership, for only a true and dedicated leadership can bring the economy into development. The leadership's position is precarious because of the opposing forces seeking power. But a leadership having the ability to motivate the people, can succeed in keeping the citizens united in the common goal of development, in spite of their differences which often divide them. The pride of tribal sovereignty, of sectorial sovereignty, and of historical sovereignty cannot survive together with economic development. Not that they should be eliminated; indeed, they should be developed as sources of internal strength. But they should be allowed to flourish only within the common objectives of building the economy, and ridding the country of starvation, illiteracy, and debilitating diseases. In a sense, these countries are "testing grounds" to determine the extent that humanity has evolved in our era; for if the test of development determines that these countries have overcome their difficulties—that their struggles, their confrontations with danger, and their sacrifices were worth the effort—and they have moved into development, then they have become integral parts of our contemporary era. Should they fail in the test, the opportunity will not be offered to them again, and the big powers competing in their regions will affect their independence. The darkness of starvation will be subject to the big powers' goodwill; the control over nature will depend on how the big powers dispense with their technologies. These countries will continue to rely on the good sense and humanity of the developing and advanced countries; they will be battered by the ravages of war, of the forces of nature; they will cry out for assistance and aid, and will be looked down upon as the poorest of humanity. They must have leaders to come to the fore to work with both internal and international forces in building their countries. This is their challenge and it is one that embraces the world.

As this writer has stated elsewhere, the alternative to an ineffective leadership is "famine, illiteracy, military and ideological war, reliance on the conscience of the developed countries—in other words, more of the same." [2] World stability and development depend to a large extent on how the emerging countries develop, for they are significant sources of instability in an era of vast potentialities for destruction. "More of the same" involves the entire world, so that the issues of the emerging—and to some extent the developing—countries cannot be neglected nor delayed. We in the developed, post-industrial countries have the means of achieving vast economic growth, and these economies have to acquire these means. This requires the leadership that can stop fragmentation, stress diversification and development, and unify the forces of the country into the important goal of development. This is certainly one of the great problems confronting our world today, and the manner in which it will be approached will, indeed, determine how the world progresses socially and economically in our contemporary era.

# 15

# Concluding Remarks

There is one set of policies which cannot be easily judged merely as to efficiency in reaching widely accepted, comparatively uncontroversial goals: I refer to those which seek to redistribute income.

George J. Stigler
"The Economist as Preacher"

When discussing the issues of welfare economics, there is probably a touch of the preacher in every economist,[1] for the economist is not only dealing with the "dismal" science—of unemployment, profits, interest rates, and the efficiency of capital. In welfare economics there must be moral considerations as well. These, as the economist *qua* scientist knows, must be augmented by scientific theory for the greater good of the discipline. But the very topic of *welfare economics*—of the concern for the betterment of the individuals in the various socioeconomic and political systems—is certainly one which cannot ignore the moral obligation of bettering the positions of all citizens and all other members of the systems.

Hence, the "problem of problems" in welfare economics *is not* the redistribution of income, for this, too, would be unfair to those who earn high incomes for their work. Nor is it the supporting of those who do not work, for this would prolong the existence of an insufficient economic sector without any long-term gains to society whatsoever. The "problem of problems" in welfare economics is the formulation of a theory that can make the economy more efficient without the redistribution of income as such, so that the wealthy may continue to earn from their work, while at the same time removing the causes that allow for the maintaining and regenerating of poverty and unemployment—and of street people, slums, hopelessness, despair, and of mankind's being subdued by the forces of nature instead of controlling these forces and using them for the benefits of humanity.

Excessive taxation as a means for income redistribution is inefficient, because taxes will not be paid at the "official" rate. Social security payments relieve some of the economic burden of poverty, but they are insufficient, nor can they ever become sufficient, so long as government payments are involved.

Moreover, economic theories that emphasize only one aspect of the economy fall far short of the mark in dealing with the problems of welfare. No "optimum," nor any "substitution effect," can deal with the intricacies of the contemporary economy, and the indifference-curve approach to welfare can only relate to individuals or groups in the bargaining process, and not to the economy in general.

What discipline other than economics can discuss poverty, unemployment, high interest rates, international trade, development of markets and the efficiency (or inefficiency) of money? This does not mean that economists are "dismal scientists" by their very personalities, natures, or concerns. Indeed, most economists were and are drawn to this discipline because of their very compassion for their fellows—motivated to find ways to rectify the injustices of finance and economics. Hence, the economics of welfare is a discipline that not only deals with the dole, with taxation and social security, but is also a discipline that seeks theories for eliminating the dole and make the economy efficient to the extent that poverty and its consequences can be abolished forever. This is a noble goal, but is it within our ability to achieve?

Part of the difficulty is that we have not yet begun to understand our contemporary economic situation. We continue to live in the shadow of the Great Depression, and our economics is Keynesian in orientation. But the Great Depression is over and circumstances that perpetrated that crisis belong to an earlier era and will never occur again. One does not have to be granted the gift of prophecy to realize this; one has to understand our current economic situation and the safeguards against conditions that can lead to depressions.

Keynesian economics has, since the Great Depression, served as an economic paradigm, but for all its beauty and past effectiveness, it should be relegated to history, just as Adam Smith's theory, for all its beauty, and effectiveness, and revolutionary power has been so relegated. What is now required is a theory that accounts for our contemporary economic situation, and this writer's earlier economic work is such an attempt. However, a theory of contemporary economics without the consideration of welfare is incomplete and this is an attempt at completeness—at filling the gap in that theory. This is one purpose of this present work and the other purpose is that this economist, like so many others, is drawn to the profession in order to rectify, or at least to try to do so, the diseconomies that perpetuate poverty, be they inherited from the past economic era, or from our current economic era.

Perhaps because of the Great Depression our political leaders are more attuned to economists' messages, and to today's academic writers' theories. Perhaps because of the specter of the Great Depression, new theories are given their due now. For welfare economics the goal is not the redistribution of income, but the elimination of poverty and its consequences. This has certainly been the reason for the extension of the theory in *Contemporary Economics: A Unifying Approach,* from which the theory of welfare economics stated here has been derived.[2]

# Notes

## CHAPTER 1

1. Wassily Leontief, "Theoretical Assumptions and Nonobserved Facts," Presidential Address delivered to the eighty-third meeting of the American Economic Association, Detroit, Michigan, Dec. 29, 1970. Quoted here from Leontief, *Essays in Economics* (New Brunswick, N.J.: Transaction Books, 1985), p. 282.

2. See Joan Robinson's Richard T. Ely Lecture, Dec. 1971. Her theme was "The Second Crisis of Economic Theory." Her lecture was printed in *American Economic Review* vol. 72, no. 2 (May 1972.)

The first crisis was the massive unemployment of both labor and machinery that existed in the Great Depression. With respect to this: see this present writer's work, *Contemporary Economics: A Unifying Approach* (New York: Praeger, 1986).

3. See Karl Marx, *Capital* (Moscow: Foreign Languages Publishing House, 1961).

4. See John Stuart Mill, *Principles of Political Economy with Some of Their Applications to Social Philosophy* (London: Longmans Green, 1909). Also, see *The Essential Works of John Stuart Mill,* ed. Max Lerner (New York: Bantam Books, 1961).

See Mary Warnock, ed., *Utilitarianism* (London: Fontana Books, 1962), and *Jeremy Bentham's Economic Writings* (London: Allen & Unwin, for the Royal Economic Society, 1954).

5. For example, see the comments on Marx in Tibor Scitovsky, *Welfare and Competition* (Chicago: Richard D. Irwin, Inc., 1951), pp. 198–203.

6. This writer maintains that the Great Depression was the termination of the previous historical era of the Industrial Revolution, and was followed by our present historical era of knowledge. See David Z. Rich, *The Dynamics of Knowledge: A Contemporary View* (Westport Conn.: Greenwood Press, 1988).

7. See Rich, *Contemporary Economics: A Unifying Approach,* pp. 120–144.

## CHAPTER 2

1. Adam Smith, *An Inquiry into the Nature and Causes of the Wealth of Nations,* ed. Edwin Cannan (London: Methuen, 1950).

2. The emphasis on the healthy working force is to point out that those persons who are so severely handicapped and cannot take their places in the development of economic activity are excluded. Hospitals and other institutions dealing with the chronically ill and dependent are also in the mainstream of economic activity, however, and are therefore subject to welfare considerations.

## CHAPTER 3

1. John Maynard Keynes, *The General Theory of Employment Interest and Money* (London: Macmillan, 1947), pp. 383–384. With the development of ideas and theories in our era at a rate greater than ever before, Keynes's comment that age restricts the learning of new political and economic theories is questionable, if only that people's jobs require such an awareness.

2. See, for example, Robin Marris's work, *The Economic Theory of "Managerial" Capitalism* (London: Macmillan, 1967). See also this present writer's work, *Contemporary Economics: A Unifying Approach* (New York: Praeger, 1986). Part 1, especially pp. 18–25, for a critique of Marris's approach to dynamic equilibrium.

3. See Francis Ysidro Edgeworth, *Mathematical Psychics: An Essay on the Applications of Mathematics to the Moral Sciences,* London School of Economics, tract no. 10 (London, 1932, originally published by Kegan Paul, London, 1881).

4. F. Y. Edgeworth, *Mathematical Psychics,* Ibid., pp. 7–8. Quoted here from Guy Routh, *The Origin of Economic Ideas* (New York: Vintage Books, 1977), p. 241.

5. After Tibor Scitovsky. See his *Welfare and Competition* (Chicago: Richard D. Irwin, 1951), p. 52.

This is often called the Edgeworth–Bowley Box, after Arthur L. Bowley, an economist concerned with the mathematization of economics, a trend certainly popular today. See his *The Mathematical Groundwork of Economics* (Oxford: Oxford University Press, 1924).

6. See Paul A. Samuelson, *The Foundations of Economic Analysis* (Cambridge Mass.: Harvard University Press, 1955), p. 223. Quoted here from Morgan Reynolds and Eugene Smolensky, "Welfare Economics: Or, When Is a Change an Improvement?" in *Modern Economic Thought,* ed. Sidney Weintraub (Philadelphia: University of Pennsylvania Press, 1977), p. 478.

7. Wassily Leontief, "Mathematics in Economics," in *Essays in Economics* (New Brunswick, N.J.: Transaction Books, 1977), p. 24. See Vilfredo Pareto, *Manual of Political Economy,* trans. Ann S. Schwier and Alfred Page (New York: Augustus M. Kelly, 1971).

8. These conditions are discussed in Morgan Reynolds and Eugene Smolensky, cited in note 6, above.

9. See, for example, R.J. Barnet and R.E. Müller, *Global Reach* (New York: Simon & Schuster, 1974).

## CHAPTER 4

1. Another significant work on welfare economics is Arthur C. Pigou's *Economics of Welfare* (London: Macmillan, 1920). This work was criticized eloquently by Keynes in *The General Theory* (London: Macmillan, 1947), pp. 272–279. The work to which Keynes refers is the 4th edition, 1932, when the Great Depression was making its full impact. The neoclassical economists discussed in this present work share a full-employment position as with Pigou—of full or near-full employment, with no involuntary unemployment.

2. See Eugin E. Slutsky, "On the Theory of the Budget of the Consumer," in *Readings in Price Theory* (London: Allen & Unwin, for the American Economic Association, 1953). Also, see Igor Pearce's comments on Slutsky's theory: "Demand Theory, Consumers Surplus, and Sovereignty" in *Modern Economic Thought,* ed. Sidney Weintraub (Philadelphia: University of Pennsylvania Press, 1977), pp. 217–245. Pearce's comments on Slutsky are on pp. 227, 231, and 233. Significant is his comment on p. 227: "Furthermore, in the aggregate, the offer for sale of an extra unit of a commodity usually generates the income necessary to buy it. This is Say's Law." Say's Law of Markets has played a tremendous role in economic thinking even in our era. For a criticism of Say's Law, see this present writer's work, *Contemporary Economics: A Unifying Approach* (New York: Praeger, 1986), pp. 5–25.

3. Thus, see *Contemporary Economics: A Unifying Approach,* pp. 111–143.

## CHAPTER 5

1. The rest of this paragraph is worth quoting:

"Eh *bien,*" —exclaimed Walras characteristically—"the difficulty is not insurmountable. Let us suppose that this measure exists, and we shall be able to give it an exact and mathematical account" of the influence and utility on prices, etc. Unfortunately, this uncritical attitude has ever since constituted the distinct flavor of mathematical economics. In view of the fact that theoretical science is a living organism, it would not be exaggerating to say this attitude is tantamount to planning a fish hatchery in a moist flower bed."

Nicholas Georgescu-Roegen, *The Entropy Law and the Economic Process* (Cambridge, Mass.: Harvard University Press, 1981), p. 40. The quote is from Léon Walras, *Elements d'economie politique pure,* 3rd ed., Lausanne, 1896.

2. R. A. Gordon, *Business Cycles* (New York: Harper & Row, 1962), pp. 197–198.

3. However, see Daniel M. Hausman, ed., *The Philosophy of Economics* (Cambridge, England: Cambridge University Press, 1985).

4. See my work, *The Dynamics of Knowledge: A Contemporary View* (Westport, Conn.: Greenwood Press, 1988).

5. John Maynard Keynes, *The General Theory of Employment Interest and Money* (London: Macmillan & Co., 1947), p. 141.

6. See *Contemporary Economics: A Unifying Approach,* p. 74.

## CHAPTER 6

1. Hence, economics as the science of the allocation of scarce resources among competing ends. Obtaining these competitive resources depends, of course, on their price

and availability. If the price is too high, or the resources are at the time unavailable, then the project will be either dropped or postponed.

2. These technologies can be acquired over time by way of the unions. This is discussed in Part 2 of this work.

3. The terms "innovation" and "imitation" were defined rigorously in *Contemporary Economics: A Unifying Approach,* pp. 30, passim. In short, an innovative firm is one that brings into the market a new product, while an imitative firm is one that enters into a market already established by the innovative firm.

4. Steven Weinberg has defined entropy as:

A fundamental quantity of statistical mechanics, related to the degree of disorder of a physical system. The entropy is conceived in any process in which thermal equilibrium is continually maintained. The second law of thermodynamics says that the total entropy never decreases in *any* reaction.

From Steven Weinberg, *The First Three Minutes* (New York: Basic Books, 1977), p. 159. However, the term is also used for information systems and refers to the breaking down of the information system's viability, performability, and utility. As used here, entropy and utility are opposites.

5. Robin Marris, *The Economic Theory of "Managerial" Capitalism* (London: Macmillan, 1971), pp. 37–38.

6. H. A. Simon, "Theories of Decision Making in Economics and Behavioral Science," *American Economic Review* 49 (1959): 253–285. Quoted here in ed., G.P.E. Clarkson, *Managerial Economics* (Baltimore: Penguin Books, 1968), p. 26.

7. H. A. Simon, "Theories of Decision Making," p. 28.

8. See J. M. Keynes, *The General Theory,* pp. 272–279.

## CHAPTER 7

1. Emmanuel Farjoun and Moshe Machover, *Laws of Chaos* (London: Verso Editions, 1983), p. 33.

2. For example, Keynes wrote:

Thus, Say's Law, that the aggregate demand price of output as a whole is equal to its aggregate supply price for all volumes of output, is equivalent to the proposition that there is no obstacle to full employment. If, however, this is not the true law relating the aggregate demand and supply functions, there is a vitally important chapter of economic theory which remains to be written and without which all discussions concerning the volume of aggregate employment are futile.

From J. M. Keynes, *The General Theory,* p. 26.

3. See, for example, Henry Steele Commanger, *Jefferson, Nationalism,* and *the Enlightenment* (New York: G. Brazillier, 1975); Merrill D. Peterson, *Thomas Jefferson and the New Nation* (New York: Oxford, 1970); and Lally Weymouth, ed., *Thomas Jefferson the Man . . . His World . . . His Influence* (New York: G.P. Putnam's Sons, 1973).

4. J. A. Schumpeter, *The Theory of Economic Development,* trans. Redvers Opie (New York: Oxford, 1969).

5. J. M. Keynes, *The General Theory,* pp. 25–26.

6. See my discussion on the Harrod–Domar model in *Contemporary Economics: A Unifying Approach,* pp. 15–18, and on Marris's model, in pp. 18–25.

7. J. M. Keynes, *The General Theory,* pp. 199–209.

8. J. M. Keynes, *The General Theory,* p. 322.

9. In *Contemporary Economics: A Unifying Approach,* the heuristic law of markets was stated. This law depends on five stages of management activity, which are: first, innovative or entrepreneurial activity, or imitative activity; second, the planning and consideration of various proposals for manufacturing the accepted project; third, the commitment of resources and the analysis of the feedback that this resource allocation provides, including the diversion of resources from other products if necessary; fourth, the managerial assessment of the product's internal development in production and the economies of scale and plant utility; fifth, the external evaluation of the product in markets it pioneers or, if imitative in the markets in which it competes.

This law of markets is a managerial imperative based on the profit motive, requiring production to meet potential and actual demand that it generates through the stages of managerial activity. The law thus states that consumption should be related directly to production in the aggregate for the firm's total output. Hence, general managerial activity is within the domain of the heuristic law of markets, thereby relegating the product cycle to second place within the overall planning and production procedures. See pp. 96–108.

## CHAPTER 8

1. Lester C. Thurow, *Generating Inequality* (New York: Basic Books, 1975), p. 33.

2. Lester C. Thurow, *Generating Inequality,* p. 33.

## CHAPTER 9

1. According to the teachings of Judaism, Malachi was the last true prophet. He spoke of returning to the values of the faith as symbolized by the Temple and the services of worship that took place there. With the Temple's destruction by the Romans and the dispersion of the Jewish people, the ethical bond that the Temple represented no longer existed, and the gift of prophecy so bound up with the centralized religious services and the ethical significance of these rituals no longer held. Instead, the Talmud served as an exposition of the teachings in the Five Books of Moses and the Temple service, maintaining the ethical force that binds the Jewish people, but without the prophecy being renewed in the written or spoken word. See Yoma, *daf Het and Tet.*

2. Even matters of defense can be directly related to welfare, because the decision for establishing a defense-based industry in a certain region can boost business in that region when implemented, thereby reducing unemployment and generating regional growth.

## CHAPTER 10

1. The welfare utility function is discussed in Chapter 12, section 2, p. 82–83 below. The dynamics of this function with respect to international trade are elaborated there.

2. *Contemporary Economics: A Unifying Approach,* pp. 134–135.

3. There are difficulties in measuring poverty levels among the countries of the world because national living standards vary from one country to the other. In spite of this, there are absolutes that can be measured without international ambiguities. These are:

Improper medical care, hunger, and malnutrition; the lack of formal education; and the presence of people sleeping in the streets.

4. This was certainly the case in the United States, where slavery as an institution was abominable and alien to the concepts, ideals, and the very Constitution that formed the principles on which that country was established.

Slavery worldwide has yet to be abolished totally, but it has been diminished in scope, although a good case can be made for considering South Africa's system of apartheid a form of institutionalized slavery. This issue, however, is outside the scope of this work and will not be discussed here.

5. J. M. Keynes, *The General Theory,* p. 383.

## CHAPTER 11

1. Emmanuel Farjoun and Moshe Machover, *Laws of Chaos* (London: Verso Editions, 1983). p. 97.

2. However, several economists have also been outstanding philosophers—Adam Smith, David Hume, J. S. Mill, Karl Marx, and John Maynard Keynes. Keynes's treatise on probability theory is perhaps a landmark in this branch of mathematical reasoning. See J.M. Keynes, *A Treatise on Probability* (New York: Harper Torchbooks, 1962).

Also, Daniel M. Hausman's book, *The Philosophy of Economics* (New York: Cambridge University Press, 1984) is significant for describing his treatment of the philosophy of science and scientific method in relation to the issues of economic reasoning. This book is a collection of essays that are important for the clarification of reasoning about economic processes.

## CHAPTER 12

1. Rep. Martha Griffiths, "Income Security for Americans: Recommendations of the Public Welfare Study," Report of the Subcommittee on Fiscal Policy of the Joint Economic Committee, U.S. Congress, 1974. Reprinted in Arthur Spindler, *Public Welfare* (New York: Human Sciences Press, 1979), p. 438.

2. In the 1980s both Japan and South Korea have experienced organized demonstrations, to the point of violence. Whereas Japan's is a developed economy, South Korea's is a developing economy in which industry is technological in orientation. With its people feeling the need to protest, it has adapted the methods of the developed economy, providing an original South Korean "touch" to them. See Hannah Arendt, *Crises of the Republic* (New York: Harcourt Brace Jovanovich, 1972). Her comments and approaches to social protest, civil disobedience, and revolutions are important even at our present time. Moreover, this author holds to the approach that the techniques of protest and civil disobedience are originated by the developed economies and copied by those less developed. For example see in South America; this view, however, cannot be discussed here.

3. See, for example, "America's 57th budget resolution," *The Economist,* 3 Sept. 1988, pp. 16–17, where the issues of Social Security and the U.S. budget difficulties are clearly discussed.

4. See, for example, James P. Marky, "The Labor Market Problems of Today's High School Dropouts," *Monthly Labor Review,* June 1988, p. 36. Training for reemployment is conducted on the basis of low pay relative to the wage scale for the knowledge

of on-the-job work situations. This is fair, but unfortunately industry cannot train people all the time, nor are people's skills and abilities those that industry requires for all training situations.

5. The problem with the workforce programs is that the opportunities for developing on-the-job skills and advancement are nil. The work offered is menial and, while skilled people who are unemployed take these jobs, the nature of the work itself provides nothing more than a salary; but this, too, is important in difficult times.

These programs have proven difficult to monitor with regard to work attendance and performance; moreover, establishing such programs can be costly because of the need to develop work sites. This is an example of government's good intentions leading to questionable programs.

6. Not that the problems of alcohol and drug abuse are not serious, but the funds directed toward their programs were taken from those funds relegated to assist the poor. The funds for higher education, for example, were not so directed and the middle and upper classes benefit from this funding.

7. While post-school training is impressive in the U.S., the worker bears the cost usually in the form of lower wages. But these wages will be represented statistically with the Bureau of Labor Statistics, and will be reflected in wage growth after the training period is completed, no matter where employment will then be found.

8. Laura Castaneda, "Poverty Rampant in U.S.," *Jerusalem Post,* 16 Nov. 1988, p. 10.

9. From the *Economic Report of the President* (Washington D.C.: U.S. Government Printing Office, 1988), "Human Capital" section, pp. 165–177; quoted here from page 171.

10. The issue of taxation, and the form it is to take, is again being discussed. When the cycle moves downward, reducing taxes is one accepted manner for increasing consumer liquidity and hence consumption, thus stimulating production and at least reducing the momentum of the cycle's downward movement.

However, with the U.S. economy in a fairly strong yet somewhat unstable position, and with the large trade imbalance and the restriction of the zero budget deficit by 1993, the imposition of higher taxes is one possible method for reducing consumption. Moreover, the middle-and upper-middle-class social security recipients would also be included in the taxable category—if not through direct taxes on their pensions and Social Security payments, then through the imposition of a value-added tax. See Andrew Kupper, "The Case for a Consumption Tax," *Nation's Business,* Aug. 1988, pp. 36–38; and A.J. Cook, "The Roof is Off Tax Shelters," ibid., pp. 42–44. For the position of the aged and the aging in modern American society, see Thomas Cole, "The Specter of Old Age: Politics and Culture in an Aging America," *Tikkun,* Sept./Oct. 1988, pp. 14–16, and 93–95.

## CHAPTER 13

1. R.I. McKinnion, "Optimum Currency Areas," *American Economic Review* 53, pp. 717–724. Quoted here in *International Finance,* ed. R.N. Cooper (Baltimore: Penguin Books, 1972), p. 227.

2. This is the standard textbook model used for explaining trade; its advantage is that it concentrates on the interrelationship between a nation's pattern of international trade and its endowment factors of production, including capital. See Richard E. Caves, *Multinational Enterprise and Economic Analysis* (New York: Cambridge University Press,

1985), pp. 46–56; see also, Charles P. Kindleberger, *International Economics* (Homewood, Ill.: R.D. Irwin, Inc., 1963), p. 246.

3. In *The Dynamics of Knowledge: A Contemporary View* (Westport, Conn.: Greenwood Press, 1988), this present writer distinguished among three different types of society: The future-oriented society; the present-oriented society; and the past-oriented society. These distinctions are made on the basis of a country's economic status, its political and social development, and its direction with respect to its attitudes and goals. These distinctions are important with respect to trade. See Part 3.

4. Zaire, for example, is one of the world's most heavily obligated debtor countries, having outstanding debts in billions of dollars and seeing no possible way of repaying this debt financially.

## CHAPTER 14

1. Peter T. Bauer, "The Grail of Equality," in *Equality, the Third World, and Economic Delusion* (Cambridge: Harvard University Press, 1981). p. 8.

2. *Contemporary Economics: A Unifying Approach,* p. 186.

## CHAPTER 15

1. George J. Stigler, "The Economist as Preacher," in *The Economist as Preacher and Other Essays* (Chicago: Chicago University Press, 1982), p. 10.

2. Further works being considered by this writer are in international economics and the economics of developing countries. In both works, the concepts of dynamic disequilibrium and the welfare utility function will be employed.

# Selected Bibliography

Ansoff, H. Igor. "An Action Program for Diversification." California: Lockheed Aircraft Corp., 1955.

Arrow, K.J., T.E. Harris and Marshack, J. "Optimal Inventory Policy." *Econometrica 19,* 1951, pp. 250–272.

Bell, Daniel and Irving Kristol ed., *The Crisis in Economic Theory.* New York: Basic Books, 1981.

Buchanan, James, and Gordon Tullock. *The Calculus of Consent.* Ann Arbor: University of Michigan Press, 1962.

Cairncross, A.K. *Factors in Economic Development.* London: George Allen and Unwin, 1962.

Cooper, R.N. *The Economics of Interdependence.* New York: McGraw-Hill, 1968.

Dahl, Robert, and Charles Lindblom. *Politics, Economics and Welfare.* Chicago: University of Chicago Press, 1976.

Dansinger, Sheldon, and Daniel H. Weinberg, eds. *Fighting Poverty.* Cambridge, Mass.: Harvard University Press, 1986.

Davenport, Herbert J. *Economics of Enterprise.* New York: Macmillan, 1913.

Eichner, Alfred S., and J. Kregel. "An Essay on Post-Keynesian Theory: A New Paradigm in Economics." *Journal of Economic Literature* 13 (Dec. 1975), pp. 1293–1314.

*Employment and Training Report of the President.* Washington, D.C.: U.S. Government Printing Office, 1983.

*Encyclopedia of Social Work.* Vols. 1 and 2. Silver Spring, Md.: National Association of Social Workers, 1987.

*Federal Housing Assistance: Alternative Approaches.* Congressional Budget Office. Washington, D.C.: U.S. Government Printing Office, 1982b.

Fishman, Robert. *Criminal Recidivism in New York City.* New York: Praeger, 1977.

Goodwin, L. *Causes and Cures of Welfare.* Lexington, Mass.: Lexington Books, 1983.

Gordon, David M., ed. *Problems in Political Economy: An Urban Perspective.* Lexington, Mass.: D. C. Heath and Co., 1971.

————. *Theories of Poverty and Underemployment.* Lexington, Mass.: Lexington Books., D. C. Heath and Co., 1972.

Hennipman, P. "Pareto Optimality: Value Judgement or Analytic Tool." In J. Cramer, A. Hervite, and V. Venekamp, eds. *Relevance and Precision: From Quantitative Analysis to Economic Policy, Essays in Honor of Pieter de Wolff.* Amsterdam: North Holland Publishing Co., 1976, pp. 36–69.

Hillenbrand, Martin, and Daniel Yergin eds. *Global Insecurity.* New York: Penguin Books, 1982.

Hollis, M., and Neil, E. *Rational Economic Man: A Philosophical Critique of Neo-Classical Economics.* Cambridge: Cambridge University Press, 1975.

Irick, Christine. *An Overview of OASWI Revenue, Expenditures, and Beneficiaries, 1974–1985.* U. S. Department of Health and Human Services. Washington, D.C.: 1986.

Isard, W. *General Theory: Social, Political, Economic and Regional with Particular Reference to Decision-Making Analysis.* Cambridge Mass.: M.I.T. Press, 1969.

Kahn, Herman. *World Economic Development: 1979 and Beyond.* New York: Morrow Quill, 1979.

Kinzer, D.M. "Care for the Poor Revisited." *Inquiry* 21, no. 1 (1984), pp. 5–16.

Lerner, Abba P., and David C. Colander *Map: A Market Anti-Inflation Plan.* New York: Harcourt Brace Javanovich, 1980.

Linker, R. *The Human Organization: Its Management and Value.* New York: McGraw-Hill, 1967.

Morris, Michael and John B. Williamson. *Poverty and Public Policy.* Westport Conn.: Greenwood Press, 1986.

Nikaido, Hukukane. *Convex Structures and Economic Theory* New York: Academic Press, 1968.

Nurske, Ragnar. *Lectures on Economic Development.* Istanbul: Faculty of Economics and Political Science, Ankara University, 1958.

Okun, Bernard, and Richard W. Richardson, eds. *Studies in Economic Development.* New York: Holt, Rinehart and Winston, 1962.

Paglin, Morton. "The Measurement and Trend in Inequality," *American Economic Review* 65 (Sept. 1975), pp. 598–609.

Pechman, Joseph A. *The Rich, the Poor and the Taxes They Pay.* Boulder, Colorado: Westview Press, 1986.

Reynolds, Lloyd G., Stanley H. Masters, and Colletta N. Moser. *Labor Economics and Labor Relations.* Englewood Cliffs: Prentice-Hall, 1986.

Ross, Stephen A., and Michael L. Wachter. "Wage Determination, Inflation, the Industrial Structure." American Economic Review 63 (Sept. 1973), pp. 675–692.

Sidel, Ruth. *Women and Children Last.* New York: Viking Penguin, 1986. See especially chapter 4: "Welfare: How to Keep a Good Woman Down," pp. 77–99.

Smith, Charles W. *A Critique of Sociological Reasoning.* Oxford: Basil Blackwell, 1979.

*Social Security Programs in the United States* vol. 50, no. 4. Washington, D. C.: U. S. Government Printing Office, 1987.

Solon, G. "The Minimum Wage of Teenage Employment: A Reanalysis with Attention to Serial Correlation and Seasonality.'' *Journal of Human Resources* 20 (1985), pp. 292–297.

Sowell, Thomas. *Knowledge and Decisions*. New York: Basic Books, 1980.

Tinbergen, Jan. *Income Distribution: Analysis and Policies*. Amsterdam: North Holland, 1975.

Vernon, Raymond. ''Foreign-Owned Enterprise in Developing Countries.'' In Therberge, J.D., ed. *Economics of Trade and Development*. New York: Wiley, 1968.

Weintraub, E. Roy. *General Equilibrium Theory*. London: Macmillan, 1974.

Weintraub, Sidney. *An Approach to the Theory of Income Distribution*. Philadelphia: Chilton, 1958.

Worcester, Dean, ''John Rawls' Justification of Unequal Income and Wealth,'' University of Washington Institute of Economic Research Discussion Paper no. 74–4, (Seattle, 1975), pp. 25–29.

# Index

## ABOUT THE AUTHOR

DAVID Z. RICH serves as economic consultant to a number of business firms and international corporations. A resident of Israel since 1969, he is the author of *Contemporary Economics: A Unifying Approach* (Praeger, 1986) and *The Dynamics of Knowledge: A Contemporary View* (Greenwood, 1988). Mr. Rich received a B.S. degree in economics and philosophy from Florida State University and did graduate work at the London School of Economics. He is translator of a book on economic efficiency and its applications in Israel by the late Abba P. Lerner and Professor Chaim Ben Schacher of Tel Aviv University.